Practicing Pilgrimage

Practicing Pilgrimage

ON BEING AND BECOMING
GOD'S PILGRIM PEOPLE

Brett Webb-Mitchell

CASCADE *Books* • Eugene, Oregon

PRACTICING PILGRIMAGE
On Being and Becoming God's Pilgrim People

Copyright © 2016 Brett Webb-Mitchell. All rights reserved. Except for brief quotations in critical publications or reviews, no part of this book may be reproduced in any manner without prior written permission from the publisher. Write: Permissions, Wipf and Stock Publishers, 199 W. 8th Ave., Suite 3, Eugene, OR 97401.

Cascade Books
An Imprint of Wipf and Stock Publishers
199 W. 8th Ave., Suite 3
Eugene, OR 97401

www.wipfandstock.com

PAPERBACK ISBN: 978-1-62032-948-1
HARDCOVER ISBN: 978-1-4982-8870-5
EBOOK ISBN: 978-1-5326-1404-0

Cataloguing-in-Publication data:

Names: Webb-Mitchell, Brett.

Title: Practicing pilgrimage : on being and becoming God's pilgrim people / Brett Webb-Mitchell.

Description: Eugene, OR : Cascade Books, 2016 | Includes bibliographical references.

Identifiers: ISBN 978-1-62032-948-1 (paperback) | ISBN 978-1-4982-8870-5 (hardcover) | ISBN 978-1-5326-1404-0 (ebook)

Subjects: LCSH: Christian pilgrims and pilgrimages.

Classification: BV5067 .W43 2016 (print) | BV5067 .W43 (ebook)

Manufactured in the U.S.A.   NOVEMBER 8, 2016

All Scripture quotations are taken from New Revised Standard Version Bible, copyright © 1989 National Council of the Churches of Christ in the United States of America. Used by permission. All rights reserved.

Contents

Acknowledgments vii
Introduction xi

PART I: FRAMING PILGRIMAGE
1 A "Pilgrimage" and the "Pilgrimage of Life" 3
2 The Story of Pilgrimage 17
3 Pilgrimage as Biblical and Theological Practice 36
4 Pilgrimage among Different Faith Communities 53
5 Characteristics of Pilgrims and Pilgrimages 65
6 The Art of Hospitality on Pilgrimage 82
7 Being and Becoming God's Pilgrim People: Worship and Pilgrimage 93

PART II: PRACTICING PILGRIMAGE
8 Labyrinths 110
9 Teaching the Pilgrimage of Life 120
10 A Pilgrimage of New Beginnings 129
11 Pilgrimage of Remembrance 137
12 A Pilgrimage of the Earth 146
13 A Pilgrimage of Justice and Peace 155
14 Pilgrimages of Advent and Lent 164
15 A Daily Pilgrimage 172

Epilogue: "The Church as Resident Pilgrims" 191
Bibliography 197

Acknowledgments

Going on a pilgrimage and writing a book have many things in common. First, there is a beginning, middle, and end when walking a pilgrimage and in writing a book. Second, pilgrimage and writing are both processes that are filled with adventure, fun, frustration, joy, challenges, deep satisfaction, and even deeper sighs on tired days (whether one is walking one more mile or writing one more page). Third, going on a pilgrimage and writing a book are not solo activities. Granted, the pilgrim and the writer alike may not necessarily see or be aware of the community that surrounds one while walking or writing. After all, pilgrimage, like writing, tends to be a solitary activity and not a group project per se, depending on the scope of either the pilgrimage or book. Nonetheless, when walking or writing, we are accompanied by both a visible and often invisible community of people, along with all of creation around us. Let me explain this a little further: while there are times on pilgrimage when one hits the trail and is all alone on this adventure, nonetheless, there is usually a community of people from the very get-go of the journey. For instance, there are those who are part of the discernment process in assisting a pilgrim to figure out everything from the call of the pilgrim to the logistics of doing the pilgrimage. Likewise, in writing, we play with ideas for a book in our conversations with friends and strangers alike. Once on the pilgrimage, there is the encouragement that individuals and a community might send or communicate to the pilgrim along the pilgrimage route itself. In writing, the author will need to push away from the task of writing and simply hang out with others, checking in to be sure one is on target with one's book. Oftentimes, if a pilgrim starts walking a pilgrimage alone, there is not only the company of other possible pilgrims one will inevitably meet along the way, but God's very creation joins in the happy yet arduous melee of the pilgrim life itself, whether one can welcome a mosquito or mouse in one's sleeping bag or not. Earlier in life, my dogs were the ones who heard the first draft of my writing for the

Acknowledgments

morning. And finally, there are the relationships that one comes back to on a pilgrimage. For a writer, there is nothing like sharing our writing, once edited and polished. And be prepared for the unexpected in walking or writing a book! Both the pilgrim and the people waiting for the pilgrim will have moved on in life, and there is always time to share the stories of great joy and even deeper challenges that confronted the pilgrim or pilgrims along the way. So too with writing a book: the writer has been nourished by new waters and adventures in writing that will inevitably shape the very character of the writer's self going forward.

In writing this book, I was joined by many pilgrims on various pilgrimages—pastors, priests, religious leaders, people in religious orders, congregations, strangers in pubs, college groups, friends, associates, acquaintances, grown children, our dogs, and partner. I bow deeply to all of you and thank you for your encouragement in going on pilgrimage with me, picking me up after a pilgrimage as well as tolerating life with me as a writer. Since writing the essays for *Follow Me* and *School of the Pilgrim*, I have been on more pilgrimages, broadening my understanding of the nature of pilgrimage and pilgrim life, and of a surprising faith and unearned grace while on pilgrimage. The list of names is long, and, with regret, I will forget to mention you by name, so my apologies.

This book was conceived and plotted out with help from one of the grants administered by Dorothy Bass of the Lilly Endowment and Valparaiso University, looking at this connection between intentional pilgrimage and the pilgrimage of everyday life. For that project I worked with and am thankful for the company of Matt Norvell Sr., Stef Weisgram (OSB), Rita Bennett, and Rob Hagen (formerly Fr. Aelred). It was during our pilgrimage between Charleston and Mepkin Abbey, in Moncks Corner, South Carolina, that many of the ideas in this book were born.

My pilgrim comrade, Jaqui Tutt of New Zealand, not only walked with me on the last half of the Camino de Santiago de Compostela but has been in constant contact with me as she goes on pilgrimages around the world—while walking to Rome from Canterbury, England, and while on the Shikoku pilgrimage, where the pilgrim visits eighty-eight Buddhist temples. Our correspondences throughout the years have provided great fodder for thought and reflection on the nature of pilgrimage and what keeps a pilgrim ticking (and walking).

On my pilgrimages to Chimayo, I am indebted to the hospitality always shown to me by Fr. Ed Savilla and the people of the archdiocese

Acknowledgments

of Santa Fe, New Mexico. Fr. Ed has always graciously welcomed me, my questions, thoughts, opinions, and provided great care when I have come as a happy-go-lucky gringo from North Carolina to walk along one of the five paths to Chimayo. To all my friends, *peregrinos* and *peregrinas*, many thanks for the lessons you've taught me along the way. Many of the practices included in this book come from our time together.

Sr. Stefanie Weisgram, Sr. Agatha Zwilling, and the sisters of St. Benedict Monastery in St. Joseph, Minnesota, along with Richard Bresnahan at St. John's Abbey and University in Collegeville, Minnesota, have always shown me the warmth of Christian hospitality, especially when I needed to focus on finishing this book. Our conversations, our times of prayer, our shared Eucharist—along with convivial conversations over a meal with various libations—gave me the energy to write this book.

I am also indebted to the spirit of Christian hospitality and time to write that the folks at St. Andrew's Presbyterian Church (USA) have given me during my time as the interim senior pastor. From the very first days of my tenure at St. Andrew's, I was given plenty of opportunities to talk and reflect upon the nature of pilgrimage, from book clubs to adult forum events. The congregation has heard me call Jesus "the Pilgrim God" in more than one sermon.

To my partner, Dean Blackburn, and my children and in-laws, Adrianne and Scott Anderson and Parker Webb-Mitchell, Liz Mitchell, a.k.a., Mom, along with my friends Wally Hannum, fellow pilgrim Paul Fukui, Charles Airey, Bruce Whiting, artists Julia Kennedy and Shannon Bueker, Eileen and Ric Parfrey, Larry Russell, John Rogers, and the young women and men of the Presbyterian Campus Ministry of University of North Carolina-Chapel Hill. Thanks to Michele Ware, who was chair of my department at North Carolina Central University (NCCU), in Durham, where I taught for almost five years. Michele made it possible for me to teach a course on world religions once a year that gave me the time and intellectual space I needed to explore pilgrimages of many world faiths and belief systems with the students at NCCU. John and Trina Rogers and I led a group of wonderful students who had recently graduated from the University of North Carolina-Chapel Hill on a memorable pilgrimage across England along Hadrian's Wall, from Bowness-on-Solway to Newcastle upon Tyne. I am thankful for the guidance, teachings, and friendship of Henry Carse, Dr. Rabia Gad, and his assistant Moussa Abdel Sayed, who taught me much about the Holy Land and pilgrimage. Lately, on my many pilgrimages

Acknowledgments

to India and Nepal, I have learned a lot about pilgrimage in South Asia through the expert instruction of Bharat Singh Chundawat and his brother Gajraj Singh Chundawat in India, and Nawaraj Khatiwada in Nepal. I am grateful to have talked about pilgrimage many times with the Reverends Jill and Rick Edens of United Church of Chapel Hill, North Carolina; Mary Francis of the Franciscan Center of Portland, Oregon; and Richard Rodriguez—many thanks for walking, laughing, thinking, and loving me as I went on pilgrimage and wrote this book. I could not have done it without your belief in me and your enthusiasm for all things related to pilgrimage. Finally, thank you Charlie Collier and Wipf and Stock Publishing for working with me on this book.

As you, dear reader, take time to read this book, please take it with you on your pilgrimage of life. And perhaps you can smile someday, as it seems appropriate, and wish others well on their pilgrimage of life as you share with them what is uttered countless times every day on Spain's Camino de Santiago de Compostela: *Buen camino!*

Good journey, to one and all!

Introduction

"Solvitur ambulando" —Diogenes of Sinope
"Follow me." —Jesus of Nazareth
"Show me your ways, teach me your path." —Richard Rohr

The First Pilgrimage

My friend Stephanie Friggo once told me that the first sentence of an article or book should be like one's first kiss with someone you love: "You never forget your first kiss." Similarly, those of us who are ardent pilgrims might admit something similar: "You never forget your first pilgrimage."

My first pilgrimage was almost twenty years ago, in 1999, and I have been walking ever since. I read the book and saw the musical based on Geoffrey Chaucer's *Canterbury Tales* in high school, enjoyed travelogue documentary movies or Bob Hope's and Bing Crosby's "on the road" films, watched Rick Steves' European adventures on public television, grew up in a family that took incredibly long car trips for summer vacations, and I started writing about pilgrimage in my writings about the church and people living with disabilities. Two friends, both of them Roman Catholic, told me the following on two separate occasions: while I wrote beautiful passages about pilgrimage in my books, it was too bad I never took a pilgrimage. They were correct. For example, in my books on children living with disabilities I compared people living with disabling conditions to pilgrims, for they both often stood in the middle of the public square of medieval towns, stranded, with no one showing them hospitality—not even churches. Sadly, churches, inns, and monasteries were often closed to people with disabilities in the medieval ages. The words I wrote were academically and poetically powerful, they said, but lacked the heart or panache of a seasoned pilgrim. With the encouragement of these friends,

Introduction

I arranged to go on a pilgrimage to El Santuario de Chimayo in northern New Mexico right after Pentecost, joining up with the Pilgrimage of Vocations held annually with the Catholic Archdiocese of Santa Fe. There are usually four to five groups of pilgrims, with each group made up of thirty-five or so people. Pilgrims go to Chimayo because of the sacred soil that is at the heart of the small chapel. This soil has certain curative properties for what ails people in mind, body, or spirit. For hundreds of years, people seeking a cure have gone on pilgrimage to this place.

Unbeknownst to me at the time, this inaugural pilgrimage would transform my understanding of the mystical body of Christ. Being on an actual pilgrimage strengthened my understanding of the theology of the church as the body of Christ by introducing me to the idea that this is a body *in motion*. Being a pilgrim helped me in getting a firmer toehold in what can only be considered the mysterious spiritual life of a follower of Jesus. Personally, the pilgrimage gave me the language and metaphor I needed to better understand the process of leaving my gay closet and walking out of fear into hope. This singular pilgrimage consisted of walking more than 120 miles in six days in the hot, sunbaked desert of New Mexico. A group of us followed a fellow pilgrim carrying a cross with the figure of a gnarled, bloody Jesus; next came one holding up a flag with the imprint of Our Lady of Guadalupe, then one carrying a weirdly shaped block of wood that was part of a larger wooden puzzle of the heart of Jesus, and finally one carrying a bag of soil from various locales on the pilgrimage. Our pockets were filled with scraps of paper with prayer requests written on them. All of this was new to me as a Presbyterian clergyperson. As a Caucasian male who spoke very little Spanish, my group of *peregrinos* (pilgrims) quickly dubbed me *el gringo loco*, both because of the multitude of questions I asked out of ignorance and because of my sense of joy at the end of each day. While I had a rudimentary knowledge of Catholic theology, nothing had prepared me for this immersion into the ins and outs of Catholicism in northern New Mexico, with its focus on Mary the mother of Jesus and the blending of Spanish, Mexican, and Native American spirituality. Walking from Costilla, on the border between New Mexico and Colorado, through Taos Pueblo to Chimayo, breathing was hard because of the change in altitude. While I had hiked long distances in the Pacific Northwest and sung Christian camp songs around an open fire, I was not prepared for all the songs and prayers in Spanish, praying the rosary morning, noon, and night, eating food that was far spicier than bland Caucasian fare, and sleeping on the floors of

Introduction

schools, armories, and churches, all with communal showers. Rising at 3:00 a.m., being on the road by 5:00 a.m. before the sun rose, and going to bed at 9:00 p.m. was a new rhythm. My senses were easily overwhelmed by the smells of incense and candles, by the stunning beauty of the landscape, by trying to translate a new language, by the taste of new spicy foods, and by walking with blister upon blister. I was also enthralled with the understated simplicity of pilgrimage; it begins with the musical two-beat footstep: heel-toe, again heel-toe. Like a march, we walked in 4/4 time, but the speed of the pilgrimage changed depending on who was leading it. Essayist Robert Macfarlane quotes writer-philosopher Nan Shepherd, who writes that the two beats of a step is her version of René Descartes' "I think, therefore I am": "She celebrated the metaphysical rhythm of the pedestrian, the iamb of the 'I am,' the beat of the placed and lifted foot."[1] For Nan Shepherd, her eyes were in her feet.[2] It was simple: move the foot forward, heel and outside of the foot hitting the dirt road, calf squeezing, body leaning forward, foot rolling from heel to toe and then the next foot, leaving our imprint upon the roadway until wind, rain, or snow mad it vanish. "I walk, therefore I am." That works for me!

I still remember our first morning, beginning the pilgrimage at 5:00 a.m. and watching a large moose lazily walk off the roadway a few minutes after we had started. At 8:00 a.m., I was in awe of the expansive blue sky, which looked like a large blue bowl turned upside down, covering the earth. Because there were so few trees in that desert land, and from such a high locale, I swear you could almost see a slight curvature of the earth. At night, the sky was like a black velvet cloth with starry jewels strewn across it, with seemingly no obvious pattern.

While amazed at the expanse of land before us—my eyes fixed on the road ahead—and wondering where we were going, my mind was challenged theologically during our discussions about the differences between Catholicism and Protestantism. Many of my fellow pilgrims had never met a Presbyterian before. My heart grew larger as I welcomed new friends, friends I would stay in touch with over the years, walking with a few of them on future pilgrimages to Chimayo. And my body was challenged as I learned exactly which toes tend to blister and the blessings of cornstarch in my underwear. I now add pads and bandages to my toes and heel before I

---

1. Macfarlane, *Old Ways*, 201.
2. Ibid., vii.

Introduction

go on pilgrimage to avoid painful blisters—the mark of a pilgrimage—and wear shoes that support my aging body.

Lessons Learned from an Actual Pilgrimage about the Pilgrimage of Everyday Life

After that first pilgrimage I learned to love going on a pilgrimage. Why? Because it provided a chance for me to leave the seemingly routine life of going to church, teaching, and home, and to rediscover that I live a life of choices both on pilgrimage *and* at home. In a dramatic awareness, to go on pilgrimage is an opportunity to throw down my metaphorical gauntlet and challenge the Spirit to teach me something new about living a life dependent upon God, questioning the ins and outs of life, dying, death, and resurrection. Coming home from an actual pilgrimage time and again, I slowly started to envision my entire life as a pilgrimage. In a transformational moment, I realized that the Christian life in all its fullness *is* a pilgrimage—and the body of Christ is a moving body on pilgrimage.

I can identify with writer Gideon Lewis-Kraus—a pilgrim himself—who writes that on pilgrimage, he is more conscious of what is going on in ordinary, everyday life, recognizing that "whatever we are doing is something we have, for the most part, chosen to do . . . with some limited knowledge of what's at stake; and though we worry that perhaps there are costs we have ignored or underestimated, we understand that there is no way to know how we feel about this decision down the line."[3] Pilgrimage becomes a time of vulnerability and thus intimacy with myself, others, and God as parts of life are stretched, while other parts are constricted, thus making me uncomfortable. Pilgrimage near and abroad led me to new experiences that dashed old boundaries and raised new horizons. I am more *present* and aware after a pilgrimage than I am during an experience of Sunday school, youth group, seminary training and teaching, or most Sunday morning worship, even when I'm leading worship. To quote Lewis-Kraus again, on pilgrimage I live between the "blurry function of choice and necessity . . . between saying 'I felt like it' and saying 'I had to.'"[4]

Leaving Chimayo for home in Chapel Hill after that first pilgrimage, I was just beginning to learn the many lessons that would come to me over the years while strolling (and crawling) among Buddhist and Hindu shrines

---

3. Lewis-Kraus, *Sense of Direction*, 237.
4. Ibid., 238.

Introduction

in Thailand, Cambodia, India, and Nepal; lost in the Shinto shrines of Japan; walking barefoot around the basilica in the middle of Lough Derg and Croagh Patrick in Ireland; wandering on camelback in the deserts of the Sinai Peninsula; walking alongside the remains of Hadrian's Wall in England; sweltering in the heat on a pilgrimage between Charleston and Mepkin Abbey; interviewing pilgrims in Mexico City, Esquipulas, Guatemala, and Costa Rica; and strolling along the last 190 miles of the Camino in Spain. These pilgrimages changed not only what I taught at Duke Divinity School but the very pedagogy I practiced, or how I taught. Not only did they influence my approach to teaching, but they transformed my understanding of ministry in general. At Duke I began teaching a course on religious education as pilgrimage. On a personal level, both at work and at home I was suddenly a very round peg that refused to be squared and could no longer fit in the square hole I had occupied, though I did not comprehend the many ways this was true. Walking to Chimayo and being a pilgrim gave me the language and tools necessary to grasp flickers of insight into the complicated process of coming out of a suffocating gay closet, which I had constructed with society's encouragement. In my ministry, I couched my work with churches in the language of "change process" as pilgrimage. In 2007, I began a religious nonprofit, the School of the Pilgrim, to create a gathering of other interested people who were open to co-learning and co-teaching the ins and outs of pilgrimage. Creating this nonprofit included constructing the necessary elevator speech: "We invite you out of the 'religion of rush' like rush hour, to find the inward path and call to be a pilgrim in the world today." And my partner challenged me to take the symbol for the School of the Pilgrim and have it tattooed on my left shoulder with the charge, "Now you have to live into being a pilgrim."

More importantly, I call myself a "pilgrim," or a "Christian pilgrim," and find myself using in my everyday life the very language, symbols, and rituals I would use on an actual pilgrimage. Using such language in my daily life reminds me that I am a pilgrim. The pathway forward is sometimes obvious to one and all, though sometimes it is not readily seen or perceived. Sometimes, I agree with poet Antonio Machado: "There is no road, the road is made by walking."[5] My courage to walk forward when the pathway is hard to distinguish comes from Holy Scripture and meditation using a book of Benedictine prayers at morning and evening, Eucharist, worship, and a nudge by the Holy Spirit. Suddenly, briefly, the map for a

5. Ibid., 236.

Introduction

stretch of road ahead of me appears, and I soldier onward. Other times, I make the decision by gut feeling, and the grace of pilgrimage seems to have carried me forward.

This is now my daily routine as a pilgrim of God in the everydayness of life: from my first waking stretch to my final sleepy yawn, I thank God for the beginning and ending of each day, no matter how wonderful or awful this stretch of life's pilgrimage has been, using the Benedictine morning and evening prayers for holding me up and keeping my act together. During the day, I earnestly try to live out and take up the invitation of Jesus, the Pilgrim God, to "follow me" right where I live today and into tomorrow. Weekly, I take Sabbath or mini-Sabbath rest from the journey to attend worship with other pilgrims in a local faith community or to go to a movie, a most necessary luxury at times. Throughout the day I strive to "be where my feet are planted," rather than being focused on tomorrow and the days to come. And who knows, there may be a day in which I may be drawn out by God to a place I've never been to before, never to return.[6] What was revealed to me in the actual pilgrimage to Chimayo is that often my ordinary life can be as extraordinary as going on a far-flung, exotic international pilgrimage. My daily life is a pilgrimage, a thoroughly absorbing experience, a true wandering, which involves discipline and attention, prayer and conversation, time alone and moments of great conviviality with companions, in which I learn daily to reflect upon and use gestures to embody the practices of the Christian faith as I follow Jesus, the Pilgrim God. And *that truth* has made all the difference.

How Intentional Pilgrimage Reveals the Extraordinary Pilgrimage of Ordinary Life

The focus of this book is simple: being on an actual pilgrimage can help Christians understand that our everyday life is a pilgrimage. In creating or going on an actual pilgrimage at home or abroad, the underlying theme of the Gospel is revealed: that Christians are people of the Way (Acts 9:2), following Jesus, who is the Way (John 14:6), otherwise known as the Pilgrim God. In order to sustain our faith, and for our faith to mature into the truthfulness of this Spirit-inspired reality, there are certain practices that we may individually and communally engage in daily and weekly that will enable us to respond to the call of Jesus to "follow me."

6. Dillard, *Teaching a Stone to Talk*, 41.

Introduction

I write all this from the vantage point of a veteran pilgrim. I have walked, led, and coordinated numerous pilgrimages since 1999. I come back from each pilgrimage refreshed, with renewed eyes and ears, heart and mind, capable of re-discovering and re-claiming that the ordinary Christian life is an extraordinary pilgrimage. My ordinary life is now shaped and informed by the language and practice of pilgrimage. When I wake up in the morning, after sipping a hot cup of coffee and wolfing down oatmeal, I embrace or kiss my partner goodbye; he goes on his pathway and I on mine as we travel to our respective jobs. We hope we will see each other at the end of the day, but you never know what may happen along the way . . . just like an actual pilgrimage. That's why at night we catch up with each other, sharing the experiences we had while apart, the unexpected conversations and texts, the new insights, our aching feet and sore backs ready for bed . . . just like an intentional pilgrimage.

On this Christian pilgrimage of daily life, on this our journey of faith, the faith community also has a responsibility to prepare us and support us. We are publicly welcomed to the trail of the Way through the waters of baptism, fed by the Eucharist, meeting friends, family, and strangers alike with whom we share in the experiences of creation, relationship, faith, sin, penance, redemption by grace, love, birth, dying, and death, and the hope of resurrection. On pilgrimage, there are times of solitude as well as walking with the present company of saints in the shadow of the unknown cloud of witnesses, with our share of successes and failures, and the opportunity to make a difference in this world. What a pilgrim lives out during an actual pilgrimage is an intensification of what we pilgrims of God live out every day on the pilgrimage of faith. But more about that in the next chapter.

What Makes This Book Different from Other Books on Pilgrimage

In my books *Follow Me* and *School of the Pilgrim*, I shared stories of the pilgrimages I've been on around this world, near and far away, and laid out the theological, sociological, and psychological framework of pilgrimage. Since the publication of those books, I've been on several more important pilgrimages as noted above. I've also conducted many workshops with groups of people on the pilgrimage of life in various church groups. And what I keep learning and relearning is that in this pilgrimage of life, there is

Introduction

always this rare mixture or alchemy of knowing and faith, faith and knowing, in which there isn't one without the other.

In order to be sure that others may have the advantage of knowing what I mean, my purpose in writing *Practicing Pilgrimage* is to provide a way to assist others in embracing and heeding the call to follow Jesus right where we are. As mentioned earlier, I began this book with the assistance of four friends: Matt Norvell, Rita Bennett, Robert Hagan, and Sr. Stef Weisgram. With a Lilly Grant in hand, we walked from downtown Charleston to Mepkin Abbey in Moncks Corner, South Carolina—roughly forty miles in four days. The hope was that a book would come out of the pilgrimage. Some of the ideas in this book come from our walk and work together, and in those parts of the chapters where I can use their material, I will acknowledge that this is their idea or inspired by our conversation. However, much has happened since that pilgrimage to Mepkin, and most of the material is new. Nevertheless, I am thankful for their joining me on that pilgrimage.

Outline of This Book

While there may be multiple kinds of pilgrimages—not only various sites but also diverse ways of going on pilgrimage, and as many causes or reasons for why people go as there are people—there is one constant in all pilgrimages: at the end of the day I've never met a person whose life wasn't changed or altered to a certain degree. This ancient practice continues to evolve and be found adaptable to every generation of people of various faiths while retaining some solid characteristics that never change. What people find attractive about pilgrimage is that by doing something exceptional, they find something new about themselves and their relationship with others, the land, or God.

The greater purpose of this book is to make it possible for everyone who wants to go on pilgrimage to become a pilgrim wherever one lives. A pilgrimage need not take place in an exotic, faraway locale. It need not take a whole week or two. It can take place in our backyards, in our neighborhoods, around our churches and retreat centers. One doesn't need to be wealthy to be a pilgrim. One simply needs to have a purpose and place in mind where one can go to in order to experience the Holy.

The first part of this book covers the theological, sociological, and psychological framework for pilgrimage. In chapter 1, there is the deeper exploration of an actual pilgrimage that informs our daily pilgrimage. Chapter 2

Introduction

is a brief exploration of what a "pilgrim" is in general and what "pilgrimage" is from a Jewish and Christian perspective. Chapter 3 is a Christian theological reflection on pilgrimage, with the focus on Jesus as the Pilgrim God. Chapter 4 draws from lessons of pilgrimage from other faith communities, including indigenous faiths, Judaism, Islam, Hinduism, Shintoism, and Buddhism. After all, the major world religions all recognize and honor the practice of pilgrimage. We have much to learn from one another. Chapter 5 provides a general list of characteristics that compose or are in play for a walk or journey to become a pilgrimage. Chapter 6 addresses the art of hospitality, which is central to pilgrimage. And chapter 7 examines the subtitle of this book, *Being and Becoming God's Pilgrim People*, and covers how worship in a faith community follows a paradigm of pilgrimage.

Part II of this book is dedicated to examples of pilgrimages that could be used by any group for various purposes. Chapter 8 looks at a brief history of the labyrinth, a way of doing a pilgrimage for many generations of Christians who could not afford to go to Jerusalem in the Middle Ages. Chapter 9 is an outline for a workshop session on pilgrimage, teaching a small group about the basics of pilgrimage over a one- or two-day event. Chapter 10 is the first pilgrimage that follows a theme, specifically, "New Hope." For example, consider a pilgrimage around the theme of baptism, which is always a time of new hope in the life of a congregation and parish. Chapter 11 is a pilgrimage of memories. Imagine during a time of a death in a family or congregation, or in the wake of a momentous event in society (such as 9/11), the need for people to walk through this time in order to understand that this is part of the journey of life. Chapter 12 considers the place of the earth, sky, and water in our pilgrimage. Chapter 13 is a pilgrimage of justice. The great walk between Selma and Montgomery, Alabama, in 1965, as civil rights leaders sought protection of voters' rights for *all* people, was a pilgrimage of justice. The North Carolina Moral Monday marches that have taken place in 2013 and 2014 include an element of pilgrimage of justice. There is power in seeing a group of people walking in the name of a cause greater than themselves. Chapter 14 lifts up the seasons of Advent and Lent, when the church immerses itself in the language of "pilgrimage" and "journey," yet usually without any explanation of what a pilgrimage or sacred journey is. Chapter 15 is a set of practices that may be used when going on a pilgrimage, though there is no set of explicit pilgrimage exercises that must be used along the way. For example, on the Camino de Santiago de Compostela there is no explicit guide for what to say or do along the way. This chapter provides some suggestions on how to focus the mind, body, and spirit during this sacred time. The Epilogue is an exploration of congregational life as a gathering of God's resident pilgrims.

Finally...

To reiterate: the aim of this book is to show the many ways an actual pilgrimage can be the portal that enables us to understand that our ordinary life is anything *but* mundane, but rather is an exciting, breathtaking, jaw-dropping, yet also long, drawn-out pilgrimage. This book includes guides to creating actual pilgrimages with hopes that the reader and user may more readily understand and perceive life as this mystical yet real quest. And by coming to the awareness that the Christian life *is* a blessed pilgrimage and that our name is *pilgrim*,[7] our very understanding of faith, grace, and love may be renewed, if not expanded. This possibility was made clear to me in Gideon Lewis-Kraus's book on walking the Camino as well as Shikoku's eighty-eight temples, and the journey to Uman, Ukraine. Lewis-Kraus writes that the power of renewal that comes from the many rituals of pilgrimage, which are all filled with stories, "leaves the pilgrim feeling somehow renovated, even if he's hard-pressed to articulate why. Part of it, in fact, is probably just that: it's an exercise in freedom from the necessity of articulating your motives with too much exactness, an opportunity to be broad-brush about why you're doing what you're doing, to just do what you're doing without worrying that maybe your reasons aren't good ones, that maybe you should be feeling bad about your decision."[8] The personal rituals of daily life on our life's pilgrimage, along with the rituals of the community of faith we belong to, with its set of ritualistic practices found in worship, service, fellowship, education, and outreach, contain within them a refreshing way of putting into context what we experience daily.

In the next chapter, the focus is on the interplay or conversation between an actual pilgrimage and the pilgrimage of everyday life. It is often the case that it is on an intentional pilgrimage that we become aware of the pilgrimage of our everyday life in the body of Christ.

---

7. I'm fully aware that actor John Wayne used to call certain people "Pilgrim" in *The Man Who Shot Liberty Valance*, as well as the tendency for some to consider the "pilgrims", a.k.a., Puritans of yore.

8. Lewis-Kraus, *Sense of Direction*, 122.

PART I
Framing Pilgrimage

1

A "Pilgrimage" *and* the "Pilgrimage of Life"

O teach your wandering pilgrims
by this their path to trace,
Till, doubt and striving ended,
they meet you face to face.
—William Walsham How[1]

I am a pilgrim, but my pilgrimage has been wandering and unmarked. Often what has looked like a straight line to me has been a circling or a doubling back. I have been in the Dark Wood of Error any number of times. I have known something of Hell, Purgatory, and Heaven, but not always in that order. The names of many snares and dangers have been made known to me, but I have seen them only in looking back. Often I have not known where I was going until I was already there. —Wendell Berry[2]

Three Stories of Pilgrimage

There was a chill in the morning air as my partner and I parked my car close to the starting line of a march that was to take place in Raleigh, the capital of North Carolina. We walked to the actual starting line of the 2014 Historic Thousands on Jones St. ("HKonJ") march, which, at the end of the day, would involve anywhere from two thousand (the police estimate) to eight thousand (the march organizers' estimate) people. We were surrounded by people with placards, buttons, T-shirts, clergy stoles and collars,

---

1. How, "O Word of God Incarnate."
2. Berry, *Jayber Crow*, 133.

banners, and handheld bumper stickers raising issue with the budget cuts in the recent state legislative sessions, which would have a big impact on the long-term unemployed, on women's health, on public school and university education, and on those receiving Medicaid. There was an African American gentleman dressed as Uncle Sam, American flags pinned here and there to his costume, standing on a large city-owned electric box and lecturing us on the problems with North Carolina's government; from time to time he broke out into patriotic songs, with the crowd cheering him on. Various people handed out bottles of water in case anyone got dehydrated after the one-and-a-half-mile walk downtown. Our destination was a raised platform in front of North Carolina's early nineteenth-century capitol building, where speaker after speaker named the injustices being brought upon the citizens of North Carolina by the Republican-controlled General Assembly and musician after musician sang with Gospel swagger, reminding us that God's justice will prevail in the end. Even though it was a cold day, the rain that was predicted did not come. Instead, later in the morning, the sun actually shone as if to bless the crowd of walkers, rewarding us for our small yet noble efforts.

This march in Raleigh was a kind of pilgrimage.

⁓

The small group gathered together in the large fellowship hall of University United Methodist Church. Composed primarily of officers of the church, the group was to take a walk of reflection on the past and discernment for the future. The church had recently received a generous gift of a large parcel of land in a yet-to-be-developed part of Chapel Hill, North Carolina, and the church's leaders were struggling with what they could or should do with this gift. So we took a pilgrimage from the church to the new plot of land, which (thankfully) was within easy walking distance. We kept our ideas for the purpose of the property and God's will for the property front and center as we walked. Walking behind a cross used in the church's worship, we followed the cross and cross-bearer to the land, walking either single file or two by two as we prayed, discussed, laughed, and talked openly about visions of what could be done with the land. Along the route, I would stop the group occasionally and ask the pilgrims to think out loud about their ideas, or to pray quietly about the use of this land. On the land itself we saw a little white tent set up in the middle of the lot. Under the white tent was

A "Pilgrimage" and the "Pilgrimage of Life"

the original Lord's Supper table used by the church when it was founded in the early 1800s. They were looking into the possibility of opening a satellite campus, and this seemed a good opportunity to use the table again as the church considered a new venture. What might rise here? A house for youth ministry, or a retreat center of sorts within the Chapel Hill area, or perhaps a house for people living with intellectual challenges? We closed with a chance to break bread and share from a common cup in remembrance of Jesus, ending with a singing of the Doxology, all the while contemplating what vision God would have for the land.

This was a pilgrimage too.

~

At the beginning of the semester, I would take the general ethics class I teach at North Carolina Central University (NCCU), a historically black college/university, on a pilgrimage. We began the pilgrimage in the large lecture classroom, where I usually set the stage for a pilgrimage with a discussion about what happened in the modern civil rights movement for the African American community in the American South prior to February 8, 1960. We talked about the U.S. Supreme Court decision of *Brown v. Board of Education of Topeka*, handed down in 1954; Rosa Parks sitting in the front of the bus in Montgomery, Alabama, in 1955; and the integration of Little Rock Central High School in 1957, in which nine students were given the task of being the first black students in an all-white school. The last example I gave the students from the civil rights movement was the sit-in at the F. W. Woolworth diner in Greensboro, North Carolina, on February 1, 1960. As a national policy, Woolworth neither sanctioned nor condoned separate eating sections in their diner. Each store in every region of the country could make that decision. The managers of the Woolworth stores in Greensboro and Durham chose to segregate. With that background, I asked the students to close their books and follow me. We made our way to the James E. Shepard Memorial Library, the main library on campus. Once there, we walked under the main stairwell in the building, in which there is a portion of the Woolworth diner that students from then-North Carolina College (NCC, now NCCU) and some students from Duke and CORE (Congress of Racial Equality) occupied on February 8, 1960. Like the students at North Carolina A&T, the students from NCC also walked and sat on similar plastic seats with aluminum backs and were jeered at, spat upon, and worse—they had hot coffee thrown in their faces, ketchup or milkshakes poured over their heads, all because they sat in the "whites only" section of Durham's Woolworth diner. Even though current students often passed by this exhibit throughout their days at NCCU, none of them ever took the time to read the plaques and realize the significance of the historic items. "This is not your history or my history, but *our* history," I told the students. Most important was this: we were honoring those who went on a pilgrimage of justice in 1960, marching from NCCU's campus to the downtown Woolworth's. Those students walked to the Woolworth diner every day for more than six months. Martin Luther King Jr. heard of their sit-in and gave a historic talk at the old White Rock Baptist Church in downtown Durham a week after the sit-in began. He told the students not to fear jail or arrest for doing what was right. The students were emboldened by Dr. King's presence and admonition, and continued until the Woolworth management at each store in the South agreed to let people sit where they wanted to sit, thus ending segregation at the Woolworth diner counter. The faded plastic seats in orange and teal blue shades with their aluminum backs, and the countertop with a menu from the Woolworth diner of the 1960s, have become historic not because they are replicas or made to be historic. They are historically significant—indeed a kind of relic—because of the civil and holy action that took place as people resisted injustice and worked to overturn a bad law. Thankfully, justice prevailed.

This class expedition was also a pilgrimage.

Scholar Larry Russell writes that pilgrimages involve simple, repetitive acts with deep consequences.[3] According to this description, each of the examples given above was a pilgrimage. And each one of these pilgrimages embodied consequences that went beyond the personal to the communal, from being a mundane act to becoming sacred ritual.

The Pilgrimage Begins Right Where You Are

Participating in a march to North Carolina's capitol building in Raleigh with other marchers and pilgrims, walking in prayer with a church group to a new piece of land, and going to see the historic relics of pioneers of justice are all pilgrimages. For some, pilgrimage is going annually to Graceland in Memphis, Tennessee, visiting the musical relics of none other than the late 1950s icon Elvis Presley. For others, taking a ride in a vintage

---

3. Russell, "A Description of Pilgrimage."

convertible—preferably a '63 Chevy Impala—along Route 66 may be a religious pilgrimage of sorts, with nostalgia ushering memories of the past to the present. Visiting or walking to the church that holds the iconic painting of the Black Madonna in Częstochowa, Poland, lighting votive candles and praying intercessory prayers in the presence of the icon is a pilgrimage. In the American South, returning to the church of your childhood for an annual homecoming celebration, after being away from that church (or any church) for years, is a kind of pilgrimage too. Going to a high school class reunion may be considered by some a pilgrimage. People stream year round to a place like El Santuario de Chimayo in New Mexico, or crawl on bended knees for over a mile to venerate the statue of El Cristo Negro in Esquipulas, Guatemala, or go to great lengths to celebrate Mass at the Basilica of Sainte-Anne-de-Beaupré in Quebec, Canada, seeking healing of mind, body, and spirit. Perhaps, dear reader, you've already been on a pilgrimage, but you just didn't realize it.

What makes each one of these people "a pilgrim"? Or the route one is on an example of a "pilgrimage"? One of the best responses I have received after leading a workshop on pilgrimage was given to me by a young middle school student who said that a pilgrim is someone who is seeking or looking for something important, while a pilgrimage is a "holy hike . . . just like the people in *The Lord of the Rings!*" While I laughed at his response at first, the more I thought about it, the more I came to agree: the Hobbits were pilgrims, returning the ring to the place of its origin, and a pilgrimage is a holy hike, a sacred walk, or a spiritual journey. After all, a pilgrimage involves a movement of body, mind, and spirit from one's current location (point A) to one's destination (point Z). As one person in essayist Gideon Lewis-Kraus's book on his pilgrimages around the world says, "[Pilgrimage is] a vacation. Okay, well, not exactly a vacation, but it's a religious reason to tell my wife and three kids that I need to be away. You know, to go and pray for our family so that we have a good and successful year."[4]

"It's a religious reason"—we go on this walk or move between two points with a certain sacred goal in mind. Pilgrimage is spiritual. This is a critical distinction marking the difference between a traveler and a pilgrim, between travel and pilgrimage. On a vacation or trip, one merely wants to get to the locale in order to play or rest, depending on the purpose of the vacation. When flying to Kona, Hawaii, my partner isn't "into" the flight; he simply longs to be on Hapuna Beach in a beach chair, stretched out,

---

4. Lewis-Kraus, *Sense of Direction*, 273.

listening to the surf and watching the sunset in the distance. Likewise for a hiker who wants to hike, a walker who wants to go at a certain pace, a flaneur who wants to roam merely for the sake of roaming, a runner who wants to better her time, or a biker who wants to ride a number of miles on his bike: there is a goal that has nothing to do with the journey itself. A pilgrimage is more than *just* a hike, a walk, a run, a bike ride, a vacation, or a journey. The spiritual quest or religious purpose makes a pilgrimage more than a vacation or a holiday jaunt by oneself or with one's family (hopefully a respite). Pilgrimage is the state of mind *and* heart or spirit that changes the vacation, the hike in the woods, the long kayak journey along an intercoastal strip of water, the ride out into the country, the walk to a friend's house, the errand in the middle of the day, the walking of a dog, the 5k run or marathon . . . *into a pilgrimage in which one encounters the Holy*. Benedictine monk David Steindl-Rast describes this very sentiment: when the pilgrim sets her foot on the ground, every step is a goal, and the pilgrim says "now, now, now"; she is living in the present and claiming the presence of the Holy God now in her midst, upon this soil, fully cognizant of the sacred land she walks upon. Steindl-Rast reminds us that the essence of pilgrimage is love, which is realized in each step the pilgrim takes in her life. And when we say "we love" or "I love," what we are saying is that we belong. Who do we belong to? God. For God is love. In other words, if a church—part of Christ's body—is on a pilgrimage, then every step the pilgrim people make forward, moving towards God, is a step or movement of love.[5] Whether we are on an actual pilgrimage or perceive that the road of life we are on is our pilgrimage, each step, each move one makes is blessed by the Spirit. For both an actual pilgrimage and the pilgrimage of everyday life is a journey of faith.

An Actual Pilgrimage and the Pilgrimage of Life

This is where pilgrimage gets interesting. Typically, a pilgrimage is perceived or constructed by many in religious communities as a set time for an individual or group of people away from one's ordinary, typical life. As a result, a pilgrim and pilgrimage is considered quite exotic. The pilgrim is someone who has been called to spend time away from the ordinary, and is financially able to take the time off or away from work or life to be on a

---

5. David Steindl-Rast, a leader in interfaith dialogue, shared his thoughts on love and forgiveness in his opening address to the Fetzer Institute's "Global Gathering: A Pilgrimage of Love and Forgiveness," in Assisi, Italy, on September 19, 2012.

pilgrimage. But the line between an actual pilgrimage and the pilgrimage of life is not only blurry or porous per se, but is a line that is constructed in the mind or imagination of the individual pilgrim. The actual pilgrimage is a special time *set within* the great pilgrimage of life itself. Because, as David Steindl-Rast reminds us above, wherever we are, whether on an actual pilgrimage or walking around our neighborhood church, going on a peace march, or making our way to church, a pilgrim is a pilgrim when one simply says in one's mind and repeats those words of "Now, now, now," aware of the sacredness of every step or movement one makes right where we are.

To be fair, an actual pilgrimage can be a sacred time, setting off for a set period of days, starting from a certain locale, walking or traveling over a certain geographic region to a certain location that is considered a holy place (destination), with or without a group of other pilgrims. This intentional pilgrimage may take place either in and around where one lives or in a more exotic locale, like Spain's Santiago de Compostela or the Holy Land. But what is interesting is that an actual pilgrimage may then become a catalyst for helping one reframe or reimagine one's ordinary life as a lifelong pilgrimage. Consider this: like an actual pilgrimage, as a member of a congregation we start off and have a set period of time (birth to death) for the walk, starting from a certain place (the place we were born), traveling many miles over a certain region of this earth, to a place where we will eventually die. For those of the Christian faith, the journey continues in the afterlife. Like an intentional pilgrimage, along the way we sometimes walk with a host of other people, or maybe with one companion, and at other times we walk alone, following Jesus the Pilgrim God. What the actual pilgrimage does to us is set us up to be pilgrims in everyday life with unexpected consequences, in which we can either construct or discover a life that is an ongoing, ever-expanding sojourn, in which we meet the Holy in unexpected ways.

Discovering Pilgrimage in the Pilgrimage of Life

Consider some of these examples in which the actual pilgrimage is discovered amid the pilgrimage of life. The title character of the novel *The Unlikely Pilgrimage of Harold Fry*, by Rachel Joyce, is Harold Fry, a retired executive who lives in southern England. One day he receives a note from a former colleague, Queenie, who lives and is dying in a hospice in Scotland. He writes a note to her, leaves his wife in a house to post the letter, only to start walking to Scotland right then and there, dressed as he is, with none of the pilgrim attire.⁶ It is only along the way to the hospice where Queenie lives that Harold slowly becomes the pilgrim that he is. Once a person or a group of people are doing something that is dedicated with a known or explicit sacred, spiritual, religious goal, or purpose for the greater good, or to serve a higher power, then everything about the person participating in the journey, one's very being, and the very character of a group of people on pilgrimage, changes dramatically (and sometimes comically) over time. The very route is no longer a walkway, path, trail, byway, highway, road, or avenue, but is transformed into a pilgrim path. Out of one's ordinary life, one becomes a pilgrim of life on a pilgrimage, a sacred journey, in which all the known world is the pathway of the Holy, and every day we walk on sacred ground.

Outside of this literary example, there is also the rise among the number of ordinary people who, unexpectedly, one day, out of the blue, identify themselves as pilgrims going on pilgrimage in this world. The essayist Robert Macfarlane writes eloquently about this change of view: "'we have been,' wrote the poet Edmund Blunden in 1942, 'increasingly *on* pilgrimage.' We are once again increasingly *on* pilgrimage."⁷ Macfarlane sees a rise in the number of ordinary, average people who, one day, suddenly find themselves going on pilgrimage throughout Europe, even though the number of people who are going to church is dwindling. Or many people randomly start constructing life itself as a pilgrimage. Macfarlane agrees that words like "pilgrim" and "pilgrimage" have become to many, especially secular people, a tiresome piety. Nonetheless, the pilgrims Macfarlane met were using words like "walking" or "pilgrimage" to make meaning of *this* world, where they lived, and their very average lives, in which one day people realize that they couldn't help calling themselves "pilgrims": "I couldn't find a better name for them than pilgrims."⁸ For some of Macfarlane's subjects who see everyday life as a pilgrimage, a pilgrimage is purely religious. For others, a pilgrimage is more social, political, familial, or cultural; but it is still, for them, a pilgrimage because the purpose of the trek is for the greater good of the group, however it defines the "good." In other words, in the religious and sacred alike, there is a sense of purpose in these pilgrimages, these journeys, in which the pilgrim is aiming for something greater

6. Joyce, *Unlikely Pilgrimage of Harold Fry.*
7. Macfarlane, *Old Ways*, 235.
8. Ibid., 236.

A "Pilgrimage" and the "Pilgrimage of Life"

than one's self. Life had become a pilgrimage, and the person, a pilgrim. According to Macfarlane, there is an understated movement occurring in this modern world of "quiet pilgrims," undertaking one's own kind of "slow travels" around the world. Macfarlane writes about people who simply walk along the moor paths of Lewis, England, tread a track between circles of stones set up by ancient people, sail sea roads through storms, try to understand the politics of geology, sleep in woods between Paris and Jerusalem for over a year, and follow old paths in the county of Northamptonshire (home of Britain's boot industry).[9]

Consider one man that Macfarlane meets from Dorset, England, who took a long walk, following chalk paths that disappear over green hills into the uncertain distance; his life has never been the same. "Once walked . . . the old ways inhabit us. Even here, now, in the green and low southwest, I often find myself looking high for a beaten chalk path, recalling those days of strange liberation." Later, MacFarlane met up with a man who had set out from London and walked to "St. Gallen in Switzerland, where he grew up as a child, carrying his father's ashes with him, sleeping in a small tent by the sides of vast alfalfa prairies and crop fields in northern France."[10] In one's ordinary life, a person simply may discover one day that she or he is living or has been living a life of pilgrimage! Sometimes being on an actual pilgrimage reveals this "aha" moment that opens others to the realization that everyday life is a pilgrimage. Other times, it is the slow realization of what is happening as we walk that road, travel that path, drive that blue highway, or ride that waterway that lets us know we are on a pilgrimage in our everyday life.

That's the thing about being on an actual pilgrimage and the pilgrimage of life: on an actual pilgrimage, sometimes we need a *credencial*—the passport book given to those on the Camino de Santiago de Compostela—to remind ourselves we are on a pilgrimage, craving or needing the "official" designation that we are a certified "pilgrim." And there are others who quietly are or are becoming pilgrims, and get on their pilgrimage right where they are. Hape Kerkeling, a German comedian who happened one day to simply start walking toward the Camino from his home in Germany, wrote, "'I'm off then!' I didn't tell my friends much more than that before I started out—just that I was going to hike through Spain. My friend Isabel had only

---

9. Ibid.
10. Ibid., 237.

this to say: 'Have you lost your mind?' I'd decided to go on a pilgrimage."[11] And on that day he went on an actual pilgrimage. But as Kerkeling says at the end of the book, he now considers that in his life, he is and always will be a pilgrim.

Or consider this example from my walk across England. I co-led a pilgrimage along Hadrian's Wall in England with a group of people who expressly went out to walk on a pilgrimage from the University of North Carolina Presbyterian Campus Ministry. We walked across England. Now and then along the pathway that we followed, walking west to east with the wind at our back, we would meet up with other walkers along the way. Some people we simply caught up with and passed, while others chose the east to west route. And that's exactly who they were: they were walkers, not pilgrims. Some were taking a stroll. Others were clearly enjoying the day hike. Still others were researchers, doing studies on the historic remnants of Hadrian's Wall. But our group? It took us awhile to figure out that we called ourselves "pilgrims on a pilgrimage." At first, we were simply a group of individual people from the Chapel Hill area, but slowly throughout the week of walking together we became pilgrims on a holy pilgrimage. Granted: there weren't a lot of sacred sites on the western end where we started near Bowness-on-Solway. But what made the pilgrimage a pilgrimage was not necessarily the places per se, but the people whose hearts and minds were dedicated to being and becoming pilgrims. And here's the thing: when the students went home, some of them discovered that the pilgrimage continued. Not only did they think *about* the actual pilgrimage they went on, but they also started to think about themselves as one of Jesus's followers, one of the pilgrims of the Pilgrim God, and the life before them was becoming a pilgrimage of sorts.

Finally, in the interplay between going on an actual pilgrimage and the lessons learned on the road of life, right where we are, on this pilgrimage of life we live daily, in both cases we do not walk alone, but are most often visited by the presence of the Holy. When a person starts an actual pilgrimage or realizes that life *is* a pilgrimage, no longer does one necessarily control the outcome of the specific journey or journey of life. Nor do we control the ways of the Holy who may interrupt our very lives. Sometimes, we may be able to negotiate what happens along the way. But there may be variables or exigencies that are simply out of our control, leading us to a place that takes us far out of our comfort zone on an actual pilgrimage or

---

11. Kerkeling, *I'm Off Then*, 1.

the pilgrimage of life. Annie Dillard writes of eighteenth-century Hasidic Jews who acted as if every day was a pilgrimage, of sorts—at any moment they could be called by God to leave their family and friends:

> A rabbi refused to promise a friend to visit him the next day: "How can you ask me to make such a promise? This evening I must pray and recite 'Hear, O Israel.' While I say these words, my soul goes out to the utmost rim of life . . . Perhaps I shall not die this time either, but how can I now promise to do something at a time after the prayer?"[12]

I can no longer count the times that the unexpected presence of the Holy Spirit was and is made present during a long or short pilgrimage, or the pilgrimage of my daily life. The Holy Spirit simply shows up, often when least expected, yet usually when most needed and necessary, or so I have learned after the fact. The presence of grace is often known retrospectively, rather than prospectively. Though I've not been taken yet to the utmost rim of life, wondering if I would ever physically return, there is no doubt that I've been on actual pilgrimages after which my life was never the same again. And I've found myself in the everydayness of life's pilgrimage, surprised by God's immanent presence within my life. The Spirit is often recognized if I just get out of the way of trying to control my lifelong pilgrimage. To quote my 12 step friends: God often does for us what we cannot do for ourselves.

Why We Go on Pilgrimage

During a conversation on the way to one of the eighty-eight temples of Shikoku Island, Japan, a pilgrim tells Gideon Lewis-Kraus that they had to go on pilgrimage to get through grief: "So I searched for a sacred walk, and this has been just what I needed."[13]

As a Christian, I discovered that I am on a pilgrimage every day of my life, a pilgrim of God following Jesus, after going on an actual pilgrimage, or set time aside in life to seriously be a pilgrim. To this day, I go on an actual pilgrimage to, first, experience the Holy on pilgrimage. More precisely, I know I will encounter Christ's Spirit, who is also known to me as the Pilgrim God. In order to do that, I need to leave behind the hurly-burly of my daily life. I enjoy the work of being a professor, consultant, writer, preacher,

---

12. Dillard, *Teaching a Stone to Talk*, 41.
13. Lewis-Kraus, *Sense of Direction*, 199.

workshop leader, parent, partner, dog owner, gym user, yoga practitioner, and all-around cultural gadfly. On pilgrimage, I find new life as I get away from it all and reflect about where I've been in my daily life. I focus on more spiritual matters of the heart, mind, and body (often with focus on the heart). Sometimes I go to challenge my body to do the impossible by walking long distances.

The second primary reason I go on pilgrimage is to reset my daily routine and habits of where I live every day of my life, asking myself, "What will I experience in today's pilgrimage life?" Soon, I will keep forgetting to ask myself this question. I quickly get sucked into the quotidian moments of life. I easily find myself in ruts, making little progress at all, and need the physical time on the road, walking, making progress each day, to recognize that I am moving, progressing, not standing still. That is why I then set off on another pilgrimage to reorient my life to remind me that life is a pilgrimage of unexpected encounters with the Holy.

Third reason for pilgrimage? I go on pilgrimage in order to relearn what it means to be open to the unexpected, meeting up with the stranger, or being the stranger. As pastor, teacher, and speaker, I usually find myself among a group of people in a place in which I am the host, welcoming the stranger. On pilgrimage, I push myself out of a routine of the expected and known as host, placing myself into the role and function of stranger, and that often makes all the difference in my life.

Why do others go on pilgrimage? I have walked with pilgrims who are Buddhist whose experience of pilgrimage is different than mine, but their experience of the sacred comes in unique expressions that I covet with them. I go on a pilgrimage outside of my Christian context to learn about other world religions and pilgrimage. My sisters and brothers who are Hindu remind me that Ganesha, the elephant, is the god of traveling, removing obstructions along the way of life. As I walk with my brother and sister who are Muslim and Jewish, especially wandering in the arid desert area of the Sinai peninsula, the birthplace of these desert religions, the stories of Abraham and Ibrahim, Isaac and Ishmael, Sarah and Hagar, come to the fore.

There are also those who go on what they would call a pilgrimage but with more of a secular tilt than sacred, which I honor. I am reminded of the pilgrims I met on the Camino to Santiago de Compostela, as they read aloud to me parts of Shirley MacLaine's autobiography in which she encountered past lives she never experienced before until she walked the

A "Pilgrimage" and the "Pilgrimage of Life"

Camino. Another German lesbian couple had been recently married, and that's why they were walking the Camino. They were not in search of God or a cause more spiritual or sacred than to walk the Camino with one another. A young man I met at dinner one night regaled a table full of pilgrims with stories of his former girlfriends. The reason he was on the Camino seven times was to forget seven girlfriends. No search for the Holy here, just trips away from the heartache in order to find a little solace and space.

Closer to home, there are those who engage every year in the 10k CROP Walk of Church World Services (CWS) in Carrboro and Chapel Hill, along with many communities around the country. Such walks are an opportunity for each person who goes on the walk to raise some money for those who are hungry and homeless. People donate money to a walker for each kilometer they walk. People who run, walk, or bike this 10k do so for a variety of reasons: some do it out of religious conviction of loving their neighbor, while others may have more humanistic reasons for the journey. In the past, I've heard the phrase that *we* walk because they cannot walk, with the purpose of walking to raise money for building a well for clean drinking water. Finally, every June, more than 150 people go on a rugged pilgrimage to El Santuario de Chimayo in northern New Mexico, under the auspices of the Archdiocese of Santa Fe. Everyone leaves the comfort of home and church, family and friends, to walk one hundred and twenty miles over a period of five and a half days. They go because a family member is going, a priest, or a dad or uncle, mom or aunt, or a grandparent, suggested it would be good. Some travel a great distance to join the throng of the faithful to be enriched, while still others go because it is a test of one's physical fitness, even though the "purpose" is one of "vocations" in the church.

The World Is a Place for Pilgrimage

While St. Francis said that the world is our cloister, the world is also a place for pilgrimage, no matter where we live. For example, I was reminded about the dailiness of pilgrimage right where I am when worshipping one morning with the members of United Church of Chapel Hill. The first aha moment came when the pastor welcomed the church's new members with the words, "Today we rejoice in your pilgrimage of faith which has brought you to this time and place. We give thanks for every community of faith that has been your spiritual home, and we celebrate your presence in this household of faith."[14] This theme of daily pilgrimage emerged again when we sang these words from the hymn "O Word of God Incarnate":

> O make your church, dear Savior,
> a lamp of purest gold,
> to bear before all people
> your true light as of old!
> O teach your wandering pilgrims
> by this their path to trace,
> till, doubt and striving ended,
> they meet you face to face.[15]

In further exploring the ties between an actual pilgrimage and the pilgrimage of life, the next things to consider are the characteristics of being a pilgrim, what a pilgrimage is, and its importance for everyday pilgrimage, which will be explored in the next chapter.

---

14. *The New Century Hymnal*, 46.
15. William Walsham How, "O Word of God Incarnate," in *New Century Hymnal*, 315.

2

The Story of Pilgrimage

Humans are animals and like all animals we leave tracks as we walk: signs of passage made in snow, sand, mud, grass, dew, earth, or moss.—Robert Macfarlane[1]

Always, everywhere, people have walked, veining the earth with paths visible and invisible, symmetrical or meandering.
—Thomas Clark[2]

I thought when I got to Santiago that the pilgrimage would be at its end—that when you're walking the Camino you keep thinking of Santiago as your goal. But once you arrive in Santiago you realize that the pilgrimage has only begun, that you will be "walking the Camino" the rest of your life. —Kevin Sessums[3]

A Pilgrimage Story

For two years, I was blessed to join Sr. Stef Weisgram, OSB, on a pilgrimage to Esquipulas, Guatemala, to the Abbey of Jesus Christ Crucified, affixed to the Basilica, which is home to El Cristo Negro (the Black Christ). Not only Guatemalans but also people from other countries in Central America, from South America, along with some from the United States, come to see and venerate Esquipulas' El Cristo Negro. This life-size statue of Jesus captures him on the cross, dying, with Mary Magdalene and John witnessing

---

1. Macfarlane, *Old Ways*, 13.
2. Quoted in ibid.
3. Personal conversation with Kevin Sessums.

Practicing Pilgrimage—Part I

the horror of his death. It is a statue carved in Antigua by Quirio Catano in 1593. It is carved out of orange wood, commissioned by the Spanish conquistadors. By 1603 a miracle had been attributed to the iconic statue, drawing more attention from the locals in the area. One of those who experienced a miracle in the presence of the statue was a young priest who, when he became the Archbishop of Guatemala, moved the statue to its present locale in the Basilica. The secret behind it may be this: because it was carved out of orange wood, the moment that the freshly carved bark of the tree was exposed to air, it began to darken almost immediately, to approximate the color of skin of the native people. In a clever way, the black wood statue of the dying Jesus was a great tool for evangelical purposes, as it brought people to the church in then-Guatemala City. There were many stories of conversion and a miracle not only by those who visited the statue in the church, but also by those who caught a glimpse of it along the way as the statue was slowly moved to its current home south of the capitol.

Esquipulas is located in the southernmost part of Guatemala, a good two hours by car from Guatemala City. El Cristo Negro is located in the white stucco Basilica, front and center of the viewing public's eye. In order to get close to the statue, people walk through a zig-zag maze, created by someone who must have worked at Disney World. The statue of El Cristo Negro is housed in a glass booth that leaves it protected in a climate-controlled atmosphere. I watched as pilgrims walked toward the glass enclosure, first passing by a large wooden statue of Jesus crawling on the ground, his whipped back red with painted blood, carrying the cross. There were crutches and canes on the wall, pointing to the evidence that some who have come here were healed. When one comes into the elevated space around the figures of Mary Magdalene, St. John, and Jesus, there is usually a variety of responses: some are quiet and reverential, while other pilgrims weep openly; some hold up an article of clothing they want blessed by its proximity to the holy figures. Out of reverence, pilgrims slowly walk backwards away from the ensemble, believing it would be disrespectful to turn one's back on the Christ.

After visiting Esquipulas, and before taking off for the United States, I spent a night at the Maryknoll house in Guatemala City. One of the members of the Maryknoll community scoffed at the idea of pilgrimage. He suggested the ease of creating a pilgrimage site with the following illustration: imagine that a donkey dies on the side of a road between modern day Jerusalem and Bethlehem. The donkey's owner buries the donkey and places a small sign on the place the donkey is buried and a wooden cross. Suddenly a group of people on pilgrimage in the area see the cross, misinterpret the sign and believe that possibly this is the burial plot of the donkey who took the Holy Family to Egypt, escaping Herod's slaughter of the innocents. Soon, other pilgrims come to this site and begin to honor this site, venerating the lowly donkey that was chosen among all the donkeys for the high task of carrying the Holy Family to a safe locale. Before you know it, a stone edifice is created, along with souvenirs honoring the lowly donkey; songs are composed to honor the donkey; a new saint honored who may have tended the donkey. "Voila! A pilgrimage site is born out of nothing!" said the Maryknoll brother. I smiled, uncomfortably, having watched and interviewed a handful of pilgrims whose lives seemed transformed, simply by venerating El Cristo Negro.

Building a Shrine 101

The Maryknoll brother has a point: there is a hunger that people have within them for physical evidence of the ephemeral holy in uncertain times. But what this points to is a deeper truth: *people* make a site holy, not the place itself. In Matthew 18:20 Jesus said, "For where two or three are gathered in my name, I am there among them." Christians believe that when two or three people are gathered in Jesus's name, Christ's Spirit is present among them. And as people gathered in Jesus's name, some believe that the very place where people have gathered is endowed with a sense of the Holy or sacred. Religion scholar Mircea Eliade wrote that what makes a rock, a tree, or a shrine in a high place holy is because something significant happened at this spot—a birth; a death; a significant milestone in one's life—thus altering the spot from being "normal" to being highly unusual. A physical place is bound up with a metaphysical event, and what is born is a sense of the sacred, as if there were a thin membrane between the initiate (human) and the Holy at this place. And once that place is designated as holy, a shrine of sorts, then expect a pilgrimage to be born, with many people coming and paying homage or venerating the site for years to come. After all, El Cristo Negro is a holy site because of the people who have experienced a miracle in their lives when venerating these figures.

Eliade's description of a shrine or temple, places where one experiences a thin membrane between human beings—the initiators—and the Holy or the sacred, are core to both secular (or profane) and sacred pilgrimage

Practicing Pilgrimage—Part I

experiences. For example, living in the college town of Chapel Hill, North Carolina, there is the "Old Well" on the campus of the University of North Carolina. There is a small marble podium that was once a drinking fountain underneath a canopy held up by white columns. The Old Well used to be a well when the college was first founded in the late 1700s. But with all the events that have taken place around the well, with people becoming engaged there, wedded around it, the site of graduation pictures and prom date photos, the Old Well has become iconic, a shrine, where generations upon generations of Chapel Hill graduates come back and sing songs, regaling each other with stories of lives changed. The site is emblazoned on T-shirts, mugs, bumper stickers, stationary, and baseball caps.

Likewise, in old town Tucson there is a shrine, *El Tiradito,* that is an old, crumbling brick wall, with several *Santos* or crosses nailed into the wall. There is a large metal rack for small burning votive candles, with plants (largely cacti) artistically arrayed, making it easy to walk from the sidewalk to the crumbling wall. In the brick wall, where there may be some mortar missing, are slips of paper that people have left with written prayers on them, much like prayers left in Israel's Western Wall. The Catholic shrine was set up for a man who once died for the love of a woman. It is the only non-consecrated cemetery with a sinner buried in the grounds. The people leave prayers asking that the man be freed from purgatory, or they may light a candle for the healing of their wounded hearts.

Key to all pilgrimages is both a *reason* for leaving and a place of departure, the genesis of the journey, *and* the destination point. I will say more about this later in the book, but the place, group of people, or more importantly the *reason* that people go on pilgrimage does not seem to have the same weight to it as does the place where they are going. The shrine, the people, the high place, the focus on the destination, is the draw, the lure, the bait, for the pilgrim going on pilgrimage. I'm aware of those who write that the journey is the thing, but one wouldn't be on the journey if it weren't for the bait of the destination. For example, in *Pilgrim's Progress,* John Bunyan's pilgrim is eager to leave the crisis within his home (Bunyan wrote these words while he himself was in prison), and the focus of the entire book is where he is headed: the gates of heaven. When a pilgrim begins the Camino de Santiago de Compostela, the focus is on getting to the Credentials Office in the city to receive a certificate that makes it official: you are a pilgrim of Santiago de Compostela. And it includes making it to the Cathedral in Compostela to hear your country's name read aloud during the following day's mass, with hopes of watching the largest incense burner in the world swing right before your eyes. A pilgrim who spends time in the Holy Land most likely focuses not on only on going to Bethlehem to see the site of the birthplace of Jesus, but is pressed to go to the Church of the Holy Sepulcher, the place of Jesus's death and resurrection. The destination is front and center in every pilgrim's mind, heart, and body, for it is the *raison d'etre* of the pilgrimage itself. Getting there is a time of celebration, exhaling, great joy, and yet also an occasion for sadness and melancholy, as a person realizes that this incredible time in one's life has drawn to a close. No more walking and seeing other sights from other vantage points. No more time with the people that we may have come to know better in the past few days. No more meeting up with strangers along the way. Time to go back to the "ordinary." However, one is never the same again after a pilgrimage.

Essayist Gideon Lewis-Kraus rightly observes that religious pilgrimage can serve as either socialization, as a "rite of passage," or as therapy, depending upon the pilgrim's wants and needs. The groundbreaking anthropologists Victor and Edith Turner, who focused on the sociology of pilgrimage, envisioned pilgrimage as a "liminal" experience, especially during times of initiation into a community or of blowing off some steam. In a liminal state, a person is on the threshold of change, being in between a phase of life, from the old to the new. Of course, this could be an argument about Christianity or other religions, in which a person lives in the "now" but also in the "yet to come," as in the time of Christ's return.

Lewis-Kraus writes that the reason religious folks go on pilgrimage is threefold: sin, penance, and redemption. The sin is because the person turned one's back to God. The penance is a way of working through the suffering brought on by the sin, as well as by the very walk itself. And the redemption is found through nothing less than amazing grace, which is experienced at the end of the pilgrimage. For secular people, Lewis-Kraus writes that these ideas might translate to the following reasons for going on pilgrimage: anxiety, austerity, and forgiveness. Being anxious comes from past decisions gone awry, with the weight of second guessing. The time of austerity comes on a pilgrimage, which is to literally strip away those things that no longer matter in one's current life. And forgiveness is a kind of resolution to accept the parts of life's conflicts that we simply cannot change. Writes Lewis-Kraus, "On pilgrimage, privation is endured, shared, and collectively encouraged as part of the aspiration to *want less*, at least for the moment—and not only to *want less* for ourselves, but, perhaps even more important, to *need less* from others and, at the same time, to be able to recognize their suffering and give them more."[4]

This leads to the next question, which revolves around a question asked in the previous chapter: What or who is a religious pilgrim? And what is a sacred pilgrimage?

What Is a Pilgrim?

The word *pilgrim* comes from the Old French *pelegrin*, Middle English *pelegrim*, and French, *pelegrinius*. The Latin *pelegrinus* refers to the wayfarer or foreigner on a journey, traveling to a shrine or holy place. One can see the roots for the modern Spanish word for pilgrim in these various languages: *pelegrino*. What is wonderful in such word play is the double meaning of some words in translation. For example, the Latin *pelegrinus* also means "from abroad," and *per agrum* can mean "through the field."[5] To be a pilgrim is to be a person on the move, where a change is afoot. One may be facing difficulties at home, or simply seeking solitude while on the journey; the reason for one's trek may be religious or secular, the destination a shrine or a landmark.

Among the many characteristics of a pilgrim, there are three that I would like to lift up.

1. A Pilgrim Is Never Alone

There are as many variations on how to be pilgrim as there are pilgrims. There are times that we find ourselves more like one of Geoffrey Chaucer's pilgrims on the way to Canterbury, chatting with many who are on the way. At times, we may walk two by two as they do in the planned Pilgrimage of Vocations to Chimayo, New Mexico, every June. And then there are the times that we *seem* to be alone on a journey, walking by one's self as many choose to do on the Camino de Santiago de Compostela. Walking alone on pilgrimage is very much in the fashion of John Bunyan's "Pilgrim" in *Pilgrim's Progress*, who leaves family, home, and the village in the "City of Destruction" to seek the "Celestial City."[6] Because pilgrimage is a blessed

---

4. Lewis-Kraus, *Sense of Direction*, 122–23.
5. Cousineau, *Art of Pilgrimage*, 9.
6. Bunyan, *Pilgrim's Progress*.

or sacred time, as the Christian pilgrim has thrown down a challenge to the ordinariness of life, one is really not alone when one undertakes an intentional pilgrimage. One is accompanied by the Spirit of Christ on such journeys, and by the rest of nature, including other living creatures, from mosquitoes to the stray dog that follows you for days on the Camino. The question: is one ever alone on a pilgrimage? The issue of being in the company of others or being alone is also pertinent to the pilgrimage of life: there are times we are surrounded by others whose company we choose to keep, and there are times we may feel all alone, even though we may find ourselves standing in a crowd of people. But are we ever really alone if God's Spirit is everywhere?

2. A Pilgrim Is on a Blessed Time, with Challenge and Joy

The root word for *travel* is *travail*, from the Latin *tripalium*, which in the Middle Ages literally meant "torture rack."[7] Granted, there are times when travel on the pilgrimage can be a challenge; it can feel more like a medieval torture rack than a blessed time, or a joke one can laugh at in the coming years. But there are stretches of the pilgrimage that challenge mind, body, and spirit, that are not to be avoided but rather embraced, because they usually lead to deeper, more meaningful understandings of pilgrimage in particular, and hold greater life lessons in general. Oftentimes, at these difficult junctures there are options. For example, we can see a challenge as a momentary "hump" that we can get over, remembering all the other times we got over similar "humps" in our lives before. Or, we are to seek the company of others, because no pilgrim makes it happen by one's self, but by the unexpected strangers, new and old friends, who pop up along the way.

The blessed time of pilgrimage was reinforced throughout the years on the pilgrimage to Chimayo. At various chapels and small places of devotions, whenever and wherever other people hosted our pilgrim group, the host group would line up single file, and as we passed them some would hug us individually, while some would put a scrap of paper in our hands with a written prayer before we left the premises. At earlier pilgrimages with this group, I remember a woman in her late eighties taking the hand of a timid thirteen-year-old boy and asking him for a blessing: "This is a time for saintly people," she asked the boy: "Bless me?" Surprised and frozen in

---

7. Cousineau, *Art of Pilgrimage*, 9.

place, she carefully took his hand and helped him trace the sign of the cross on his forehead. For her, and now the young boy, it was a blessed time.

Similarly, in the daily life of pilgrimage we experience challenges daily that catch us off guard, causing us to dig deep and embrace the challenge, finding its lesson for us. Or we have the chance to bring our troubles to our community—seeking succor from those who know us best.

3. Once a Pilgrim, Always a Pilgrim

As stated earlier, I went on my first pilgrimage in 1999. It was a life-transforming experience that changed my understanding of the very nature of the church as a more or less static organism that stays in one place and vibrates with life; I came to see it as the walking, sojourning body of Christ. Because of this change, I devoted my life to continuing to go on more pilgrimages so that I could better understand the nature of both pilgrimage and the church. But even if it had been my one and only pilgrimage, my hunch is that I would have remembered it always; I threw down a challenge to the ordinariness of life and walked away a new person. Every time I hear the word *pilgrimage* or *pilgrim* I am instantly taken back to that first pilgrimage, as would someone who only went on one journey. The memories of a pilgrimage last a lifetime.

On life's pilgrimage, I'm more aware of how much the surrounding society uses the language of "journey" and "quest." There are television shows like *Game of Thrones* that are packed with pilgrimage references, while musicians have written about journeys and "the long and winding road" (Beatles) over the years. These surprising social and cultural references from secular sources are helpful reminders of the journey of life before all of us.

Some Defining Characteristics of a "Pilgrimage"

A Pilgrimage Is an Act of Mind, Body, and Spirit

A pilgrimage is like a puzzle, in which the various parts of my life are thrown up in the air while on the journey, only to come back down and reassemble themselves, yet in a new pattern. That's how transformational a pilgrimage feels, refiguring one's very life. I say a prayer before each and every pilgrimage, knowing that I will not be the same person who started the pilgrimage by the end of the quest. Though this may sound simplistic, my mind literally fights with my spirit and body on pilgrimage, as my body may have hit a "wall," much like a marathoner hits a wall in a 26.2 mile run, but with the strength of the mind, even though exhausted, I push onward to the goal that day. I've walked with blisters on both heels, blisters on top of and in old blisters, as well as blisters on the toes, and a knee that became sorer each and every day. Often times, walking is a matter of "mind over body" at those points, in which my mind kept on trying to think of different ways of walking to alleviate the pain, or to rationalize the journey by saying, "this will all be forgotten soon, and something I will laugh at in years to come." That works too.

As an example of pushing one's body by using one's mind and spirit (with or without group effort), consider the pilgrimage along Hadrian's Wall. The group of pilgrims I was walking with was tiring quickly. After a short break, though our bodies were tired, we began to sing campfire songs together. Within minutes, our spirits rebounded and we made it to the town and pub of Once Brewed, our destination that day. Likewise, in the pilgrimage of daily life, our spirit or mind may be burdened with a certain heaviness, filled with lists of things to do, agendas (self and others), ideas, and feelings that the only outlet left to us is to walk it out. As mentioned earlier, there is something to the physical act of walking that helps sort out some of the confusion that we may feel inside.

It Is a Spiritual Act

Religion scholar Huston Smith wrote that pilgrimage is more than an act of body, mind, and spirit. It is belief in action.[8] On pilgrimage, the pilgrim makes a low bow, and at points, kneels, as women and men visit places where great heroes of one's faith may have lived or died, as well as visit shrines where people for generations say that they experienced a sense of God's presence.

As mentioned in the last chapter, for some, pilgrimage is understood in terms of sin, penance, and redemption.[9] This especially rings true for the medieval pilgrimages to Rome, Jerusalem, and Santiago de Compostela. Prior to the Reformation, the pilgrimage routes were a well-known way for a person to escape Purgatory through the payment of indulgences while on

---

8. Quoted in Cousineau, *Art of Pilgrimage*, 107–8.
9. Lewis-Kraus, *Sense of Direction*, 121.

the pilgrimage itself. One pilgrim told me that I would work myself out of going to Purgatory if I went three times to St. Patrick's Purgatory, a site on Lough Derg (the Dark Lake) in Ireland.

In the pilgrimage of daily life, sometimes the simple act of going to worship is faith in action. To worship God, to gather with others in praise of Christ, to be part of a service project, to go and practice hospitality, to "love our neighbor as we love ourselves," as Jesus commands—these are examples of how our faith is engaged, in action, on the pilgrimage of our lives.

Pilgrimage Is Treading on Sacred Geography

There are no doubt some places where people believe the land, the earth, is sacred and to be held in reverence by one and all. Such places include Taos Pueblo, Chimayo, Christ in the Desert Monastery, and Abiquiu in northern New Mexico, where Georgia O'Keefe herself said that the Spirit of Christ is draped over the land. Writer Flannery O'Connor talks about the Southeast as the "Christ-haunted" landscape, with churches dotted all over the land, and at least four churches on every street corner in small Southern towns. When on pilgrimage in the Sinai desert on camelback, my friend Henry Carse repeatedly drew my attention to the fact that the people of Israel walked this land for generations. From enjoying a lunch with a group of current-day pilgrims at an oasis where Moses and his followers encamped (mentioned in Num 33:3), to St. Catherine's Monastery, the base camp for the trek to the top of Mt. Sinai where El Shaddai gave Moses the Ten Commandments, this land is holy land, where God revealed God's self over generations of those who followed him, whether by a cloud of dust by day or a pillar of fire at night. The land itself is a sacred text of sorts, only to be understood by walking on it, or riding on camelback. Having been on the island of Iona in Scotland, along with a trek to Lindisfarne—the Holy Isle—from Melrose Abbey, one is reminded that this land is equally sacred too, as is the land around St. Patrick's Purgatory and Croagh Patrick, where St. Patrick scared the snakes out of Ireland.

What these lands have in common is a sense that "something has happened here," with and among a group of people, that is hard to put in words. To go back to Eliade's understanding that there are some shrines where there is a thin membrane where one seems to be closer to the Holy than other places, so this land almost reverberates with the presence of God. To make this point clearer, after one pilgrimage to Chimayo, in which the

Roman Catholic Church was celebrating four hundred years of inhabiting parts of northern New Mexico, one deacon of the church leaned over to me and whispered in my ear, "Yeah, but God was here a long time before the church got here."

In the South, many churches celebrate "Homecoming" events, in which former pastors, members, and friends of a community come back once a year for part celebration and part revival in the life of a congregation. People will return to the very pews they used to sit in Sunday after Sunday, as well as visit the cemetery in the back of many rural churches. The sanctuaries and education buildings, built with human hands, are also built on sacred, holy grounds.

The "Why" behind Pilgrimage

It is fair to say that there are as many reasons to go on pilgrimage as there are people who are pilgrims. Each of us has his or her own reason: curiosity; a need to break out of the ordinary rut of daily life and shake things up; a physical, spiritual, intellectual, or emotional challenge by someone else or by one's self; a crisis—or crises—at home that needs to be atoned for; or perhaps a sense of calling. I've also met people who went on pilgrimage for secular reasons, like physical exercise over a long span of time. For example, consider the people I met on the Camino de Santiago who went for a wide assortment of reasons. There were many who, like myself, wanted to go on the medieval pilgrimage because of its history and lore. As referenced in chapter 1, the German comic Hape Kerkeling is well known for starting the Camino from his home in Germany in a supine position, quickly finding transportation to St. Jean-Pied-de-Port in France, and walking the entire way to Santiago de Compostela. Writes Kerkeling, "People have undertaken the journey to Saint James when they have no other way of going on with their lives—figuratively or literally."[10] Others were lost in their addiction—alcohol, drug, sex, to name a few—and, having hit bottom, the pilgrimage gave them a chance to gain some perspective behind their addiction, leading them to an Alcoholics or Narcotics Anonymous program upon returning to their homes. I already mentioned the fans of Shirley MacLaine on the Camino, the young man who kept on breaking up with young women, and the lesbian couple from Germany celebrating an anniversary and wanting to go for a nice walk in the woods.

10. Kerkeling, *I'm Off Then*, 3.

Practicing Pilgrimage—Part I

For the life of pilgrimage, envisioning that we are all on a journey, each one of us leaves home and family every day for jobs, schools, and other obligations. Simply walking outside the door of the abode, in which we live, for whatever purpose, is an excuse for us to meet the world, and the people in it, anew. And thus, a new adventure begins.

Three general categories that many of us fall into for going on an actual pilgrimage may include the following

1. To Leave because of a Great Crisis: Genesis of the Journey

As mentioned earlier, like many stories intentional pilgrimages have a beginning, a middle, and an end. I am uncertain as to when the beginning of a pilgrimage starts, believing that perhaps it is when we get the first inclination to go on a pilgrimage (and likewise about the open-endedness of the conclusion of a journey). Nevertheless, there is a beginning, a genesis, a "Point A" where a pilgrim on the Camino can confidently say, "I started at St. Jean" or, if walking along Hadrian's Wall, "I began at Bowness-on-Solway."

But that is the *physical* beginning. There are the spiritual, emotional, or psychological reasons that one starts a pilgrimage. A classic reason to go is because one's life is messed up beyond repair where we live, that we must go and try to get distance in order to figure out what is happening. This does not mean that we are running away from problems, but merely saying that our chaos is all-consuming and that we must take a walk and process how and why we are in the place we find ourselves. As mentioned earlier, the classic case in point for such a reason is John Bunyan's "Christian," the paradigmatic pilgrim, whose reason for going on pilgrimage is because of the sense of crisis at home. Bunyan, himself, wrote the book while in prison because of religious persecution, which was reason enough for wanting to go on pilgrimage. Bunyan's pilgrim, "Christian," is the protagonist of the story, which focuses on his journey from his hometown, the "City of Destruction" or the world, to the "Celestial City," which is heaven, atop of Mt. Zion. Christian is fully aware of his sin, which he believed came from reading the book in his hand, which was the Bible. The burden is so great, that he must escape the City of Destruction or face the possibility of sinking into hell. So he leaves family and home (unable to persuade them to come) and sets off, with the Evangelist (John) as the guide to the Celestial City.

Throughout the years, I have met up with many people who express a variation on this theme in their everyday life. At home, they were lost, despondent, depressed, uneasy, hesitant about where life was going, and they needed to take a break or throw a challenge to the ordinariness of life, and go on pilgrimage. As mentioned earlier in this text, learning, reflection, processing goes on when walking or moving on a pilgrimage. What feels like a jumble in one's mind is parsed out or easier to categorize with some distance from the chaos in which one lives. With time and distance, with the physical demands of a pilgrimage, with times of solitude and times of socializing, there may be a moment of "aha," of transformation, of being freed from the cumbersome load to a sense of freedom.

2. The Journey

Each of us has our own journey of life. No two are the same. Even if two people walk the same physical or psychological path, because we are unique in so many ways, we experience the trail we are on differently. Many folks agree with Homer that "the journey is the thing," not necessarily the destination.

It is on the trail, while walking, where we create and discover the stories that will last a moment or a lifetime. It is on the pathway, in the silence, that we will find ourselves in conversation with the Holy, dealing with previously unconscious ideas, with new images, and conversation with the Pilgrim God suddenly comes bubbling forth. It is along this piece of dirt that we walk where we will meet strangers who might soon become best friends, at least for the moment. It is as we wander that we ponder and reflect on our inner biases, prejudices, patterns of dysfunction, and awkward habits that destroy others and ourselves, rather than lift up the best of us. And during the stroll we may give ourselves permission to kick up our heels and dance.

The trail we are on today will be totally different tomorrow. Even if we don't see the minutiae of growth in the flora and fauna of a trail, or the rushing water of the trail, it is all changing, as are we, the pilgrims. And it is focusing on the details of the beauty around us—whether the succulent cacti of the desert of the Sinai or the dense forest of the upper altitude of the Camino—that makes the pilgrimage unforgettable.

One experiment I like to do to awaken novice pilgrims on the pilgrimage route is to first travel over a landscape in a car or minivan, or even by bike or motorcycle. The person sees some of the beauty of the land in general broad-brush strokes, but misses the details that make up the broad, gorgeous stretches before us. It is isn't until we start to walk the land, even

Practicing Pilgrimage—Part I

walking slowly on the land, that we start to take in the beauty that is all around us.

Another practice I use on pilgrimage to awaken the eye to the surrounding beauty is as follows: Walk a certain distance of the pilgrimage headed one way, noting the beauty around and about you. Cover around a few yards or a mile (if you have the time). Then stop, and turn around and cover the same ground you just covered, taking in the new horizon, plants, and people around you. In truth, it is a wholly different trail than the one we were just on only a few minutes earlier, but our perspective has changed. We have changed. Same geography as outlined on a map, but different angle of taking it all in, which, of course, makes all the difference.

One final practice I like to partake of when on pilgrimage is silent prayerful contemplation. We may have a rosary to bring us to prayer, a rubbing stone, or a small seashell (my preference). On pilgrimage, when praying we find ourselves in the hands of God, walking alongside the Pilgrim God. Focusing on the silence, listening to feet fall upon leaves and stones, we suddenly hear the birds around us, perhaps a dog bark. Perhaps we also sense the deep presence of the Spirit, and the radical union with God that can never be taken away. My mask of hiding slips as I become more myself in the presence of the Almighty.

Sound and smell are the other important senses of a pilgrimage. Breaking out of the religion of "rush hour," away from smart phones, computers, radios, TVs, and other tools of modern society that occupy our lives, we are given an opportunity to focus on parts of life that we either ignore or take for granted. On pilgrimage, I spend some time in silence, even when walking with others, quietly walking the trail. What always fascinates me about this time is first, I usually walk faster than when I am talking with others, and second, I am aware of sounds that my talking covers, from the sound of foot hitting the tarmac or ground, to the sound of birds or planes over head, or the hum of electrical wires overhead.

Because the majority of our daily life is either at work, at school, or at church, our lives are often bookended by the start and end of the day. The journey is the pilgrimage, and the pilgrimage is the journey. During our sixteen to eighteen hours of wakefulness, we are on the go, moving, chatting, walking, driving, riding, or standing in line, sitting, relaxing, vegging, or perhaps praying. There is always a sense of adventure in our daily-life pilgrimage if we are willing to see, hear, feel, smell, and taste it. The Holy Spirit meets us along the pathway of life in our spontaneous conversations

The Story of Pilgrimage

with friends and strangers alike, our openness to nature, returning to "what matters most in life" moments.

3. The Destination

Since there is a "Point A," there is also a "Point B" or "Point C," however you understand the pilgrimage. I prefer "Point A" to "Point Z," or the British "Zed," with the rest of the alphabet in between. When wandering in the wilderness on camelback in the Sinai Desert, the goal after five days and four nights in the desert air is getting to St. Catherine's Monastery. After walking for weeks on end, the goal for those on Spain's Camino is the Cathedral in Santiago de Compostela. In northern New Mexico people walk more than 120 miles to reach the blessed El Santuario de Chimayo. The goal of the journey is ever before us, pulling us, tugging at us, promising an end to this part of the trek in which new blisters pop up for no apparent reason, shoulders ache more, knees begin to give out, and a childlike "Are we there yet?" spirit prevails.

But it is more than reaching that final destination. It is here, at the destination, where the tears flow, thankful for the blessed time, but also grieving the end of a "once in a lifetime" experience. The people we walked with may never be brought together again, and so saying "good bye" is bitter sweet. The sites we visited may change the next time we come by, if we come by that way again. Atonement may have come or not. Reconciliation may have been achieved in a broken relationship or not. A sense of the Divine was experienced, and we try to hold on to that time, picking up a relic, a remnant from where we were, maybe even a rock or a shell, reminding us where we went and who and whose we are. Hape Kerkeling, who began as one who doubted the faith, experienced God as a

> unique liberating spark that fans out indefinitely to foster and embrace self-realization. By contrast, those who get swept up in any group aimed at robbing us of our individuality and dousing the liberating spark wind up crushing themselves in the process.
>
> The creator tosses us into the air and then, to our happy amazement, catches us again at just the right moment. It is like the spirited game parents play with their children. . . . I realize that God kept tossing me into the air and catching me again. We encountered each other every single day.[11]

---

11. Kerkeling, *I'm Off Then*, 332.

Kerkeling is on to something here. The goal of a pilgrimage is similar to seeing a powerful play or movie, hearing a sermon that haunts us, experiencing a musical event that altered our world slightly, reading a great book, seeing a work of art anew, or being part of a historical event: once our closed lives are open, how do we remain where we are—with a new appreciation for life—and not succumb to the ways we have always done things? Finding ways of remaining open to lessons that may be learned on an intentional pilgrimage, and bringing that insight into our daily pilgrimage of life, are the focus of this book.

The Art and Science of Walking

To understand and get on with the pilgrimage that is our daily life, there is some "unlearning" that might be necessary, and some new learning that might take place *on* the road of life. To teach and learn the practice of the pilgrimage of everyday life, it may be best for one to participate in an actual or intentional pilgrimage in order to later transfer the language, rituals, and other activities into one's ordinary life.[12] Christians are on a pilgrimage, moving from point "A"—our birth and baptism—into the life eternal, or point "Z" (Zed). What happens between points "A" and "Z," well, isn't that where the adventure is located, where we stretch the bounds of the expected until the unexpected breaks in and the Spirit disturbs us and our world, while the entire time we are undergirded by grace and love? And we walk or move along the roadways of life as God's pilgrim people. For we are not the ones at "home." Again: God is our home, and we are making our way to the Holy.

This sense of being a believer on a pilgrimage is captured in one of my favorite verses in Scripture: "Walk humbly with your God" (Micah 6:8). This is not rocket science. There is an art to walking with God, let alone walking humbly, in humility, with the Creator. Think about it: Creature and Creator walking about the created landscape. This phrase is from a longer set of instructions of how we are to live and be known as Jewish and Christian people: "To do justice, love kindness, and walk humbly with your God." I read this Hebrew scripture recently—in ancient Hebrew no

---

12. This will be explored later in the book: having worked with people with disabilities who could not walk for many years, I am using "walk" *metaphorically* in this book, meaning "to move" or "ambulate" however one is able to, whether in a wheel chair, with a cane, with crutches, on a gurney, etc.

The Story of Pilgrimage

less—while I stood in line at the supermarket Harris Teeter. The message was in front of me, tattooed on the calf of a young man's leg. As one who has been "inked" or tattooed myself, I kind of liked it. I had already tattooed the symbol for the School of the Pilgrim, the non-profit I created. I gave thought to a new tattoo . . . as a reminder that life is a pilgrimage. The other tattoo I gave thought to was: "*Solvitur ambulando*", or "it is solved by walking." What this tattoo did for me was make me mindful, aware, that life is a pilgrimage, in which we who are Jewish and Christian walk humbly with God. That was art!

What I've been surprised by after all my years of being on pilgrimage is the almost natural urge to walk, to stroll, to take a roll in the wheel chair, to get moving, which is directly associated with teaching and learning. Since the time of Greek philosophers, many people have written of the connection between walking, thinking, writing, praying, and contemplating. This can happen when working, when facing an imminent threat, or needing to "clear one's mind," or so we tell ourselves when we are struggling. In *The Old Ways*, Robert Macfarlane writes that philosopher Jean-Jacques Rousseau wrote that "when I stop I cease to think; my mind only works with my legs." It is Danish philosopher Søren Kierkegaard who wrote that the mind "might function optimally at the pedestrian pace of three miles per hour, and in a journal entry describes going out for a wander and finding himself 'so overwhelmed with ideas' that he 'could scarcely walk.'" Wordsworth employed "his legs as an instrument of philosophy." Macfarlane concludes: "walking is not the action by which one arrives at knowledge; it is itself the means of knowing."[13] Henry David Thoreau wrote: "Methinks that the moment my legs begin to move, my thoughts begin to flow."[14] And William Wordsworth walked "as many as a hundred and eighty thousand miles in his lifetime, which comes to an average of six and a half miles a day starting from age five."[15]

The science that connects walking with thinking is found in our physical chemistry. Writer Ferris Jabr writes, "When we go for a walk, the heart pumps faster, circulating more blood and oxygen not just to the muscles but to all the organs—including the brain. Many experiments have shown that after or during exercise, even very mild exertion, people perform better on

---

13. Macfarlane, *Old Ways*, 27.
14. Quoted in Jabr, "Why Walking Helps Us Think."
15. Ibid.

tests of memory and attention."[16] Jabr notices that walking helps us organize our world, and the pace of our walking helps organize our mood: "When we stroll, the pace of our feet naturally vacillates with our moods and the cadence of our inner speech; at the same time, we can actively change the pace of our thoughts by deliberately walking more briskly or by slowing down."[17]

The practice of pilgrimage is act of learning, of knowing, of teaching us about the journey of faith as an act of faith. Robert Macfarlane continues, writing that walking is a part of the language of learning:

> The trail begins with our verb *to learn*, meaning, "to acquire knowledge". Moving backwards in language time, we reach the Old English *leornian*, "to get knowledge, to be cultivated". From *leornian* the path leads further back into the fricative thickets of Proto-Germanic, and to the word *liznojan*, which has a base sense of "to follow or to find a track". "To learn" therefore means at root—at route—"to follow a track".[18]

This connection between learning and walking is obvious for anyone who has taken a long extended walk, hike, or pilgrimage, especially over a series of days. There is learning on the trail or pathway. There is the possibility of clearing one's mind as we process thoughts and feelings as we are physically engaged in the walk.

Come to Me, You Heavy-Burdened Ones: The Promise of Rest

In the Gospel of Matthew, Jesus reportedly said, "Come to me, all you who are weary and burdened, and I will give you rest" (11:28). The Pilgrim God promises rest for our weary souls. That is why most of us go on pilgrimage: we lead cluttered, chaotic, uncertain lives, weighed down by our problems or the problems of others that we bring on or that come upon us, searching for meaning, insight, relief, and release. In this passage, Jesus invites us to sit down, take a load off of our feet, and slowly unpack the very full backpack we carry on our daily pilgrimage. "Take my yoke [my backpack] upon you and learn from me, for I am gentle and humble in heart, and you will find rest for your souls," says Jesus (Matt 11:29). This may be the best reason

---

16. Ibid.
17. Macfarlane, *Old Ways*, 27.
18. Ibid., 31.

for going on pilgrimage: coming to know the burdens we carry in life, and realizing, at the end of day, we don't have to carry such burdens with us in this life, or the next. The chance to sit down, reprioritize, or to consider restructuring our lives, unlearning old habits that drained life away from us in order to learn anew the ways of Christ, is a gift.

In the next chapter, the focus is on theological topics when reflecting upon pilgrimage. More precisely, the focus is on the image of Jesus, the Pilgrim God, who sets the pattern and map for our daily pilgrimage.

3

Pilgrimage as Biblical and Theological Practice

God for us, we call you Father.
God alongside us, we call you Jesus.
God within us, we call you Holy Spirit. —Richard Rohr[1]

The God of the Jews and the Christians and the Muslims is unbounded by time or space, is everywhere present. . . . Yet it was within the ecology of the Middle Eastern desert that the mystery of monotheism blazed. And it is the faith of the Abrahamic religions that the desert God penetrated time and revealed Himself first . . . to the Jews. —Richard Rodriguez[2]

Travels with My Family

In life, there are vacations, journeys, business trips, field trip, tours, and family visits. Growing up, my Dad largely chose what we were going to do on our "vacation," which more or less became a history field trip. We traipsed over many battlefields from the War of Independence to the Civil War. We witnessed re-enactments of wars in forts from the 1700s. Mom would make it a point to remind us we were having breakfast with Presidents when she poured cold milk into small cardboard cartons of cereal outside of Monticello before opening hours. Later in life, my Mom's idea of a "vacation" won out, and she now tours as many quilt stores as possibile in many large cities, along with quilt shows when possible, from Paducah, Kentucky, to Bend, Oregon. Later in life, I discovered that a vacation means

1. Rohr, "The Ultimate Paradigm Shift."
2. Rodriguez, *Darling*, 36

to literally "vacate," to leave premises and schedule behind, and to be away from the ordinary schedule. No work. No muss. No fuss. Today, vacation is between two palm trees in a faraway locale, an engrossing book (preferably a novel or good biography), an icy drink, a chair firmly planted in the sand or a hammock strung up between the two trees, the sound of surf, and no watch on my wrist to keep me preoccupied with what I should be doing at any hour of the day.

On business trips, tours, field trips, and family visits, time and usually the schedule are not in our control. We are usually negotiating with others for the time being spent, where it is being used, and how it will be executed. There is an implicit or explicit agenda to be met, in which hopefully "a good time is had by all," and will be hailed a "success" if all the parties meet the expectations they had either voiced or secretly coveted. Vacation, especially family vacation, is negotiated time together, in which the end result is a sense of accomplishment or maybe the acquisition of a new knowledge set. Granted, there are "down times" and fun times in between the scheduled events. But spontaneity is not the goal of the gathering. The focus is on accomplishing the scheduled events or list of items to be covered, which was the *raison d'etre* for the trip and tour.

Likewise, when one is older—with or without children—the family visit or reunion (different than vacation) can also feel like one is meeting a pre-scheduled list of expectation of how time will be spent, a schedule kept, with plenty of events commanding how our time is to be spent together. It is not that time with family could not be a restful time, but for many of us it is a rarity. Many times I have spent on a family visit leave me hungry for some alone time, looking for time to simply vacate after I return home in order to feel recharged. While I usually experience time-well-spent with family members, and see visits on a regular basis as essential for the ongoing wellness and healthiness of family systems, the time spent together is usually different from other vacations, trips, or pilgrimages I might take.

Pilgrimage shares a lot in common with the above list of travel scenarios, in which there *may* be an explicit agenda, a controlling set of expectations, specific time constraints, and forced time with others with little down time with one's self. But again, what pilgrimage has that these other times en route from one place with others in our lives do not necessarily have is the sacred, spiritual, divine, or holy aspect of a walk. As stated earlier, a pilgrimage *is* a religious hike. To quote pilgrimage writer Philip Cousineau, it is a soulful journey that ought to make the pilgrim quake as one walks upon sacred soil to a shrine.³ This is true whether one is at the shrine or on sacred soil out of a sense of reverence, veneration, or worship. To quote religious scholar Huston Smith again, pilgrimage is literally "belief in action," in which the pilgrim walks by faith (we often do not know what lies before us), comforted by grace known retrospectively, and carried forward by love in forms of hospitality.

In this chapter, the focus is on pilgrimage as a biblical and theological practice. The language and focus for much of this chapter will be Christocentric, with Jesus as the paradigmatic Pilgrim God, both man or human (Pilgrim) and divine (God). Or as Richard Rohr calls Jesus, the God-man. As Richard Rodriguez rightly noted above, many of us worship a God who is unbound by time and space, who "exists as much in a high mountain village in sixteenth-century Mexico as in tomorrow's Jakarta, where Islam thrives as a tropical religion. Yet it was within the ecology of the Middle Eastern desert that the mystery of monotheism blazed. And it is the faith of the Abrahamic religions that the desert God penetrated time and revealed Himself first—thus condescending to sequence—to the Jews."⁴ Rodriguez continues: "The Semitic God is the God who enters history."⁵ In Jesus—Emmanuel, which is literally "God with us"—God enters and has a stake in human history. God literally and figuratively sets a tent among the many dwellings of human souls in the human form of Jesus, in which God entered our time and our space, and walked among us as the Pilgrim God.

It was the late Brother John of the ecumenical Taizé community in France who first named Jesus "the Pilgrim God." After all, from what we know he owned no home, but based much of his pilgrimage around the home of Mary, Martha, and Lazarus. He called his disciples and other followers to assume the pilgrim life, carrying as little as possible, which would sustain them for the journey ahead. And to this day, the Spirit of the Pilgrim God continues to call disciples to follow the one who claimed to be the "way, the truth, and the life" (John 14:6), in which the earliest followers were called people of "The Way" (Acts 9:2). It is out of love and obedience that God's pilgrim people follow, whether the trail is well marked or not, day in and day out.

---

3. Cousineau, *Art of Pilgrimage*, 9.
4. Rodriguez, *Darling*, 36.
5. Ibid., 45.

Soulful Journey as Theological Practice

First order of business: What is a practice? Philosopher Alasdair MacIntyre defines practices as "any coherent and complex form of socially established cooperative human activity through which goods internal to that form of activity are realized in the course of trying to achieve those standards of excellence which are appropriate to, and partially definitive of, that form of activity, with the result that human powers to achieve excellence, and human conceptions of the ends and goods involved, are systematically extended."[6] For MacIntyre, practices embody goods internal to the practice agreed upon according to the *telos* or aim or purpose of a community. Virtue requires embodiment in practice. MacIntyre writes that a virtue is "an acquired human quality the possession and exercise of which tends to enable us to achieve those goods which are internal to practices and the lack of which effectively prevents us from achieving any such goods."[7] As such, practice is carried out in reference to one's relationship with other practitioners according to shared common standards. In this sense, living out shared virtues in relationship with a community is a dynamic process. In the practice of pilgrimage, virtues such as patience, charity, and the like are known and formed daily.

There are two kinds of Christian pilgrimage that may be considered a theological practice. The first is the *intentional* pilgrimage that a group of people may undertake during an exact span of time in their lives, from point A to a designated point Z. During this actual walk, the pilgrim actually practices the virtues that are core to a pilgrimage, like discipline or self-control, courage, and hospitality or benevolence, as one strives to reach the destination of one's pilgrimage. The pilgrims are inspired to do this walk because they desire time away for further reflection on the Christian life, because of life crises, or to reacquaint themselves with what it means to be a follower of Jesus on the road of life, as described in the previous chapter. The pilgrimage is *theological* because it is a journey where one's faith and understanding *of* God are put to the test as one participates in a tradition and practice that is as old as Abraham and Sarah, connecting with Jesus and his followers, and finally tying a loop around the saints of the church, like St. Francis of Assisi and Julian of Norwich.

---

6. MacIntyre, *After Virtue*, 175.
7. Ibid., 191.

The actual, intentional pilgrimage that a lone pilgrim may make will then open the walking figure to that second, larger *meta-narrative* and practice of the body of Christ, the people of God on a pathway toward God's heavenly realm (the telos or goal of life's pilgrimage) with people of faith embodying certain virtues (self-control, courage, benevolence). This is what makes Christian pilgrimage such a substantial practice in the church's story: it is more than analogy or metaphor, because the church—the body of Christ—is on a journey. It is a living, moving organism that struggles and yet celebrates the vision, the mission ahead of it, carrying or embodying the Jesus message, the good news, to other people. In part, the Bible (both Testaments), the text itself, provides a road map of sorts, and it is also a source of comfort and support for the people on the journey. But it is an actual pilgrimage that has the capacity of opening the pilgrim to understand anew the ways that the community of faith—the church, the body of Christ, of which we are members—is itself on a journey that, begun before we were baptized, will continue long after we leave this life for the final journey home. Paul himself writes about the parts of the body in 1 Corinthians 12, referring to eyes, head, hands, feet, all parts of the human body, in which we share in having the mind of Christ. To quote the United Church of Christ, God is still speaking, the Spirit is still leading, the body of Christ is still moving, and we continue to follow the Christ in doing justice, loving kindness, and walking humbly with our God (Mic 6:8). The one who connects these two levels or characteristics of earthly pilgrimage is Jesus, the Pilgrim God.

Modern pilgrimages are largely based upon the ancient practice of pilgrimage. For example, Melito of Sardis is the first identified Christian pilgrim who wanted to go on pilgrimage in the Holy Land before 190 CE. Melito's work is based upon collecting the writings for the progenitors of pilgrimage, like Abraham and Sarah, followed by Moses, not to mention the various pilgrimages that the people of Israel took between their home country and places they lived in exile. Let's continue with a further exploration of the biblical and theological practice of pilgrimage with Abraham and Sarah.

Abraham and Sarah: Pioneers of Pilgrimage Today

The paradigmatic pilgrims for Jews, Christians, and Muslims alike are Abraham and Sarah. It is Abraham—then Abram—who heard the voice of God and received this commandment, along with the promise that he would be made the father of a nation more numerous than the stars: "Go from your country and your kindred and your father's house to the land that I will show you" (Gen 12:1). And with that command, in faith, Abraham and Sarah moved their family from the land of Ur, which they knew well, following God to a foreign land more than four thousand years ago.

Having been on pilgrimage in the Sinai desert on camelback, led by Bedouins, it is a wonder that Abraham and Sarah did not get easily lost in a land that all looks the same: mountainous, with sandy valleys, with an occasional oasis dotting the land here and there. But then again, they were of the land, and the ability to be more nomadic than agrarian was not a hard transition.

Along with Abraham and Sarah, there are the sons of Jacob who wandered the land, even dumping their brother Joseph along the way, with hopes that they would be rid of the most-favored brother. And the other important biblical pilgrimage is Moses's. In the great exodus of the people of Israel out of Egypt, we read that Yahweh was transported in an ark as the people walked by foot to the promised land: "The cloud covered the tent of meeting, and the glory of the Lord filled the tabernacle" (Exod 40:34).

In the Wisdom literature of the Hebrew Scriptures, there is quite a bit about the virtue of journeying in faith, being a sojourner in the land, and the practice of hospitality. For example, Psalms 120–34 are well known as songs of pilgrimage, meant to be sung by pilgrims as they sojourned up to Jerusalem and the Holy Temple. They especially traveled to Jerusalem as pilgrims during the feasts, such as the Passover in the spring, the Feast of Weeks or Firstfruits, and the Feast of Tabernacles (Deut 16:16), which celebrated the coming in of the harvest in the autumn. When the Israelites were no longer captives in Babylon, they came rushing back on pilgrimage to Jerusalem. Maybe Jesus himself quoted Psalm 121:1–2, "I will lift up my eyes to the hills—from whence comes my help? My help comes from the LORD, who made heaven and earth." And Psalm 122 conveys the happiness of being called as a pilgrim to come to the temple to worship Yahweh.

Jesus, the Pilgrim God

As I wrote above, the late Brother John of the ecumenical Taizé Community wrote that Jesus is the Pilgrim God for the following reasons: according to the birth narrative in Luke and Matthew, Jesus is "constantly traveling to

Practicing Pilgrimage—Part I

and fro, between Nazareth in Galilee, Judaea with Bethlehem the city of David, and Jerusalem with its Temple. In Matthew, the holy family recapitulates the whole journey of its ancestors' descent into Egypt (2:14) and the return to the land of Israel (2:20)."[8]

> A pilgrim with no fixed abode in this world, Jesus is far more than a "new Abraham" or a "new Moses." These typologies, though present in the gospel portrait of Jesus, do not yield the key to his identity. At a first level, Jesus is certainly the man who answers God's call and sets out to follow in his footsteps. But he fulfills this mission in a unique way, because he is primarily the one who comes into the world to call men: like the Shekinah, he comes to chart God's path in the heart of our history. In the context of the story of Abraham, we may liken him first to the pilgrim-God who speaks, and only then to the human being who hears the divine Word and conforms his existence to it.[9]

Brother John understands that there are two aspects of Jesus's pilgrimage on earth. The first is Jesus in his pilgrimage around Nazareth and Galilee (captured primarily in the Synoptic Gospels—Matthew, Mark, and Luke), and the second is Jesus's time in Jerusalem, which is the focus of John's Gospel. When considering Jesus's life, it is easy to see how his life was defined by pilgrimage, beginning with his birth narrative, as mentioned earlier. The wandering of Jesus as an adolescent is captured in Jesus sneaking off from his parents to sit alongside the rabbinical scholars in Jerusalem, reading Torah, in which he then quotes from the prophet Isaiah in claiming his own identity. Most likely, Mary and Joseph, along with Jesus, were already on their way to Jerusalem, celebrating one of the feasts.

As an adult, the themes of pilgrimage in Jesus's life become more pronounced. To begin, consider the forty days that Jesus spent in the wilderness as a pseudo-pilgrimage, for he wandered without a home, without a reservoir of food, foraging the land for the next meal, sleeping outside under the stars. It is during this time that Jesus is tested through a variety of temptations, set for him by the evil one (Matt 4:1–11). As mentioned earlier, later in the Gospels, Jesus is well known for not owning his own home but residing with his friends Mary, Martha, and Lazarus. Jesus's attire is a model for his disciples as he sends them out, two by two, to proclaim and embody the Gospel (Mark 6:7; Luke 10:1), with a tunic, sandals, walking

---

8. Quoted in Robinson, *Sacred Places, Pilgrim Paths*, 12.
9. Ibid., 13.

stick, and not much else, relying on the hospitality of others for sustenance. And of course, over 32 times in the four Gospels, Jesus invites his disciples to "follow me."

More powerful yet is the final "Passion" week of Jesus's life, starting with the triumphal entry into Jerusalem. Jesus is celebrated as the "King of the Jews," riding on the back of the foal of a donkey. His reason for being in Jerusalem is to celebrate and remember the great pilgrimage of the Israelite people, the Passover, remembering the forty years in the wilderness as the people of God were led by a pillar of dust during the day and pillar of fire at night, fed manna by God, until they made their way over the Jordan river to the promised land of Jerusalem. Throughout Holy Week, the focus is on what we now call Maundy Thursday, the occasion in which we are given the sacrament of Christ's body and blood, followed by recognition of his death, his flight to hell to retrieve the lost, and his resurrection. But the pilgrimage does not end there; it continues in Luke 24 with the paradigmatic story of pilgrimage hospitality, breaking bread with strangers, as the two disciples flee Jerusalem to Emmaus, only to meet up with the resurrected Jesus. Finally, in Matthew 28, there is Jesus's great commission, a call to pilgrimage: "Go therefore and make disciples of all nations, baptizing them . . . and teaching them to obey everything that I have commanded you. And remember, I am with you always to the end of the age (28:19, 20).

Brother John saw that there was a second way of understanding the Pilgrim God from the perspective of the Gospel of John. In John, Jesus is a pilgrim who is human but he is not necessarily of this world (John 8:23), he has come from heaven, that is to say from God ("He who sent me", "the Father"), in order to give life to the world (John 6:33; 8:42). Sent from heaven by God in order to give life to the world (John 6:33), Jesus then also leaves the world: "But now I am going to him who sent me" (16:5; 23).[10]

Followers of the Pilgrim God

Paul and the other apostles seem bound to live a life of pilgrimage after the resurrection and ascension of Jesus Christ. Throughout the book of Acts, besides the followers of Jesus being called people of "the Way" (Acts 9:2), the stories indicate a constant movement of the apostles, with various stories of their spreading out from Jerusalem soon after Jesus's death. For example, there are stories of St. James going as far as modern-day Spain. St.

10. Ibid., 12.

Mark started one of the first monasteries in Egypt. St. Thomas was given credit for reaching out to the people in modern-day India (his tomb is in Mylapore, India). St. Peter is persecuted and buried in Rome. And Paul himself is set free to live life on the road, taking the Gospel to Macedonia, Corinth, Ephesus, Galatia, Thessalonica, and beyond, finding himself shipwrecked or in prison at one point or another, usually traveling with either Timothy or Titus, just as Jesus instructed his disciples to do during his earthly ministry (two by two).

Following the Pilgrim God Today

Today, many of the pilgrimage sites that dot the "Holy Land," especially around Nazareth, Galilee, Bethlehem, and Jerusalem, are there because of the Roman emperor Constantine and his mother, Helena, who made the journey to the land of Jesus. Helena, with the guidance of the Byzantine (Greek Orthodox) monks who took care of the sites, was responsible for the designation of what we in the modern world would call the "holy sites," from the Church of the Nativity in Bethlehem, where Jesus was born, to the Church of the Sepulcher in Jerusalem, where Jesus rose from the dead. One of the first pilgrims to also confirm these holy sites was a Spanish nun, Egeria. In her *Diary of a Pilgrimage,* she sought out monks in remote locations around the Sinai Peninsula, visiting Christian communities and recording their liturgical practices. One of the locales she visited is recorded at the end of John's Gospel, when Peter and others were fishing and drawing nothing into their nets until Christ came upon them and instructed them where to place the net. This site is near Capernaum, and to this day there is a church in that spot, and outside the church is a large, flat rock, which is reportedly the rock that the disciples gathered round and ate after Jesus cooked the fish and fed his disciples.

New pilgrimage sites also sprang up around the newly created monastic movements. Deep in the Red Sea mountains of Egypt is St. Anthony Monastery, a Coptic Orthodox monastery, established by the followers of St. Anthony, who is considered by many to be the first Christian monk. It was established by in 356 CE by the followers of St. Anthony, during the reign of Julian the Apostate. Isolation was stressed as the brothers lived in solitary cells surrounding a communal worship space. Soon after, the monastery of St. Macarius was established in 360 CE. Both of these Coptic Orthodox monasteries quickly became pilgrimage sites for many pilgrims, especially from Europe. Later, in the sixth century, Emperor Justinian helped create the current St. Catherine's Monastery, at the base of Mt. Sinai, also a modern-day pilgrimage site for many.

The Apophatic and Kataphatic Dimensions of Pilgrimage

In the area of spirituality, there is more attention drawn these days to both the kataphatic and apophatic approaches to sacred life, and both may be found in the practice of pilgrimage. To put it simply, the kataphatic approach to the religious life uses words, images, symbols, signs, ideas, and objects to point and refer to the Holy. In this sense, the use of icons, candles, and statuary, along with songs and prayers, is central to pilgrimages I've been on from Jerusalem and Santiago de Compostela to Canterbury and Chimayo. Amid churches that embody the term "smells and bells," amid figurines of saints and the blessed ones, there is a real sense that all of this clutter allows the believer to approach the throne of God, because meeting alone with the Holy is way too much for us to bear.[11]

In the apophatic tradition, the opposite is the case: all is removed that stands in the way before us and the presence of the Holy. It is the emptying of words and ideas, simply resting in the presence of God. The times that this apophatic approach is most real is in the wilderness of the Sinai on pilgrimage. Or climbing to the top of Mt. Sinai, like Elijah and Moses did, after the tourists break away from morning sunrise, taking in the barren landscape before us. As Henry Carse once reminded me, the metaphor of the mountains and hills joining in songs of joy, of rivers and trees clapping hands (Isa 55:12), may come about by a slight earth tremor, with the echo of the land moving heard miles away, or the rustling of leaves when the wind moves across the otherwise arid land. No cross is needed, nor lit candle, to absorb the immensity of the Holy and the Creator's creation when taking in the endless horizon on the top of Mt. Sinai.

Sin, Penance, Redemption: Discovering Grace on Pilgrimage

As was mentioned earlier in this book, many pilgrims have gone on pilgrimage when there was no other way to go on with life. Either the conditions at home or church were bad enough, vague, unsettled, in a rut, or had

---

11. Rodriguez, *Hunger of Memory*, 110.

hit a dead-end, such that a person simply needed to do something unusual, extraordinary, and unexpected in order to break out of an unproductive rut and move on with life. As Gideon Lewis-Kraus wrote, the divine model for going on pilgrimage included sin ("a bad decision in the eyes of God"), followed by penance, which was working out the causation of sin by going on pilgrimage, leading to redemption, the "goal of penance," and "forgiveness in the eyes of God."[12]

Among some Catholics, penance is not metaphorical but literal—one must feel the pain that one caused God in Christ to experience because of our sins. In order to appreciate that we were saved by the death of our Savior, some traditions go so far as to emulate suffering. In the case of the group of men called *Penitentes* (whose name is based on the root for our words *penitential* and *penance*) in northern New Mexico, I walked on the way to Chimayo with the brothers in the *Penitentes,* who purposefully put on shoes that hurt their feet, causing blisters, in order to feel the pain that Christ experienced because of our sins. Likewise, I stayed awake for twenty-four hours on the isle of St. Patrick's Purgatory in Lough Derg, Ireland, walking barefoot on rocky stones, following others whose feet were bleeding from stubbing and cutting their feet on the rough hewn stony pathways around the Basilica in the middle of St. Patrick's Purgatory. And some walk barefoot on "Reek Sunday" in climbing up Croagh Patrick in Galway, where legend has it that St. Patrick scared away the snakes. Catholic pilgrims walk barefoot in these places based "upon the conviction that mortification of the sole leads to amelioration of the soul. This is barefootedness as penance, maceration, test: the stones cut the pilgrims' feet so badly that blood oozes up between their toes and stains the path."[13] In these illustrative stories, there is another story of pilgrimage I find to be grace-filled time. Call me a Protestant pilgrim at this juncture of the book. Granted, many times I go on an actual pilgrimage in order to leave a place in which I have a list of "things to do" a mile long, or a time in which I may be working out life struggles with members of my family and on the cusp of making important decisions. Gideon Lewis-Kraus writes that early Christian pilgrims went on pilgrimage to free themselves up to cope with the problems facing them. Medieval pilgrims longed for a life other than the one she or he inherited. But modern pilgrims like me, who live in a fluid society with multiple choices, long to live with some of the constraints that are brought about

12. Lewis-Kraus, *Sense of Direction*, 122.
13. Macfarlane, *Old Ways*, 160.

by pilgrimage.[14] With all the choices spread before me, I long to experience some sense of direction in my life, a goal that is not necessarily one of my own creation, but of God's good will. This reprieve of having to make decisions hastily is grace. The grace of God—being welcomed, loved, and accepted as I am, and as we are—is known anew during pilgrimage, when I am given the space, time, and sense to work out my own relationship with my wants and needs, desires and longings, weighing the worth of sacrifice and the costs or consequences of my decisions, and the decision of others. Walking with the Pilgrim God on pilgrimage, with the Spirit in me, I sooner or later lean upon and fall into the hands of God, knowing I, yet not I, but Christ who lives in me, tethers me to the sure foundation of my being, which is none other than God (Gal 2:20). Such a gift of time and space to discern God's will is a gift of amazinwatg grace.

The Body of Christ, the Church, Is on a Pilgrimage

We Christians are God's pilgrim people, and the ordinary, daily Christian life is an ongoing pilgrimage. This may come as a shock to those who read this for the first time. After writing about the centrality of community and the manifold gestures of the body of Christ in *Christly Gestures*,[15] I proposed earlier that the diverse body of Christ is a living, moving entity as *we* are the hands, feet, eyes, nose, and ears of God as we take our part of the larger, cosmic pilgrimage of the body. For some, being "church" is more sedentary, expressed in how many hours are spent in a building known as "church," while for others, they are on the road of life *being* church, a.k.a., wherever two or three are gathered in Jesus' name. Or others may have fallen into the false belief that faith is something to focus on during Sunday morning hours, in which we spend much of our time sitting—around tables for Sunday school, in our coveted pews for worship, and in our usual spot for youth groups or intergenerational meals on many Sundays. We easily forget that faith is an unfolding journey, in which Sunday is our Sabbath, our day of rest, and that the *rest* of the week is meant for discovery, confirmation, and wrestling with doubts about the faith, each step of the way. We have been lulled into thinking that Advent and Lent are the sole church seasons for *discussing* and *considering* the *possibility* of the life of faith as a journey, using sojourning metaphors solely during these two periods of the church

14. Lewis-Kraus, *Sense of Direction*, 216.
15. Webb-Mitchell, *Christly Gestures*.

calendar, not necessarily realizing that this faith walk goes on 365 days a year, 7 days a week, 24 hours a day.

An experiment. While we are sure we are marching to the beat of our own drummer (apologies to Thoreau), setting our own calendar for the day, try this test. Write down all the events you have planned for a day at the beginning of day on a piece of paper. Now throughout the day, take that piece and check off what you did, along with all the unexpected events, meetings, conversations, phone calls, texts, Facebook and Instagram messages that intervened, along with all the surprising—meal, coffee with an old friend, an unexpected death. At the end of the day, tally up the "expected" events and compare them to the "unexpected" events. Usually—unless you lead a really controlled life—there are more unexpected than expected events. That's because we are living a life that is really not in our control. While we may have some ways of being proactive in making certain events happen—teach a class, prepare a meal, pick up the kids, write a sermon—there are more times that we are *active* or *reactive* to what is happening, making the best of life, come what may.

God Is the One Who Is Home, We Are the Ones Out on a Walk

This life journey, with all its steps and stages, is not our sojourn alone. As the medieval mystic Meister Eckhart wrote, "God is at home; it's we who are out for a walk." We are on a personal pilgrimage within a larger communal journey, with generations who preceded and will succeed us on this eternal quest to be with God. This is where Trinitarian theology breaks-out: In order to know the way forward to God, we follow and are accompanied by the Pilgrim God, who guides us on this incredible pilgrimage that is life giving. And it is the power of the Spirit that energizes our every step. Following Jesus, it is guaranteed to be a journey of adventure and knowledge. And where are we headed? We are on the road to God, living in the dawning reality of God's realm, a life of goodness, peace, and joy (Rom 14:17–19).

Learning and Faithfulness Meet on Pilgrimage

To walk is not only a way of learning, but might also be a matter of faithfulness. In all four Gospels of the New Testament, one of the oft-repeated phrases by Jesus is "Follow me." If you add them up, Jesus said it twenty-three times, or so it was recorded within the four Gospels. This meant that someone was expected to leave home and family, as well as vacate an occupation they used to feed and house a family, in order to follow the itinerant rabbi, healer, and prophet from Nazareth. "Follow me" was usually uttered by Jesus at the end of an actual event, like healing someone, feeding a few thousand, or providing one more parable and instruction on what challenges awaited the disciples. Such is the cost of discipleship, of faithfulness.

In all the pilgrimages I've taken, the two themes of teaching-learning and faithfulness continue to emerge. In walking there is both a time of teaching-learning the art of pilgrimage, in which we are aware of our faith as we are accompanied by the Spirit of Christ. You almost cannot have one without the other. My mind, body, and spirit have been stretched, challenged, built up, massaged, soaked, and celebrated on each pilgrimage I've attempted. My experience of walking with the Pilgrim God has graciously blessed me with safe journeys thus far—save for the expected blisters on the left foot on the small little toe and then inside of the left big toe—in which I've learned more about the land and the people I've walked with, and to interpret bits of old Scripture and poems in new ways with groups of other pilgrims and strangers alike. I've learned to apply and live out the Gospel in new ways, always challenged to practice the good news again in new and often challenging situations. I've become accustomed to welcoming strangers along the way rather than to avoid them. In a sense, to learn *about* the Triune God I find it helps to take a literal and figurative walk *with* God, to walk in faithfulness in trying to live out and follow the pattern and practices that Jesus laid out according to the Gospel writers, which is more than enough for a daily walk with the Pilgrim God.

To teach and learn the multivalent art and practice of being a pilgrim on pilgrimage *as a journey of faith* in our daily life is a constant theme in this book. We are people not on a metaphorical "journey," but an hourly, daily, grinding, joyful, mind-stretching, exhilarating, physically exhausting, awe-inspiring, spiritually depleting, life-giving sojourn of faith who are on our way. After all, the first generation of Christians weren't called "Christians" but "people of the Way" (Acts 9:2), following Jesus who called himself "the way, the truth, and the life" (*via, veritas, vita*; John 14:6).

Teaching and Learning with Our Mind, Body, and Spirit as Members of the Body of Christ

Not only are our minds stimulated by the pilgrimage, but our bodies are also learning to travel anew. It is one thing to walk a few feet every day, or to take ten thousand steps over a period of a day in order to lose weight. On a pilgrimage, one walks anywhere from a few miles a day to something like the Camino de Santiago de Compostela, which is 484 miles. On such a lengthy pilgrimage, there is the education of the body, in which the walker learns how much she can push herself in a day, the places on the foot where she blisters, new aches or old pains in the back or the knees, and the joy of a hot bath or foot massage at the end of the day.

Finally, lessons of the Spirit on a pilgrimage are multiple. Hospitality is front and center on a pilgrimage, in which one is either guest or host—or sometimes both at the same time—on any part of a trail. There is no doubt that a pilgrimage is a time of learning to depend once more upon the Spirit for every step of the journey. On pilgrimage, one always walks in sacred time, on holy ground, and that, as they so on the Pilgrimage of Vocation to Chimayo, the Lord is the companion of my journey. The Pilgrim God is present rain or shine, during the stroll on low, flat plains and on the slight rises. Opportunities to share food, to share lives, arise aplenty throughout a pilgrimage, and it is none other than the Pilgrim God that is present at these moments.

Yet here's the other connection, and the reason for this book again: an actual or intentional pilgrimage teaches us lessons about our daily pilgrimage of faith at home, with a congregation or parish, and in the public square. One feeds into the other. They are not two separate experiences, able to be categorized and set apart neatly. They bleed and run into each other until they become more or less one and the same. The only difference is the context in which we find ourselves on a pilgrimage. To those pastors and priests, religious educators and pastoral counselors, and others who participate in the religious life and are reading this book, consider the sermon "fodder" in examples that abound from pilgrimage. Consider backpack analogies, in which, on pilgrimage, there is always the habit of over-packing and having to purge somewhere along the journey. I have a habit of having to pack and repack several times on a pilgrimage, trying to figure out what is washable, what is necessary, what is frivolous, and then the "What were you thinking?" selection. Likewise, the pilgrimage of life is similar: we tend to over-pack, to be consumers, or to use the media phrase, "hoarders." In the pilgrimage that is life, what can we leave behind, and what is necessary, as we follow Jesus?

Or there is the admonition of Jesus for us not to worry about tomorrow, for tomorrow will have enough things in it to consume our days (Matthew

5). Pilgrimage can help us focus on the pathway before us, to be where our feet are planted, rather than worried about what happens tomorrow. In a rainstorm on pilgrimage, one is not worried about tomorrow, only about figuring how to get dry and warm after a day of being soaked. Likewise, how can we embrace this very attitude when we are hit by the rainstorms of our life, not worried about tomorrow, but simply focused on where our feet are planted today?

As mentioned in the Introduction, I was such a firm believer of this connection between pilgrimage, walking, teaching, and learning that I used to teach a course at Duke Divinity School, "The Education of Pilgrimage," as the "capstone course" for seniors focused on Christian religious education. Believing that true Christian religious education is the formation and nurture of disciples in creating and growing in Christian community years earlier, there was a problem. Those who I had studied with who kept banging on the theme of "Christian community" had a very static understanding of this always changing/never the same, organic yet mysterious communal gathering that is called the body of Christ. In *Christly Gestures* I spent a great deal of time discussing Paul's vision of the church, which *is* the resurrected body of Christ (Barth). But it is a body *on the move*, with legs, feet, arms, and hands, traipsing around this globe. In other words, the very body of Christ is on a pilgrimage in this land in which we live.

≈

As an oblate of St. Benedict's Monastery in St. Joseph, Minnesota, since 2000, I learned the phrase *ora et labora*, or "prayer and work." St. Benedict saw prayer and work as partners of sorts, combining contemplation with action. In a conversation with spiritual writer Kathleen Norris, she suggested that pilgrimage is monastic life on the road. So in a sense, pilgrimage—this traveling monastic life—is a perfect example of *ora et labora*, because we take the work or action of walking and combine it with contemplation, reflection, or prayer.

Let's focus a little more on the *ora* in the way of St. Benedict. In the Benedictine community, prayer may also be joined with the reflection on Scripture, which deepens a person's understanding of Scripture. This is the practice of *lectio divina* or "Divine reading," in which the person does not execute exegesis or dissection of a scriptural phrase, but rather reflects on the phrase itself, seeking a deeper understanding of the Word. In other words, pilgrimage is an opportunity for a pilgrim to use her or his theological imagining, reflecting, and praying the Scriptures through the practice of *lectio divina*, hearkening to the voice of God (which is a map in its own way) while following Jesus on the road of life.

How does this work? Consider reflecting on the Great Commission while on pilgrimage. Jesus promises to be the companion of our journey even today: "I am with you till the end of the age." This is indeed good news. We are not alone. As Jesus promises, the Holy Spirit—Christ's Spirit—is with us in this stretch of life as well. But I learned to take this even deeper while on one of the Pilgrimages of Vocation to Chimayo sponsored by the Catholic Archdiocese of Santa Fe. During the pilgrimage, one prayer prayed on the path over and over again has the refrain, "Lord, be the companion of our journey." After years of praying this prayer, that refrain is now a bedrock prayer when facing challenging times in my life, in which the stretch of road that I'm on in life feels a bit more perilous than others. It is a hopeful prayer and it is a prayer of affirmation, that with each step I take forward on an actual pilgrimage or the pilgrimage of life, even though I do not know where to place my foot in the next step, that when I go forward, the step is leading me in the right path. This stepping forward in faith is a theological move in a most concrete, visual form. It is an engagement of mind (remembering the words), spirit (grace comforts, no matter what), and body (literally moving) based upon the promise that Christ's Spirit has been, is, and will be with me until the end of the ages.

In the next chapter, I want to expand our understanding of pilgrimage by considering the pilgrimage of other faith communities and ways of living. What is phenomenal about pilgrimage is that it is a common practice among many of the world's religions, from the indigenous people of Australia, the Aborigines, whose walk-abouts are a kind of pilgrimage, to those who practice Shintoism, in which the spirits of our elderly departed as well as nature have a life of their own, to the Hindus and Buddhists whose devote followers practice a walk of devotion and veneration as well, and to Jews and Muslims. There is much to learn and consider from these other faiths that, in turn, make our walks richer.

4

Pilgrimage among Different Faith Communities

> Japanese pilgrims apparently get really into the trappings of the journey. Some people are buried with their sticks.... While you're on the walk [around Shikoku], the tradition goes, you're actually "dead to the world." This is similar to the Camino, where Catholics say that if you die en route to Santiago, you go straight to heaven.
> —Gideon Lewis-Kraus[1]

> Pilgrimages to sacred sites are also very popular forms of Jain spiritual practice.... Many of these are in Bihar, south of the Indian border with Nepal. Bihar is considered the cradle of Jainism, for it was here that twenty of the twenty-four Tirthankaras, including Mahavira, are thought to have achieved liberation.
> —Mary Pat Fisher[2]

> What's in your head—toss it away!
> What's in your hand—give it up!
> Whatever happens—don't turn away from it.
> Sufism is the heart standing with God,
> with nothing in between. —Abu Sa'id Abul Khayr[3]

The Language of Walking and Journey

The connection of walking, journey, and the Christian faith is most profound for me in the seasons of Advent and Lent. Jesus, the Pilgrim God, guides my life. And in Judaism, the Exodus of Moses and the people of

---

1. Lewis-Kraus, *Sense of Direction*, 165.
2. Fisher, *Living Religions*, 133.
3. Quoted in Holland Cotter, "The Many Voices of Enlightenment," *New York Times*, June 11, 2009, http://www.nytimes.com/2009/06/12/arts/design/12sufi.html?_r=0.

Israel is the very basis for, and remembered in, the Seder meals celebrated during Passover each year. The meal itself is symbolic of the various stages or milestones of the ancient Exodus, making its lesson real in our day and age as people eat and hear the story of enslavement and liberation. As will be explored throughout this book, Jesus himself was in Jerusalem during Passover celebrations that soon became for Christians "Holy Week." He had just finished celebrating Seder when he took the bread and wine of the Passover meal and shared it with his disciples—and with that, a major sacrament of the church was born.

Christianity and Judaism are not the only faith communities that engage in Huston Smith's understanding of pilgrimage as "belief in action." So do other world faiths. For five years I taught "Religions and the World" at North Carolina Central University, in Durham, North Carolina, reading and rereading the standard textbook we used but also some of the sacred texts of other religions. We visited Durham's Beth El Synagogue, literally touching the words of Torah on a large scroll. We held a red leather volume of the Koran with elegant golden swirls etched into the leather. We learned Buddhist contemplation after an hour lesson in how to sit cross-legged upon large black pillows. We walked around a Hindu temple in Cary, with the stories of their gods and goddesses carved in stone. What jumps out to me is the language and practice of walking, journey, sojourn among *all* the major world religions, as well as the smaller sects, cults, and indigenous faiths.

The ability to walk, along with the desire to travel by foot as a sign of belief in action, following others to venerate a god or goddess at a worship site, is part and parcel of the religions of the world prior to the establishment of Judaism, Christianity, and Islam as three of the world's five primary religions. Note the quotes above, in which Jainists participate in pilgrimage, as do Sufis. Closer to home, the Cherokee go on a Green Corn pilgrimage annually, and the people of Taos Pueblo in New Mexico go on pilgrimage of Blue Corn. And the Aborigines of Australia are well known for their walkabouts. This chapter is dedicated to the universality of pilgrimage among the religions, faith systems, and ways of life of other cultures.

Indigenous Faiths

By writing that pilgrimage is a universal phenomenon, I mean people of many faiths and cultures participate in pilgrimages, or "purposeful walking,"

Pilgrimage among Different Faith Communities

even though it may not be called a pilgrimage per se. And people have been doing it for thousands of years in all parts of the world. I want to emphasize in this chapter the global reach of pilgrimage, which is tied to religious life in particular, or to life in general in many cultures that do not divide or categorize their life into "religious" and "secular." For example, many Jews and Christians tend to compartmentalize their lives, living a life that is wide open with parties, or discussions that border on heresy, only to take a break from such a lifestyle on Sabbath or Shabbath. I kidded my college-aged students at NCCU that they go and party—including drinking alcohol and taking drugs, participating in sexual encounters—starting Thursday nights through to Saturday nights, only to stop and go to worship in a church Sunday morning, asking forgiveness for their behavior and actions for the last three nights, only to repeat this pattern the following week. And in the contemporary world, I know many Jewish people who self-identify as "cultural Jews" who participate in Hanukkah and Seder meals during Passover, but tend not to go to synagogue at any other times of the year, if at all.

Around the world, very early gatherings of human beings created rituals for their communities that enabled a group to be more or less a cohesive community, with pilgrimage as one of the important or primary ritual practices. Native people not only respected the land that they were part of, but revered that which they thought sacred, like the spirits of the recently departed and elders in a village, which, in turn, would also affirm the bonds they had with each other through their ritual observances.[4] Sometimes they celebrate the birth of life, or recognize moments of passage in a person's life like becoming an adult, by a ceremonial cutting or scarring of a person's skin. This process is called scarification. For example, circumcision of male babies in the Jewish faith is an act of scarification. Others create rituals for marriages between two families perhaps from two different tribes, while still others follow candle-light memorials upon receiving news of a tragic death of young people, or the timely passing away of those who are elderly. Each season would also countenance a new celebration, whether a group was sowing seeds in spring, recognizing the growth in summer with celebrations on summer's solstice, reaping the rewards in autumn, or praying for endurance of the longest period of darkness during winter with a solemn celebration on winter's solstice. Along with the sacred communal gatherings, native people went on pilgrimage or walkabouts. For example, in what is now Russia, ancient people known as the Buryats gathered on the

---

4. Fisher, *Living Religions*, 55.

top of Erde, which is a mountain upon which the spirit of the earth lived. They would all join hands together in order to create a circle, in which a great energy would appear in the center.[5] Meanwhile, in Mexico, the Huichol people, natives of the land, would make their way to Wirikuta, the "sacred Land of the Sun," which is where they believe that creation began. From here, they gather a yearly supply of peyote cactus, which has the power to create an alternate state of reality when inhaled, which is their way of communicating with the spirit world.[6] The purpose of these rituals is to be in touch with, remember, and honor the spiritual beings who created and help sustain the known world.

One of the best-known pilgrimage or walking cultures is the aboriginal people of Australia. English author Bruce Chatwin wrote about these "Dream Walkers" in his book *The Songlines*. Chatwin studied and wrote about the way the songs of the Aborigines are themselves a mixture of both the creation myths the people believed in, and the movement of the spirit who led and lead them, in their dreams to where they were and are to go. The dreams served as a kind of atlas of the world. The Aborigines do not have a "religion" per se as much as they have a way of life. The energy that the earth emitted in creation's beginning, this dream time, shaped not only the walking patterns of earth's people, but is captured in the very paintings of the Aborigines of Australia. These are the famous pointillist paintings that convey the creation story, with the snakes who created the water spots of the world, and the emus and other native animals who helped make the physical world as we know it.

During one trip to Brisbane, Queensland, partaking in a weeklong summer Christian youth gathering through the Uniting Church in Australia, I heard one of my favorite stories about the powerful system of a family's religious life that integrates the life of dreams and the pilgrimage or walking culture of the Aborigines even among Christians. The entire Aboriginal family joined a young person who was attending the Christian retreat because once the retreat was over, all of them would go back out on the land again and walk the land, following the dreamscape. The family had not given up their Aboriginal ways, but simply integrated them into the Christian faith system. Since dream walking or walkabouts were not a religion but part of who they are as created beings, they simply held the two worldviews in creative synchronicity without missing a beat.

5. Ibid., 60.
6. Ibid.

Likewise in the Americas, the aboriginal or native people are also well known for their pilgrimages. When I was on one of my first pilgrimages to Chimayo via Costilla, we stopped for some time with the people of Taos Pueblo. What was amazing was their annual trip into the mountains around Taos for the Blue Corn journey, or what might be called a "pilgrimage." It is an annual journey held in autumn as a sort of harvest festival, though the specifics were not shared with me, out of deference to the secret life of the Taos people. Similarly, the Cherokee people of North Carolina practice the pilgrimage of the Green Corn for the same purpose as the Taos people.

While many of these native or indigenous religions may continue to have a small band of followers today, the six more primary religions of this world also incorporate the sacred practice of pilgrimage. While covering Judaism and Christianity in the previous chapter, the rest of this chapter includes a discussion of pilgrimage in Hinduism, Buddhism, Shintoism, and Islam.

Hinduism

One of the world's oldest religions, Hinduism rose out of the Indus Valley in India, and its roots can be traced back more than two thousand years ago, according to the Vedas, the sacred writings of Hinduism. The Vedas are largely a collection of sacred hymns that are not considered human-made, but rather revealed by the eternal being. They are the "breath of the eternal, as 'heard' by the ancient sages or rishis, and later compiled by 'Vyasa' or 'Collector.'"[7]

The core ideals of Hinduism include the following: first is the concept of reincarnation, in which when the soul leaves the dead body it then enters a new body. The soul continues this pattern, advancing toward the ultimate reason for being, which is liberation for rebirth and merging with the Absolute Reality or eternal being. The process of reincarnation itself is a kind of pilgrimage, as the soul travels from being to dying to being over again, with several lifetimes before one reaches *nirvana*. Second is *karma*, which focuses upon human action, and the consequence of our actions, which shape one's future reincarnation. Third, the goal of living subsequent lives as a soul, and the overall lure of performing good actions in order to bring about good *karma*, is to achieve *moksha*, which is freedom from space, time, and matter as one lives in the full realization of the Absolute

---

7. Fisher, *Living Religions*, 77.

Being. The Absolute veils itself from us in all its entirety. The Absolute is only revealed partially by the priests or Brahmins, who make it possible for people to worship the Absolute that is largely shapeless, taking a more human form in the goddess Shakta, who is also embodied in the goddess Devi, Kali, and Lakshmi, and the gods Shiva, Brahma, and Vishnu.[8]

In Hinduism, pilgrimage is seen as a special opportunity to be personally or individually cleansed rather than as a communal or group phenomenon. There are thousands of pilgrimage routes or *tirthas*, which means "crossings" in Sanskrit. A pilgrimage begins with a *samkalpa* or declaration of intent, followed by a pilgrim pledging one's self to observe rules, including fasting and worshipping at various temples along the way. Millions of pilgrims undergo a strenuous pilgrimage that involves climbing to a certain mountain site, Amarnath Cave, which is considered blessed by the Absolute Being. This cave is 11,090 feet high in the Himalayas of Kashmir, in which glacial ice forced a large stalagmite, highly revered as a representation of the god Shiva. Pilgrims have come to this site for more than three thousand years. For those who follow the goddess Shaktas, they trek to fifty-one spots in India, which mark the abodes of the goddess, or places where parts of her body are buried. The most venerated pilgrimage sites are Kah Yuga and the Mother Ganga, the goddess of the Holy Ganges River.[9]

Before moving on further, I want to point out that the Hindu god of travel or pilgrimage is none other than Ganesha or Ganesh. Ganesh removes the obstacles that lie before us on our pilgrimage of life and blesses us on our way. He is the son of the god Shiva and the goddess Parvati. He is a happy god with the head of an elephant and is usually portrayed in a shade of blue. In various locations where I've taken a pilgrimage I've seen images of Ganesha in tattoos or figurines on keychains.

Buddhism

There once was a very devout Hindu by the same of Siddhartha Gautama. Born in 563 BCE to a wealthy father and chieftain of the Sakya clan, Siddhartha was a member of the warrior caste in what is now Nepal. His father wanted him to become the emperor of India, while his mother Maya was sure Siddhartha was a "god," giving birth to her son by miracle: from her side. Siddhartha grew up to be wealthy, with a wife and child, but yet he

---

8. Ibid., 85–89.
9. Young, *World's Religions*, 77–79.

found his life empty. He had an inner longing that wine and song, family and friends, could not fulfill. At one point, he took a chariot ride through the unclean areas of India, and while on this ride he came across "four passing sights." First was a sorrowful old man. The second sight was a man who was ill. The third sight was a man who was dead and being carried on a funeral pyre to be burned. The fourth sight was a monk walking alone in a yellow robe.[10] What is instructive about this story is that Siddhartha was a *pilgrim* on a *pilgrimage* as he moved among these four sights. A follower of Hinduism, he was acutely aware of the religious vision that was before him, and greatly disturbed by it as well.

Siddhartha finally left his wife and son—this is called "the great renunciation or going forth"—and began a six-year pilgrimage or quest. He tried to master a meditative approach to life and spent time trying out a strict ascetic life. What Siddhartha discovered by trying both self-denial and self-indulgence was The Middle Way (again, note the language of pilgrimage, "Way"). It was this path that led him to the Four Noble Truths that are the benchmarks of Buddhism:

- First, life involves suffering, a state of existence none of us can avoid experiencing, no matter how hard we try.
- Second, the cause of this suffering is desire (or craving), which leads to attachment to the impermanent, always changing things of this world.
- Third, we are not trapped—release from the suffering of life is possible.
- Finally, release may be found by following the eightfold path.

What is clear about Buddhism—in all its variation—is that there is a walking between various sites of Siddhartha's history as well as previous milestones of Buddha's story, or between shrines, a.k.a., stupas. Pilgrims flock to stupas to venerate the one who has attained enlightenment and symbolically commit themselves to follow the example of Buddha.[11]

The Island of Shikoku and the Eighty-Eight Temples

One of the most famous pilgrimages in the world is on the Japanese island of Shikoku, and involves visiting the eighty-eight temples on this small

10. Ibid., 84–85.
11. Ibid., 96–98.

island. It is largely a Buddhist pilgrimage, though there are Shinto shrines on the island as well. The shrines were created by the poet, politician, educator, administrator, writer, and priest, Kobo Daishi, who was born in 774. A convert to Buddhism after a trip to mainland China, his family hoped that he would reach great fame and fortune. But like Siddhartha, Kobo Daishi was smitten by the "Middle Way" and became a mountain ascetic, founding the Shingon sect of Buddhism, establishing 88 temples around the island as places for veneration and reverence, but not to worship any god or goddess, or emperor or empress. Instead, these temples were created to honor the common man and woman: the beggar, the fisher, the housewife, the student, and the merchant, et al. By the end of the pilgrimage, it is clear that it is the very visit of the pilgrim him or herself who makes the site special.

What is unique to this pilgrimage is, first, it is a circle. A pilgrim can start anywhere she or he wants. There is no "point A" to "point Z." That's because, second, it is a circle, without a beginning, middle, and end. This circular nature of the pilgrimage is unlike the linear nature of Western pilgrimages, such as Santiago de Compostela, St. Cuthbert's Way, Chimayo, and Lourdes, to name a few. Third, a pilgrim carries the baggage of life wherever one comes from, and this pilgrimage gives the pilgrim space to sort and dispense with some of the clutter of her or his life. Finally, this pilgrimage presents to each pilgrim the promise of days of rain and sunshine, warm and cool, and oftentimes both kinds of weather on the same day.

Shintoism

Much like Buddhism, in Japan Shintoism is not a religion in the kind of way one would call "Christianity" or "Islam" a religion. Like Buddhism, it is a practice, a way of life, founded in Japan. Shinto comes from two words: *shin* or "divine being," and *do* or "way." The great texts of Shintoism are the *Kojiki* and *Nihiongi*, which were pulled together in 712 CE and 720 CE respectively, though they are not pure Shintoism but a mixture of philosophies with hints of Buddhism and Confucianism. While the *Kojiki* lends some credibility to the spirituality of the imperial throne, the thrust of both writings tends to be pulling together a kind of spirituality of creation, the land, the oceans, nature at large, and our kinship with this created order, along with the connection of ancestral reverence for those elders who are dearly departed. As Reverend Yukitaka Yamamoto wrote, "To be fully alive is to have an aesthetic perception of life because a major part of the world's goodness lies in its often unspeakable beauty."[12] What connects the human with the spiritual through creation is *kami*. *Kami* literally means, "that which is above," referring to that which evokes amazement and thanksgiving.[13]

Though Shinto did not need shrines during the early time of its inception, since creation is enough of a monument or memorial to the spirit or *kami*, with Buddhist and Confucian influence, in the sixth century CE there was the introduction of small and large shrines. Honoring *kami* either with nature, crops, or gods, the shrines soon became a focus on pilgrimage, especially with the creation of a festival around certain aspects of ordinary life. For example, there are festivals and offerings made when a person builds a house and moves into it. There are seasonal festivals, celebrating planting or reaping harvest. On December 31, there is a ceremonial housecleaning, welcoming the *kami* into the abode, praying for good luck in the year to come, with people drawing paper lots to tell one's fortune and tying them to tree branches and asking priests to purify new cars, new buildings, new roadways and bridges, seaports, or building plots.[14]

Judaism

As has already been referenced in the previous chapter, the Jewish people are not only the People of the Book, or Torah, but are also a pilgrimage people. The progenitors of pilgrimage among the Jewish people are Abram and Sarai (later, Abraham and Sarah). The practice of pilgrimage continues for forty years in the Sinai wilderness with Moses as the leader, who guided the people from Egypt to the land of the Canaanites, which is commonly known as the Exodus. Throughout the Hebrew Scriptures there are other pilgrimages that the Jewish people participated in as they were taken from what had become their "homeland" to Babylon, for example, as part of their sojourn with God. The Jewish people have gone through a series of diasporas, finding themselves taken away from their homeland to a faraway locale as a result of turning away from Yahweh and receiving a judgment and discipline. For proof, simply read the prophets Isaiah or Jeremiah, or one of the minor prophets like Amos or Malachi to see how this pattern played itself out for generations of Israelites.

---

12. Quoted in Fisher, *Living Religions*, 224.
13. Ibid.
14. Ibid., 231.

Practicing Pilgrimage—Part I

Those of the Jewish faith celebrate many festivals throughout the year, which is based upon a lunar calendar. There are three annual pilgrimage festivals, in which Jewish males were once required to travel to Jerusalem for special temple rituals. The first takes place fifty days after *Pesach*, and it is called the celebration of *Shavuot* or weeks. It is customarily also the feast that celebrates the first fruits of the harvest or a Pentecost (Deut 16:9–12). It is a true celebration of the one who brings the first fruits of the harvest to the temple and the reception of the Torah from Yahweh.[15]

The second pilgrimage is *Sukkot*, or the festival of booths, which lasts for seven days. This is typically held in autumn and recalls the time the people of God were nomadic pilgrims, wandering in the wilderness and living in portable dwellings known as *Sukkot* or roughly built lean-tos (Deut 16:12–15). The eighth day is *Simhat Torah*, or the day of celebrating Torah, with people carrying the Torah in a pilgrimage, kissing the very scrolls and dancing with them in thanksgiving for the wisdom and guidance of Torah.[16]

The third festival is probably the most meaningful and powerful to this very day: Passover, otherwise known as *Pesach*, which means "lamb." This is the festival of the people's exodus from slavery in Egypt, being led by Moses and Aaron through the Sinai wilderness, to the time of coming up to Mt. Nebo and crossing the Jordan into the promised land. Along with a special meal, a *Seder*, the people gather in Jerusalem for this high holy day, recounting the horrors of captivity and their deliverance from their Egyptian bondage (see Exod 12 and Deut 16:1–8). In honoring Passover, Jesus himself entered Jerusalem in his final week of human life, which is why Easter and Passover coincide. Jesus actually used the leftover wine and unleavened bread or *matzah* (or matzo) as the basic elements of what Christians now call the Last Supper.

Islam

Like Judaism and Christianity, Islam is also a desert faith of the Middle East. Islam is born of its founders being a people on the move. The prophet Muhammad, born in either 570 or 571 CE, was soon orphaned after birth and adopted by his uncle, Abu Talid, a leader of the Quraish tribe of Mecca. Muhammad was soon well known for his mature spirituality and belief in the one true God, Allah, rejecting the idolatry of other Arab faiths. Besides

---

15. Young, *World Religions*, 194.
16. Ibid.

spending a long span of time in the hills surrounding Mecca in spiritual retreat and study, along with living in Medina, organizing his followers in that city, in 629 CE Muhammad established the new faith, using Mecca as a place for a pilgrimage. After conquering Mecca, he forgave his enemies, and destroyed all the idols in the Kaaba, leaving only the black meteoric stone and its enclosure. This is because it was believed that the prophet Ibrahim (Abraham) and his son Ishmael established the Kaaba. Soon, Muhammad established the rite of pilgrimage to Mecca, which Muslims believe was initiated by Ibrahim.

There are five major "pillars" of Islam: the first is the repetition of the creed *shahadah* or bearing witness, a creed recited daily in Arabic by all Muslims, regardless of one's native tongue. The second is a daily prayer or *salat*. Muslims are to pray this prayer five times a day. Third is almsgiving or *zakat*, which is a kind of tax from the rich to provide for the poor. Fourth is fasting or *sawm*, which is done during the entire month of Ramadan.[17]

The fifth pillar is pilgrimage to Mecca, the *Hajj*. The Koran (*Quran*) requires women and men to go on one pilgrimage to Mecca once in a lifetime. It is considered the holiest of cities in Islam. Roughly two million people partake in this pilgrimage every year. It is based on Muhammad's pilgrimage to Mecca shortly before his death in 632 CE. The *Hajj* takes place in the twelfth month of the lunar calendar. When the pilgrims take their place in the pilgrimage, they remove the clothes they are wearing and put on two pieces of clothing, which are symbolic of the robe of Abraham. One part is seamless white cloth covering the top, and the other cloth covering the bottom.

There are certain rites around particular stations of the Kaaba in Mecca, which reenacts parts of the faith, including not only Muhammad's life, like the focus on the meteorite that is central to the pilgrimage to Mecca and the revelation to Muhammad about his role in the faith. There is also the reenactment of the important events in Ibrahim's, Ismael's (Ishmael's), and Hagar's lives. There is also a leg of the pilgrimage in which pilgrims go to Mina, the last place that Muhammad spoke to his followers. On the last day of the pilgrimage, the pilgrims return to Mina for the Day of Sacrifice, making themselves clean through offering up the sacrifice of an animal, as Allah had done as a substitute when Ibrahim almost sacrificed the life of Ismael. At the end of this ritual the heads of male pilgrims are shaved, the women's hair cut short, nails are trimmed on all as a way of purifying

17. Ibid., 244–45.

one's self and showing that one had made the *Hajj*. There is one more walk around the Kaaba, and throughout the pilgrimage the pilgrims avoid pork, wine, and gambling. Hopefully, one returns to one's home as a changed person, renewed in the faith, renewed to more closely follow the teachings of Muhammad in praise of Allah.

Pilgrimage: A Blessed Time

It is important to acknowledge that pilgrimage is more than a "Christian thing." It is one of the most ancient religious or spiritual practices of human beings since our forbearers knelt or bowed down to a higher power, or holy other, in their personal and communal life. Above is a short list and brief descriptions of some of the faiths, religions, and lifestyles that choose to understand the present and hope for the future by honoring the past. All devotees draw strength and courage for the journey ahead by realizing how those who were pilgrims before us made it through challenging times, with celebrations of today that honor—with a sense of reverence—the implacable nature of being a pilgrim.

In sum, what these pilgrimages remind us is that, first, the earth—land, water, and wind—is the place of the holy or divine for many faiths. We tread upon not mere dirt, but sacred ground, right where we are. Second: there is time for renewal, cleansing, centering in all world religions. Third: some pilgrimages are solo adventures while other sojourns are openly communal. But even the solo treks are communal, for we are not alone but embraced by God's creation. Fourth: an actual pilgrimage is meant to influence and have an impact upon how one understands the pilgrimage of life in one's daily life among the other world's religions, especially among those faiths that see belief as part and parcel of daily living. Finally: there is a call and need for us not only to practice our own rituals and prayers of faith. Because most of the major world religions hold pilgrimage as one of the core or central religious practices, there is an opportunity here for a conversation or discussion the people of faith and religious practice may have with one another literally and figuratively on the road of life.

In this next chapter, I will outline the various characteristics of pilgrimage that are central to our understanding of an actual pilgrimage, and of the pilgrimage of daily life.

5

Characteristics of Pilgrims and Pilgrimages

My Lord God, I have no idea where I am going. I do not see the road ahead of me. I cannot know for certain where it will end. Nor do I really know myself, and the fact that I think I am following your will does not mean that I am actually doing so. But I believe that the desire to please you does in fact please you. And I hope I have that desire in all that I am doing. I hope that I will never do anything apart from that desire. And I know that if I do this you will lead me by the right road, though I may know nothing about it. —THOMAS MERTON[1]

A pilgrimage has to be completed alone, or at least begun alone. . . . Rhythm and pace are what separate most people on the trail. . . . I've resolved to walk this trail, and once I begin something, I usually finish it. . . . Actually, I begin my pilgrimage anew each day. I don't feel as though I'm on one continuous journey, but rather on a thousand short trips. . . . Just be yourself, no more and no less! —HAPE KERKELING[2]

Knowing When You Are on a Pilgrimage

Simple question: what makes a pilgrimage a pilgrimage? To answer it quickly as I did earlier in this book, it is a religious hike, a spiritual trek, or a sacred journey. But these terms are thick descriptions that may take a lifetime to explain. As stated earlier, this question, "What is a pilgrimage?" has been bouncing around in my head since I first saw the Broadway musical based on Geoffrey Chaucer's *Canterbury Tales* at Beaverton High School, and it reappears with each reading of *The Unlikely Pilgrimage of Harold Fry*,

---

1. Merton, *Thoughts in Solitude*, 79.
2. Kerkeling, *I'm Off Then*, 101–2.

a book I come back to often. *Canterbury Tales* made me toss back my head and laugh, then weep, then ponder deeply the meaning of life, all while tapping my foot to the bouncy show tunes. I was intrigued by *all* the reasons why the various characters went on pilgrimage, trying to figure out which character more or less resembled my life story.

I once went on pilgrimage with a group of five men who were part of the first class I taught on pilgrimage and education at Duke Divinity School. We went on a two-day pilgrimage, from White Cross, North Carolina, to Durham, spending a night at a Presbyterian church in Chapel Hill. Our first day was adventurous: we were met with stares by those who lived in a small African American community as six white men walked through their neighborhood with a cross, and we were pulled over by the county sheriff because of concerns raised about our group in the neighborhood. With *Canterbury Tales* as our inspiration, we ate a big dinner and bought some beer with the challenge of telling each other stories about our lives that we had never told to anyone before, with the promise that whoever told the best story could have the remaining beer. The stories we told were mind-blowing. Truly revelatory. We were unusually open, candid, vulnerable, and intimate with one another. We went beyond the "teacher-student" relationship and became pilgrims among pilgrims. I still remember some of the stories to this very day. Our morning walk to Durham was a wholly different experience as we walked with companions of the journey and not as teacher-students.[3]

I was pulled into the the surprisingly funny and yet moving novel *The Unlikely Pilgrimage of Harold Fry* by the spontaneous nature of Harold Fry's pilgrimage, which simply began one day after receiving a note from a dear lost friend. From there, the story grows from a simple walk to visit a sick friend and former coworker who was in hospice in Scotland, to a full-fledged, all-out pilgrimage. Or the way Harold is described in one brief scene from the book:

> "The unlikely pilgrimage of Harold Fry" read the caption. The article described how a retired man from Kingsbridge (also home to Miss South Devon), in walking to Berwick without money, phone, or maps, was proving himself a hero for the twenty-first century. It ended with a smaller photograph captioned "The feet that would walk five hundred miles," and showed a pair of yachting shoes similar to Harold's. Apparently they were enjoying record sales.[4]

3. Webb-Mitchell, "Six Men and a Cross," in *Follow Me*, 76–87.
4. Joyce, *Unlikely Pilgrimage of Harold Fry*, 210.

Characteristics of Pilgrims and Pilgrimages

What is interesting in the story of Harold Fry is that the professional pilgrims who try to make "Harold" their hero or earth-bound saint turned off Harold. He rejects them. He resists their efforts and continues to go on pilgrimage just as he is, with yachting shoes falling apart, the clothes on his back, and an indomitable spirit.

In Chapel Hill, when I was practicing for my philgrimage to Chimayo, all I would do is put on my T-shirt, shorts, socks, and shoes, and walk out the door on a spring morning. I know that walking from my house, northwest of Carrboro, to the easternmost limits of Chapel Hill, is around ten miles. While I drive this direction at least five days a week, there is something about putting on a pair of shoes and socks and walking it. I carry a bottle of water with me and simply walk out the front door. What happens next is anyone's bet: friends who are driving by in their cars honk and wave; lots of dogs are petted; lots of stores with drinking fountains are visited to get more water; I enjoy the aroma of baked goods coming out of Sugarland cupcake store and the whiff of freshly ground coffee at Open Eye Coffee Shop. Hitting the eastern limit, I know I could go further, but turn toward home, yet wondering, "What would happen in my life if I walked further? If I continued to walk to Wilmington, dipping my toe in the Atlantic Ocean?" Oh, the stories I could tell, relying totally on the graciousness of others. It is the spontaneity of it all, the sense of complete abandonment, that lures me forward, to test out God, and see if my needs would be met with little else than my wits and the love of God.

These stories—both fictitious and real—are all comprised of the various parts of what makes a pilgrimage a pilgrimage, and a pilgrim a pilgrim. Having already looked at the sociological, psychological, anthropological, biblical, and theological aspects of pilgrimage and pilgrim life previously in this book, in this chapter I will look at the various descriptive characteristics that make up a pilgrimage and the pilgrim's life, both on the road and in life as pilgrimage. No one of these characteristics is more important than another. They are all important in their own ways. To exclude one of the characteristics would affect the entire fabric of pilgrimage. Each one is accentuated a little bit more, depending on where we are as pilgrims on a pilgrimage.

The Whole Person on Pilgrimage: Body, Mind, and Spirit

On my first pilgrimage to Chimayo, and every subsequent pilgrimage since then that involves an overnight stay, I am reminded how much pilgrimage is an act of mind, body and spirit, that involves a kind of discipline in order to do the work of pilgrimage. Body, mind, and spirit work in coordination on pilgrimage, with a lot of pushing and pulling among body, mind, and spirit. For example, one's mind and spirit have to at least consent to moving legs, arms, and body forward from a sitting position. The body, responding to the will of the mind and spirit takes the first nonchalant step upon the ground, usually with little ceremony. It can be a first step that starts leaving a house, or from a circle of other pilgrims who have gathered to go on pilgrimage, all done in a spirit of prayer as one fights the inner impulse to question the sanity of the pilgrim.

This trinitarian concept of the body, mind, and spirit working together in going on pilgrimage is usually left out of our perspective in terms of learning and growing in the context of a faith community like the church. For example, I am a child of the church, a veteran of Protestant Sunday schools and youth groups, worshipper in myriad churches, participant and leader in evangelical rallies, participant in many Bible studies throughout college, seminary trained in three seminaries, teacher and leader of mainline Protestant conferences and retreats, and participant on too many academic panels to name (they're on my curriculum vitae). Without reservation, I can attest to the fact that most education in these contexts is of the mind primarily, and perhaps of the spirit as a byproduct, but rarely of the body. As a Presbyterian, an heir of the Reformed tradition, I realize that the focus on the mind and, secondly, the heart falls in line with Reformed theology.

Scholars who focus on pilgrimage and pilgrims have long understood that there is a connection between an outward bodily or physical experience of pilgrimage, and an internal, inner, or mystical experience of pilgrimage, write anthropologists Victor and Edith Turner.[5] Another anthropologist, Michael Sallnow, writes that a pilgrimage is a kinesthetic experience—motoric and movement-based—mapping space and charting bodily movement of the contours of the religious or Christian landscape as it rises upward from the peripheral homeland to a sacred center, such as a shrine.[6] The body does not merely carry around the heart and mind of the pilgrim. The walking experience actually connects mind with body as was covered in the Introduction to this book, along with the heart, the soul, of the pilgrim. Indeed, the Benedictine writer Joan Chittister observes that it

---

5. Victor and Edith Turner, *Image and Pilgrim in Christian Culture*, cited in Webb-Mitchell, *School of the Pilgrim*, 50.

6. John Eade and Michael Sallnow, eds., *Contesting the Sacred*, cited in Webb-Mitchell, *School of the Pilgrim*, 50.

is when the pilgrim is least prepared, when the pilgrim finds one's self lost on the pilgrimage and unsure of the next step, that the Holy Spirit arrives and guides our unsteady feet.[7]

Community and Companionship on Pilgrimage

On the various pilgrimages I have taken around this world, whether planned as a solo walk or scheduled to be a group gathering, I'm amazed at how a kind of community forms around the pilgrim. Sometimes that community is sought out, and other times it happens spontaneously. For example, on a pilgrimage on the Camino de Santiago de Compostela, I arrived about mid-way of the pilgrimage route by myself at 4:00 a.m. on a train from Madrid. I had no plans to go with anyone or to meet someone along the way. I waited in the train station awhile, until the sun started coming out and I could make my way to the Albergue or "pilgrim inn," where I opened the door and met a host of pilgrims on their way out just as I was walking in. What I did not know at the time was that this randy group of strangers would soon become friends within the next few days as I caught up with them that evening at another Albergue down the road. They displayed hospitality with an easy line, *Buen camino* or "good journey," followed by an introduction of who they were and an invitation to join them for dinner and a bottle of red wine.

Likewise in Cambodia, on a pilgrimage around the various ruins surrounding Angkor Wat, in which I was taken to various sites by a tuk-tuk driver who knew more about the hidden remains of the ancient culture of this place than the *Lonely Planet* tour books. What impressed me at the time were not the absence of the human community, but the inclusion of the animal community that surrounded me in these various historic sites. Besides the usual bugs and spiders, there were other animals like dogs, cats, chickens, and other birds that I met along the way and that kept me company.

There is no "Lone Ranger" approach to doing a Christian pilgrimage or being a Christian pilgrim. I am a Christian, and a Christian pilgrim, by the grace of God, which I know through faith, made manifest in the storied lives of the people with whom I worship, work, pray, play, serve, study, and walk with in life. The community of faith in which I reside and have

---

7. Joan Chittister, *Scarred by Struggle*, cited in Webb-Mitchell, *School of the Pilgrim*, 53.

my being provides support and ability to nurture me in the faith through mutual relationships with others, the reading of Scripture, the telling of our story, and the practice of the sacraments—reminders that I am a member of Christ's body, and that we are, individually, members, one of another (Rom 12:5). This doesn't mean that we are constantly in the presence of one another. Instead, it implies that we are continuously aware of our membership in the body of Christ, a body in which there are our friends, our associates, acquaintances, and even strangers who, through Christ, are members with us in this body.

The word *companion* comes from the French *compagnon*, with *com* meaning "with" and *panis* meaning "bread or food." In French, the word *compagnon* means either "a bread fellow" or a "messmate," one with whom we break bread. The importance of this word is given a rich overlay when we read the story of the disciples on the road to Emmaus. Jesus the stranger is revealed as the Christ in the breaking of the bread among the disciples.[8] It is our companions, those with whom we walk on an actual pilgrimage and on the pilgrimage of life, who share with us what is vital for human life—love. John Dunne writes that we have a choice in how we want to come to know God. Dunne prefers to learn of God from the friends of God who walk and speak with God, experiencing a love that is "from God and of God and towards God":

> The to-and-fro with God in which they live seems to be the only real knowing of God that man [and woman] has reached. To actually know God ourselves we will have to enter ourselves into the to-and-fro [of life with God]. It . . . has to do with experiences: floods, storms, earthquakes, afflictions, and in fact everything that happens.[9]

In this kind of companionship, perhaps philosopher Martin Buber's supreme "I-Thou" relationship, between oneself and the Holy, takes hold of our life and imagination. By our walking with others who walk and speak with God, we, in turn, find ourselves in the company of the Holy Spirit.[10]

We enter a new communion with others, through our companionship with those who walk with us. And among these new companions in the community of pilgrims, we discover new friendships as our barriers and

---

8. Webb-Mitchell, *School of the Pilgrim*, 59.

9. John Dunne, cited in Webb-Mitchell, *School of the Pilgrim*, 63.

10. It can be construed as an "I-Thou" experience as well if we don't consider the "I" an individualistic phenomenon, but that the group gathers in solidarity and becomes a grand "I." See Rodriguez, *Hunger of Memory*, 110.

fears of the "Other," the "stranger," are broken down. Aristotle's three types of friendship are made known. There are friends of use or usefulness, in whom we simply make a short acquaintance to meet the immediate needs of the moment or day. There are also friendship of pleasure, with whom we enjoy a meal at the end of day, sharing our innermost secrets, never to see this person again in our life. Finally, there are those friends with whom we have a meaningful, longlasting relationship—friendships of the good. It is with these friends that we will continue to find ourselves walking with daily, with a sense of mutuality and reciprocity in the relationship, in which both our lives are fed and nurtured deeply. These friends are at the core of our understanding of community.

Importance of Saints, Memory, and Remembrances on Pilgrimage

It is said that dogs can smell the past, the present, and the future. With their nose, they can smell out a bone dug into the ground days before. I've watched my chocolate Labrador retriever scout around the yard for his favorite toy with his nose in the present. And when dogs lift their nose into the air, they smell what is coming from our collective future.

In a similar way, pilgrims—who walk in the present—have an eye on the future, usually by looking forward. But they also experience the past through being reminded that we who walk today are but the latest pilgrims, usually walking in the footprints of those who have come before us. For example, on the way to and from Lough Derg and St. Patrick's Purgatory in Northern Ireland, along with side treks to Croagh Patrick and Knock, Ireland, there were simple shrines dotting the roadside, sometimes with a small statue of the Virgin Mary or a small crucifix. On the isle of St. Patrick's Purgatory, I was reminded of St. Brendan of Ireland, praying prayers purported to be authored by the saint. After being on pilgrimage on Lough Derg, the Dark Lake, for three days and nights with a mixture of fasting and prayer myself, I made it to Croagh Patrick, a.k.a. the Reek, on the summit of which, it is said, St. Patrick fasted for forty days and then drove out all the snakes (in which demons lived) from Ireland. As I mentioned previously, some pilgrims choose to walk up to the top of Croagh Patrick barefooted, for the expiation of sins.

On pilgrimage, especially Catholic pilgrimages such as those to Chimayo, St. Patrick's, and Santiago de Compostela, my life was filled with learning new stories and appreciating the stories of pilgrims past. The relics of saints, like St. Catherine's finger bone in the monastery that bears her name, are visual and physical reminders of those who came before us. What I learned to appreciate about these saints—these mortal women and men who came before us, and survived if not thrived when facing adversity of life and faith—is that they lived lives similar to our own, with many of the same questions and experiences, and lived to tell us about what they learned. Their stories become lessons from which we can draw succor, knowing that we are not alone, nor necessarily the first, to experience many of the challenges and joys of living the pilgrim life daily. And it is the communion of saints, which the writer of the Letter to the Hebrews (see 12:1) refers to as a "great cloud of witnesses," who are the dearly departed who are supportive of us, and for us, in a world that is at times seemingly against us. These saints before us were the ones whose footsteps we place our feet into. Again, to quote Antonio Machado, "Traveler, there is no path. Paths are made by walking."[11] The stories in the Bible, and the stories of those who preceded us on this path, are saints (and sinners) whose footsteps illuminate our steps, reminding us of what alternatives we have in life's daily pilgrimage, especially when the way proves hard to negotiate. For the saints before us, teachers of pilgrimage, we are eternally thankful.[12]

Education and Pilgrimage

A few years ago, many glossy brochures trying to sell ministerial education programs at various seminaries in the United States used the same word to describe their wares: *transformation*. Regardless of denominational pedigree, from United Methodist institutions to Presbyterian higher education contexts, the development offices were using that one word, *transformation*, to advertise their programs. They were suggesting that one would be "transformed" as a result of going through their program, or that simply by being part of the educational context one would experience a "transforming moment."[13]

On pilgrimage, transformation or a change of life and the way we perceive what is important in life may transcend our expectations. This seems to be normative for those who go on pilgrimage. And the changes in one's

---

11. Machado, "Proverbios y cantares XXIX."
12. Webb-Mitchell, *School of the Pilgrim*, 80.
13. One of my mentors, Jim Loder, wrote a book titled *Transforming Moment*. While he focused on individual psychological and spiritual change, I don't think seminary education is what he had in mind.

life may not be grasped until after one returns home from a journey, not during the actual pilgrimage itself.

The theme of learning and pilgrimage has been covered in the Introduction to this book. The nexus of learning in the process of the pilgrimage itself often falls between those who are pilgrims and the pilgrim guides. Sometimes these relationships are arranged, but most often they are spontaneous, both on an actual pilgrimage and in the pilgrimage of life. In Paulo Coelho's book *Pilgrimage,* a barely fictional story of his time on the Camino, the pilgrim is taught by Petrus, a man who has walked the Camino before. Petrus imparts an important lesson on how one learns best about pilgrimage—by taking another person on a pilgrimage that one has already taken and teaching the novice pilgrim the lessons of the pilgrimage life. Petrus says,

> You can learn only through teaching. We have been together here on the Road to Santiago, but while you were learning the practices, I learned the *meaning* of them. In teaching you, I truly learned. By taking on the role of the guide, I was able to find my own true path . . . life teaches us lessons every minute, and the secret is to accept that only in our daily lives can we show ourselves to be as wise as Solomon and as powerful as Alexander the Great. But we become aware of this only when we are forced to teach others and to participate in adventures as extravagant as this one has been.[14]

The education of pilgrimage is a kind of conversion of sorts, in which a person is continually dying to self, turning to God, and becoming more authentically human: the person that God created her or him to be, with no apology.

Virtue and Character on Pilgrimage

Within the practice of pilgrimage, lessons abound regarding the practice of moral virtues, which are key to participating in a successful intentional pilgrimage and the pilgrimage of life. In my experience on the Camino, one of the unexpected parts of the pilgrimage was the way that pilgrims could change from being a group of individuals walking on their own journeys to a living, breathing, communal organism, in which people start to look out for one another out of a spirit of camaraderie, simply because they were all focused on the goal of finishing the Camino and entering Santiago de

---

14. Quoted in Webb-Mitchell, *School of the Pilgrim,* 86.

Compostela. They trusted each other, showed compassion and benevolence at a moment's notice, displayed self-controls when need be, and showed courage at points where the faint of heart would've shrunk from their sense of duty.

What I appreciated about the pilgrimage of the Camino was the kind of bond and trust that developed spontaneously. For example, if someone left an article of clothing, a book, a piece of jewelry, or a walking stick behind in an Albergue or a restaurant, someone would pick it up and carry it with them, letting those walking faster know that they had something that was lost or left behind, and if someone was suddenly aware of the loss, to let others know until the owner was found. Same with news along the Camino: even though we had cell phones, if there was news of someone becoming ill, or a note of celebration, the news was shared up and down the length of the pilgrimage. A community of character formed serendipitously!

Above, I described Aristotle's three kinds of friendships. An argument has been made in theological and philosophical circles that it is in friendships that we learn the virtues or dispositions that build and nurture the very character of a person of faith. One learns courage not from a textbook on courage but by watching others perform courageous acts against opposing forces, like standing up against the injustices of racism, ableism, or homophobia. There is no doubt that Aristotle's understanding of virtues (such as honesty or truthfulness, trust, courage, and self-control, to name a few) and their accompanying vices (lying, cowardice, slothfulness) is part and parcel of pilgrimage. The Apostle Paul's understanding of the fruit of the Sprit like love, joy, peace, long suffering (Gal 5:22–23) are also taught and learned repeatedly on the pilgrimage of life.[15] On an actual pilgrimage and the pilgrimage of life, I experience all three kinds of friendships daily, as well as learn and relearn the moral virtues that shape not only individuals on the journey, but the very pilgrimage itself.

Rituals of Pilgrimage: Contemplation and Prayer

I like Kathleen Norris's description of pilgrimage as the monastic life on the road, only because I appreciate the rituals of monastic life, which reveal to me the mystical body of Christ. Granted, on any pilgrimage there is the normal, human, individual ritual of waking up from a deep sleep, rubbing sleep out of the eyes, preparing the body for the day ahead with a splash

---

15. Ibid., 112–16.

of water on the face, and going in search of a cup of coffee to start things off. If I'm on an actual pilgrimage, there is also time set aside for applying bandages and eating certain foods, drinking lots of water to lubricate the joints, taking multivitamins, grabbing bananas and energy bars to keep the body, mind, and spirit going all the day long. Throughout the day, there are more rituals to follow, along with a series of set practices that are used at night to slow down the body, mind, and spirit in hopes of getting a good night's sleep.

On pilgrimage, along with my individual ritual-like practices of daily life, I incorporate the prayers, songs, and other activities of the monastic life of pilgrimage introduced to me by the brothers of the Chimayo pilgrimage in New Mexico. Since the pilgrimage to Chimayo is under the auspices of the Catholic Archdiocese of Santa Fe, there is a Catholic framework that I quickly adapt to, which undergirds the very pilgrimage itself. From Saturday night, when we all first arrive to go on pilgrimage, we begin with lots of rituals, from worship to devotion to prayers around meals to evening prayers and then prayers with a small group. Prayers begin on the first day we gather for pilgrimage, which is usually a Saturday afternoon. On Sunday morning, even before breakfast at 4:00 a.m., we are praying; this is followed by praying the Angelus at 6 a.m. and noon, along with prayers for every meal, ending with more prayers in the evening. Did I write already about the prayers prayed along the route itself? Songs sung? Meal prayers again. By the end of this weeklong pilgrimage I knew most of the songs and prayers by heart having sung and prayed them numerous times throughout the day. But the prayers and songs gave structure to the day, even minimizing the sense of time we walked (usually from 5:00 a.m. to 2:00 p.m.), because our lives were filled with prayers. And I haven't mentioned the prayers and rituals that would be practiced around visiting the various churches and chapels along the way to Chimayo. What was fun on the Camino is that I took the Chimayo prayers and used them on the way to Santiago. Though I was the only practitioner throughout the day, it was not uncommon to find evening song or Eucharist being celebrated in a chapel somewhere in the late afternoon on the Camino. What these set rituals provide on pilgrimage is the framework in which I find the contemplative time, place, and space I crave in an otherwise cluttered life. I often discover that in my life at home, I spend far less time in prayer or contemplation than I desire.

In the *Institutes of the Christian Religion*, Protestant Reformer John Calvin writes, "Christ teaches us to travel as pilgrims in this world, [so] that our heritage may not perish or pass away."[16] It is in the rituals we practice in our faith communities that we are able to maintain and pass on the heritage we have received. Calvin refers to us as "pilgrims in this world," because pilgrimage was a more common practice in his day and age. All rituals reek of meaning, depending upon bodily gestures in specific, narrated contexts, with certain patterns of gestures that are often stereotypical in nature being repeated time and again. Ritual scholar Catherine Bell writes that every ritual comes "fully embedded in larger discourses," such as religion.[17] Both intentional pilgrimages and the pilgrimage of everyday life find a human framework or scaffolding in our use of simple or elaborate rituals. Rituals set the boundaries, are reminders of where we were, where we are, and where we are going. Scholar Tom Wright writes that pilgrimage is like a sacrament in and of itself, in which the act of pilgrimage involves "looking back"—as an act of great remembrance—yet also looking forward to a time of final redemption and completion. It is also open to abuse, treated as if it involved fairy dust, as a way of earning a jewel upon the crown that we will wear in heaven. Nothing can be further from the truth. Rituals on pilgrimage—like baptism and remembering our baptism and the Eucharist—are, first, reminders that our time here on earth is a pilgrimage. Each day is a new beginning for the thousands of days of pilgrimage ahead of us and soon behind us. Second, pilgrimage rituals mark us as God's people in this world. On an actual pilgrimage, we are known as pilgrims for the way we dress and the rituals we practice on the road. This is true in the pilgrimages of life, in which we honor Sabbath, pray before meals, and participate in communal rituals. Third, pilgrimage rituals, which are the rituals of a church or faith community, light the way forward. We know where we are to go, the direction, through the rituals of devotion and contemplation on the way.

What rituals help create is a setting that is conducive to contemplation and prayer, which is essential to pilgrimage. My first experience of deep solitude and contemplation was on my first pilgrimage to Chimayo. The first time I walked thirty minutes in utter silence, with a set of rosary beads thrust into my hand, I was like a person drowning in an ocean, with no boat, let alone life preserver, being thrown out to me. After running through a litany of prayer requests, the silence enveloped me. But then I watched others around me, listening to their prayers muttered softly. Walking by myself

16. Quoted in ibid., 95.
17. Quoted in ibid., 98.

in the loose linkage of pilgrims, silently, I discovered a place that is like a personal sanctuary, to which I could escape from the clamor and distractions of daily living. As theologian W. Paul Jones wrote, I discovered the healing touch of quiet, and began to reduce life to its basics.[18]

A well-known prayer on pilgrimage is that of the anonymous nineteenth-century Russian peasant in *The Way of a Pilgrim*. The pilgrim in this story wants to find the way of prayer, because he has found that true knowledge and wisdom are practiced by those who know the ceaseless prayer, otherwise known as the Jesus Prayer, which is simple: "Lord Jesus Christ, have mercy on me." This short prayer contains the summary of the gospel, and the hope of the pilgrim is that by ceaselessly reciting it, we employ the scriptural injunction to pray always.[19] Change and growth will occur in the life of all pilgrims through and with the assistance of prayer. Our Russian peasant pilgrim is deeply in love with God not because he always gets his way but because God never tires of him, and the pilgrim is simply overwhelmed.[20] The pilgrim reminds us that the message is this: prayer is both the first step on the pilgrimage and the crown of devout life, and the gospel directs us to pray constantly. For this peasant pilgrim, the pilgrimage is more than walking: it is all about prayer.

The Land, Water, and Sky on Pilgrimage

My introduction to the work of writer Annie Dillard was *Pilgrim at Tinker Creek*. Thanks to Annie Dillard, I've never seen my backyard, let alone nature itself at a micro- or macrocosmic level, the same again. From a distance, and with a quick glance, I see no "life" per se: I see different colors of green in a bush or tree, the freshly cut flowers in a vase on a table in front of me, and walk quickly down a set of stairs constructed crudely out of old railroad ties, with nothing but dirt for a step. But if I'm still and look real close, the bush in front of me is teeming with the life of birds and bugs of all shapes; the freshly cut flowers give off an aroma that is sweet, and the mound of dirt I dig up is alive with bugs, ants, and worms. And the sky above? Also teeming with life, with birds during the day and bats at night, flying insects everywhere, surrounding me as I walk.

---

18. See ibid., 132.
19. Quoted in ibid., 134.
20. Ibid., 135.

Practicing Pilgrimage—Part I

I am reminded of the centrality of earth, sky, and water in the Christian faith through the practice of pilgrimage. A helpful prayer to look around me and appreciate the world in which we live is the Navajo prayer of walking or pilgrimage:

> With beauty before me, may I walk.
> With beauty behind me, may I walk.
> With beauty on my right, may I walk.
> With beauty on my left, may I walk.
> With beauty above me, may I walk.
> With beauty below me, may I walk.
> With beauty inside me, may I walk.
> Wandering on a trail of beauty, lively, I walk.[21]

The beauty of this prayer is that it helps the mind and heart focus on not only the beauty *inside* the pilgrim but also the beauty *outside* the pilgrim. Whether being on pilgrimage in the inner city of Santa Fe, New Mexico, or Charleston, South Carolina, or walking into the large square in front of the cathedral in Santiago de Compostela, or strolling down Nablus Road in Jerusalem, or taking time to enjoy the historic relics along Hadrian's Wall, or taking in the breadth of so many hilly peaks from the top of Mt. Sinai, the focus of pilgrimage is on the surroundings of earth, water, and sky.

The beauty of the land is that *terra firma* is what we rely upon for our journey. We walk, sit, and sleep upon it; we use it for comfort and support as we lean against it. We rely upon it to feed us, to nurture our spirits, and to handle our waste. Our beginning has something to do with land. The creation story of Genesis more or less literally and figuratively grounds us, a point Christian are reminded of when they participate in an Ash Wednesday service as we are reminded: "To dust you shall return" (Gen 3:19).

The land on pilgrimage also holds a key to the change that we experience on pilgrimage. In the book *The Ritual Process*, anthropologist Victor Turner writes about a stage of change that a human being goes through when moving from one fixed sense of self to a new way of being.[22] This stage of change is known as liminality, in which a person is separating from one state of being to a new way of being in the world. Henry Carse reminds us that the land is a kind of portal or threshold of liminality when one is

---

21. "A Navajo Prayer of Seven Directions," in *Archdiocesan Pilgrimage of Vocation*, 25.
22. Turner, *Ritual Process*, 94.

Characteristics of Pilgrims and Pilgrimages

on a pilgrimage.[23] For Henry, the desert is the place, the land that holds the creative tension of liminality. It is the wilderness of the desert that is "voice and silence, form and formlessness, origin and vocation, revelation and annihilation. This 'in between' nature of the desert is both postmodern and ancient, poised on the edge of an a/theology defying distant doctrine with the sheer throb of our own nerves and blood, while simultaneously denying our desire for a deity who will pamper us with providence."[24] Again, like the desert of the Sinai, Egypt, the artist George O'Keefe observed that the land of New Mexico is covered with the veil of Christianity. This observation is echoed in the writings of Flannery O'Connor who believed that the American South is, itself, a "Christ haunted landscape." They all point to a convergence of the spiritual, the holy, touching and being embedded in terra firma—land, sky, and water—the very environment or setting for a pilgrim's pilgrimage.

Water on pilgrimage is also a gateway towards a liminal experience. As land nourishes the pilgrim, water refreshes the pilgrim. When asked what is needed on a pilgrimage, I am often quick to add: "Water!" Our bodies being composed of 60 percent water, and our brains 75 percent water, is it any wonder that we are drawn to the water's edge on pilgrimage? Whether I'm walking the Camino or traipsing alongside Hadrian's Wall, whenever possible I like to walk alongside a creek or river, listening to the flow at night as I walk along the edge.

But water is more than merely something to replenish us when on pilgrimage. Water is itself a pathway of pilgrimage. Writer Robert Macfarlane reminds us that when we think of paths we usually think of the land. But the seas, the waters, also have paths, "though water refuses to take and hold marks."[25] The seas and the lakes and rivers were once the fastest means of long-distance travels. While I've often walked on a river's edge or on the coast, I know others who have gone on a pilgrimage using a kayak or canoe. And on the open seas and oceans, the sea roads are not arbitrary, writes Macfarlane: "There are optimal routes to sail across open sea, as there are optimal routes to walk across open land."[26] It is just a matter of knowing the shape of the coastlines and the ocean currents that help transport a person along the water's edge. In a sense, our following the currents is not

---

23. Carse, *Sinai*, 20–21.
24. Ibid., 22.
25. Macfarlane, *Old Ways*, 88.
26. Ibid., 89.

unlike dolphins and whales, sea turtles and sharks, who follow what, for us, seems a circuitous route, but for them is nonetheless, through instinct, a way home. So the waters can also hold within its boundaries a route for pilgrimage.

Finally, there is the sky, the horizon, with "Brother Sun" during the day and "Sister Moon" at night (to quote St. Francis of Assisi from one of his canticles). I can never get my fill of gorgeous sunrises and sunsets on pilgrimage. Because the pilgrimages to Chimayo begin with a 3:00 a.m. wake up call in order to assure that we are on the road by 5:00 a.m., it is dark, still, and cold since the sunshine has been gone from the land for the last seven or eight hours. I am always in awe as I watch the sun, like a pinprick shining through black construction paper, grow quickly in size, breaking over the horizon in the forrested expanse near this holy site. Within an hour I've shrugged off coat and long pants for my more comfortable T-shirt and shorts, feeling the warmth of sun warm up my chilled bones . . . all before 7:00 a.m. During the day, whether I am in the desert of New Mexico or the Sinai desert, I am always struck by the expanse of blue-sky overhead. Spirituality writer Kathleen Norris compares such open skies to a bowl that has been turned over, and we are lost in the immensity of the openness all around us. When sleeping in the Sinai desert, out in the wide-open spaces, I marvel at the immensity of stars overhead, watching the play of stars with shooting stars going hither and yon above me. During daylight, it is the wide-open spaces that make my little life feel almost insignificant, given the expanse of sky above. And at night I look for redness in the sky, a good omen for the next day's push toward the destination, repeating to myself, "Red sky at night, sailor's delight." The fire of the sun during day and the reflection of the moon at night guide and illuminate the pilgrim's daily path.

And Maybe More

As I wrote earlier, the contexts of our pilgrimage, and the various nuances that shape our lives as pilgrims, are multivalent. The dynamics of the pilgrim's life change daily, as it is shaped by the context in which we walk. As no two pilgrims are alike, no two pilgrimages or pathways are alike. Each one is different, garnering a different set of experiences. Each day we may practice a certain set of rituals that are practiced every day at about the same hour, giving us a context to think, imagine, and pray "on the go." When walking the Camino de Santiago de Compestela, I found myself praying at about the same hour morning, noon, and night. I watched others and soon found myself practicing the sign of the cross. I said, "*Buen camino!*" to others with little to no thought, as it was part of my pilgrimage. I ate certain foods at particular times of the day to face the challenge ahead in terms of energy. And I tried to practice the gestures of hospitality hour by hour, regardless of how different the context was from day to day.

What sustains us amid the challenges of pilgrimage each day is hospitality, which we now turn to. I set hospitality aside as a separate, short chapter because it is central to being on an actual pilgrimage, and to the pilgrimage of life.

6

The Art of Hospitality on Pilgrimage

The door is open to all, sick or well,
Not only Catholics, but pagans also,
To Jews, heretics, idlers, the vain.
And, as I shall briefly note, the good and worldly too.[1]

All guests to the monastery should be welcomed as Christ,
Because He will say, "I was a stranger,
And you took me in." —THE RULE OF ST. BENEDICT

I often knew more about a fellow sojourner after a day's walk than I did about many colleagues I'd worked with for years. —JOHN SPALDING[2]

The Kindness of Strangers

In his book *I'm Off Then*, German comedian Hape Kerkeling is having a conversation with a new friend, Anne from England. At first, she is put-off by his bigger-than-life personality. She later apologizes to him for her stand-offish behavior: "Sorry, Hans Peter, for being so rude to you today . . . but you know . . . pilgrims aren't necessarily nice just because they're pilgrims. But *you* are nice."[3]

I agree with Ann: having walked the Camino, not all pilgrims are nice. All pilgrims are not created the same. And being on a pilgrimage can often

---

1. A message left on a door in an Albergue where pilgrims stay on the Camino, quoted in Lewis-Kraus, *Sense of Direction*, 59.
2. Spalding, *Pilgrim's Digress*, 220.
3. Kerkeling, *I'm Off Then*, 72.

The Art of Hospitality on Pilgrimage

make one a bit ill-tempered during the first few days as one's body and mind adapt to the challenge of walking long distances day after day. On my first morning on the Camino, I was under the illusion that all of us would be pleasant with each other since we were all in the same boat, beyond the almost perfunctory "*Buen camino!*" when wishing each other well on the trail. Instead, pilgrims were already in their bands of friendships and acquaintances, and no one except the Albergue innkeeper was friendly to me (his friendliness made all the difference). Of course, there was no reason to believe others would *have to be* nice for any special reason. There was nothing novel about me as a pilgrim in a land awash with pilgrims. That's why the practice of hospitality on the Camino was a welcome practice: because of its rarity! With thousands streaming along the Camino each year, there was no reason for anyone to be nicer to one person than to another.

Without fail, there is always a moment on a pilgrimage in which I am at the mercy of strangers who help me out of one pickle or another. Let me pick up on the story I began above. When I began the latter portion of the Camino de Santiago de Compostela, I walked into the pilgrim inn, the Albergue, at 7:00 a.m., right when most everyone else in the Albergue was on their way out. I watched as a large group of pilgrims were shuffling around the dining area, some dressed and others half dressed, scarfing down breakfast with one hand while trying to tie a shoe with the other. I waited until the roar of the crowd died down some before I finally got up the nerve to ask the person who managed the Albergue how one begins the Camino, besides following the yellow scallop shell signs: "First, give me your *credencial*," he said brusquely, but with a slight smile from the corner of his mouth. I complied dutifully, handing him my credential, the passport for the Camino. Then the hospitality started to come more explicitly. "Want a cup of coffee? With or without cream?" he asked in broken English. In other words, did I want a *café con leche*? "Sure!" I said. He then looked at my blank credential. "Let's see . . . why, you're a novice! Well, let me stamp your book and tell you a little bit about the trail ahead of you today." And with that generous introduction, at that very moment, many of my trepidations of being on the Camino died down. While he was brusque with the rest of the veteran pilgrims, he treated me as if I mattered! He extended care out of the goodness of his heart. There were more acts of kindness that would follow that day: I walked among a field of tomato plants, and as I walked through, one of the women who worked the field invited me to come over, holding out in her hand a ripe tomato. Simply saying "wow," she then took her knife and sliced it open for me in her open hand, then handed me the

83

ripe tomato slices. It was heaven: thick, juicy, and tasty. There was nothing plastic about the taste of this fruit of the earth. That was just on the first morning! Help with bleeding blisters, crepes cooked right in front of me by a farmer's wife outside her barn, too many bottles of red wine to count, hugs morning, noon, and evening after a fine meal . . . all of these acts of hospitality were daily fare.

It would not be too farfetched to say that when I am on a pilgrimage I often depend upon the kindness of strangers. Me, alone, will not survive, let alone thrive, on a pilgrimage when I am out walking by myself and not walking with a preselected group of friends or with a group I've been hired to lead, or if I don't find myself a part of an ad hoc community of pilgrims. I only find myself able to walk the way of a pilgrim because of the presence of others who are ready, willing, and able to help out. In other words, we walk in solidarity often with others.

Another story of hospitality. One of the most beautiful experiences of sustained hospitality is with the New Mexican *Penitentes*, or the brotherhood of the Penitential ones, which I mentioned earlier in this book. This brotherhood of Catholic laity have lived in parts of the American southwest for over four hundred years, since the land was first colonized by the Spaniards. During a period of time when the priests were not present in the country, the men of the *Penitentes* maintained the Spanish Catholic culture. My experience of the *Penitentes* comes from various pilgrimages to Chimayo. I first met the *Penitentes* and their wives gathered in a *Morada*, a house that is owned by the *Penitentes*. It is usually a large room with a kitchen and bathroom as part of it. And it is filled with religious—or more specifically Roman Catholic—icons and *Santos*. My first visit to a *Morada* was on a day in June 1999, outside of Rancho de Taos, in which our band of pilgrims were fed hot dogs and hamburgers, with all the trimmings. Inside their *Morada*, where the beverages were located, I entered the small ranch-style house, and first came upon a life-size wood statue of Jesus in a room lit only by candlelight and small Christmas tree lights. The wood carved figure of Jesus was stripped bare, save for the loincloth. Around his head was a crown of thorns. His body seemed to be painted all red because of the wounds from the whippings. Bathed in red light from numerous strings of Christmas tree lights around the room, there was almost a haunted feeling around this image of Jesus. I've been to other *Moradas* since that first trip. Many have a life-size wood carved or fiberglass figure of Jesus, almost crawling on the ground, a cross upon his back, a crown of thorns on his head, and wearing what looks like a simple white alb. I've been captivated

The Art of Hospitality on Pilgrimage

by all the various *Santos* and images of Mary and Jesus in tall votive candles on tables and sconces within the *Moradas* themselves. What is memorable about visiting these *Moradas*, the households of the *Penitentes*, is not only the interior design of each house, filled with Roman Catholic icons from floor to ceiling, but the hospitality of the *Penitentes* and their family members, who served us incredible New Mexican food, with a choice of green or red chili at the dining table. At one evening BBQ, I had Mexican food that left me only wanting more, from tortillas to pulled pork, and all the other dishes that were fit for a queen or king. At another *Morada* on the way from Bernal to Chimayo, I had a meal that was incredibly filling, with black beans and refried beans, eggs and bacon, sausages and sweet rolls, pots of coffee, with no end in sight. But it was not only the food, but also the singing of songs, the warm embrace of women and men as they paid special attention to us as "blessed ones," given this rare opportunity to be pilgrims, *peregrinos*.

In this chapter, the focus will be on the essential practice and art of hospitality. This is an essential virtue—benevolence—that creates character, and is a highlight of pilgrimage. After all, hospitality more or less holds a pilgrim and pilgrimage together. Without it, the pilgrim would be lost, and the pilgrimage doomed. Yet time and again, the pilgrimage is sustained, maintained, and celebrated through the literal and figurative "kindness of strangers." And it takes at least two for hospitality, with the interaction between the two being the "stuff" of hospitality. It is the interaction of the gentle word said, the massage of the foot, the intention of giving and receiving food, the sharing of clothes, the hug, the kiss, the ride, the support of the other when a pilgrimage gets long and the body grows weary—that's the hospitality that holds the pilgrim and pilgrimage together. More importantly, in pilgrimage is the possibility of conversion, in which stranger becomes friend as we welcome angels unawares in an actual pilgrimage as well as the pilgrimage of life.

My examples will come from both actual pilgrimages as well as the pilgrimage of life, for it is here that I've learned the lessons on pilgrimage.

What Is Hospitality?

Hospitality is more than what we experience at a Holiday Inn or nearby bed and breakfast, though they are places with people who practice hospitality, most often going the extra yard. For example, following my pilgrimage to Chimayo, I stayed at a DoubleTree hotel where the young receptionist, who likewise had gone on the pilgrimage to Chimayo, filled my hands with chocolate chip cookies and coupons for alcoholic beverages at the bar, gratis! In many colleges and universities today there are courses where instructors teach "hospitality" as a professional trade, with students becoming managers of chain hotels from Disney World theme parks and golf resorts, to working on a cruise ship and opening up a bed and breakfast. It is the "warm welcome," the "Glad you are here!" and "Come back soon!" messages that we yearn to hear at these places, no matter how sincere or insincere the one expressing such sentiment.

In most dictionaries, the word *welcome* is connected to the word *guest* and oftentimes *host*. In other words, in order to have "welcome" there is the need for a "guest" and a "host." In her book *Making Room*, theologian Christine Pohl writes that hospitality is a fundamental moral practice for communal life. It is "necessary to human well-being and essential to the protection for vulnerable strangers."[4] Pohl looks at the word "hospitality," citing the ancient Greek word for hospitality, *philoxenia*. This word is a combination of the word for love or affection for people who are friends—*philia*—and the word for stranger, *xenos*. Pohl states that this word for hospitality shows how closely it aligns love with the stranger: "Because *philoxenia* includes the word for stranger, hospitality's orientation toward strangers is also more apparent in Greek than in English."[5] In a sense, hospitality is a combination of love of God and love of stranger, even when the neighbor is a stranger, since this love—*philia*—is a practice that we learn from God first loving us.[6]

Important in the practice is not necessarily or only the host, but the stranger. What is interesting in this interaction is that the host is a "stranger" to the guest who is visiting. After all, even if one is "at home" or in "one's church" as a pastor or lay person, when a person comes to an abode like house or church as a "stranger," the house owner or church member is also a stranger to the one visiting or choosing to come into one's house or church. Being the stranger simply designates someone who is foreign to us. The word "stranger" comes from the French, *estrangier*. The stranger is the one who does not know or is unaccustomed to or unacquainted with

---

4. Pohl, *Making Room*, 28–29.

5. Ibid., 31.

6. Some of this material comes from my book *Beyond Accessibility*, especially the section "Practicing Hospitality" (82).

someone, a group of people, or a place. Sometimes we are the strangers; at other times, we are ones in the "know," as it were, and our task as Christians is to perform the gesture of welcome, of hospitality, to those who are strangers in our midst.

Biblical Roots: Hebrew Scripture and New Testament

In Hebrew Scripture, the root word in Hebrew for pilgrim or sojourner was *gur* and *ger*. The verb "gur" means to dwell for an indefinite or definite time, or to dwell as a newcomer—"ger"—without original rights.[7] To be a sojourner is to be a newcomer in the land with no rights in terms of inheriting the land.[8] "Ger" and "gur" were used to describe Abraham's situation when he fled to Egypt to escape the famine in Canaan (Gen 12:10); Lot's stay in Sodom (Gen 19:9); and then there is the non-citizen who is dwelling in a foreign land and who is also sojourner or pilgrim. Now, "pilgrim" or "sojourner" does not necessarily mean that one is constantly on the road in Hebrew Scripture. It more or less points to the idea of one being a newcomer, a resident alien, a foreigner in the land. For example, Jacob describes his life as a pilgrimage when he stood before Pharaoh in Egypt, not meaning that he was literally "on the road" but that he was a new person in a strange land that was not the land of his birth (Gen 47:9).

Throughout the Hebrew Scriptures, it is clear that the Israelites were to welcome strangers who came to them, with never an attempt to hurry the stranger away. One was expected to open one's house with the kind of hospitality that is rarely practiced in this day and age. For example, in Deuteronomy the people were told to welcome strangers, "for you were once strangers in the land of Egypt" (10:19), including food and shelter. There is a similar command in Leviticus: "The alien who resides with you shall be to you as the citizen among you. . . . I am the Lord your God." Both of these commands reminded the people that Jacob, a.k.a., Israel, and his family were brought to the land of Egypt during the time of famine, and because of Joseph they received welcome and hospitality, and stayed for a generation. Because they were once strangers in the land of Egypt, the people of Israel are to always welcome those who are strangers in Israel, or in their homes or places of worship, with open arms.

---

7. Brown, Driver and Briggs, *Old Testament Hebrew-English Lexicon*. Online: http://lexiconcordance.com/hebrew/1616.html.

8. Ibid.

Practicing Pilgrimage—Part I

In the New Testament, this tradition of welcoming the stranger on the road and providing hospitality is key to the ministry of Jesus, the Pilgrim God. To recap: Jesus began his earthly life as a pilgrim, with his family depending upon the hospitality of strangers when they fled to Egypt in order to avoid certain death. And in his earthly ministry, over the three years that the Gospel accounts cover, Jesus never owned a home that we know of,[9] and was dependent upon strangers and friends alike—like Mary, Martha, and Lazarus—to provide hospitality and welcome him in their midst. Throughout Christian Scriptures, the stranger, the pilgrim, the sojourner becomes an almost saintly figure because Jesus took on the role of the stranger. This is especially true in light of the story of the road to Emmaus in Luke 24. In this story, the risen Christ comes upon the disciples Cleopas and his unnamed friend who are on the road to Emmaus, seven miles from Jerusalem, having left behind the place of Jesus's death. Jesus was hidden from their recognition, so they did not know whom they met on the road. And the disciples still feared the authorities would arrest them as accomplices and friends with the crucified Jesus. So Christ comes upon them on the road and asks them, "What are you discussing with each other while you walk along?" Cleopas answers, "Are you the only stranger in Jerusalem who does not know the things that have taken place there in these days?" Jesus asks, "What things?" Cleopas then shares all that has happened in Jerusalem during the past few days. Cleopas called Jesus "stranger," highly exalting the stranger in their midst who is the Christ. Similarly, in Matthew, in the judgment of the nations, the Son of Man declares, "I was a stranger and you welcomed me" (Matt 25:35). Jesus names himself the stranger among us, exalting those who welcome the stranger while condemning those who fail to welcome the stranger as Christ: "I was a stranger and you did not welcome me" (Matt 25:43).

Jean Vanier, cofounder with Pere Thomas of the religious communities of L'Arche that welcome people who live with disabilities, cites Jesus in such passages as the paradigmatic stranger, who comes to us as an alien of sorts, an otherworldly presence:

> The stranger is a person who is different, from another culture or another faith; the stranger disturbs because he or she cannot enter into our patterns of thought or our ways of doing things. To welcome is to make the stranger feel at home, at ease, and that means

---

9. There are some current archeologists who suggest that Jesus may have owned a home or been in residence in Capernaum.

not exercising any judgment or any preconceived ideas, but rather giving space to *be*. Once we have made the effort of welcoming and accepting the disturbance, we discover a friend; we live a moment of community, a new peace; a presence of God is given. The stranger is frequently prophetic; he or she breaks down our barriers and our fears, or else makes us conscious that they are there and may even strengthen them.[10]

Likewise, the disciples were commanded to take a similar position in life in order that they would be, like Jesus, dependent upon the hospitality of others. For example, in Mark 1:38–39, Jesus and his disciples go on an earthly pilgrimage, "proclaiming the message in their synagogues and casting out demons." Later, he instructs them to go out two by two, with the authority given to them by Jesus, to cleanse people of unclean spirit. He orders them to take nothing for their pilgrimage except a staff, no bread, no bag, no money in their belts, wearing only sandals, and not to put on two tunics: "wherever you enter a house, stay there until you leave the place. If any place will not welcome you and they refuse to hear you, as you leave, shake off the dust that is on your feet as a testimony against them" (Mark 6:7–11).

Today, being a stranger, a pilgrim, a sojourner provides an occasion in which Christians may practice hospitality with one another. The pattern is clearly set by Jesus as the stranger, the pilgrim, who then welcomes and makes hospitality possible. For example, we see this played out in the Apostle Paul's conversion process. Soon after Paul's conversion, Paul finds his way to the house of Judas where the reluctant disciple Ananias will find Paul, and lay his hands on him, restoring Paul's sight (Acts 9). Paul himself depended upon the hospitality of others in his ministry and mission work following his conversion, as did the other disciples. In an important way, extending hospitality became a way of evangelism for the young church, in which time and again, when disciples were often welcomed into the homes of strangers, there was a high likelihood of conversion.

Hospitality and Pilgrims: The Rule of St. Benedict

I'm writing this chapter while at Studium, a place of study, at St. Benedict's Monastery in St. Joseph, Minnesota. On the nameplate of my office and guest room door are written these words: "Welcome, Brett Webb-Mitchell! May all be received as Christ, RB 53 [Rule of Benedict, Chapter 53]."

10. Vanier, *Community and Growth*, 265.

Practicing Pilgrimage—Part I

Verses 1–2 of chapter 53 of the Rule of St. Benedict read: "All guests who present themselves are to be received as Christ, for he himself will say: 'I was a stranger and you welcomed me' (Matt. 25:35). Proper honor must be shown to all, especially to those who share our faith (Gal. 6:10) and to pilgrims."[11] St. Benedict is one of the largest all-women Benedictine monasteries, and up the road in Collegeville is St. John's Abbey, one of the largest all-men's Benedictine monasteries. Both of these monasteries grew out of one of the earliest Christian monasteries, established by Benedict of Nursia, Italy, who's sister was Scholastica. Years later, Benedict would become "St. Benedict," and he and his brothers, along with St. Scholastica, became well-known in the world for their practice of Christian hospitality. St. Benedict established a touchstone of the practice of hospitality in Christian contexts, and Benedictines are well known for their hospitality. In the Rule of St. Benedict, which provides order for the Benedictine community, Benedict writes: "As soon as the arrival of a guest is announced, the superior and members of the community should hurry to offer a welcome with warm-hearted courtesy. First of all, they should pray together so as to seal their encounter in the peace of Christ."[12] Furthermore, rules of fasting may be broken by the superior (prior/abbot or prioress/abbess), to entertain the guest, and the superior pours water for guests to wash their hand and then washes their feet, with the whole community involved in the ceremony. As the stranger, the pilgrim, when I first visited the Abbey of Christ in the Desert (Benedictine) Monastery in New Mexico, I was always seated next to the abbot, a place of honor, and not among the brothers per se, and fed first, for "the superior's table should always be with the guests and pilgrims."[13]

In this act of praying together and sharing in the life of the community, the body of Christ—be it a monastery, an intentional Christian community, or a church—is working from two main axis of faith, which are central values to pilgrimage: praying and sharing. The late Brother John of the Taizé community writes that by praying and sharing life together in this way we are "enlarging to the scale of God's people the experience which many are living, and have been living for years. To go out to one another, beyond the

---

11. This statement is located on an outside kiosk, between the Great Hall and Abbey Church at St. John's Abbey and University, Collegeville, MN.

12. St. Benedict, *Rule of St. Benedict*, 53.

13. Ibid., 67. Much of the information in this section also comes from my book: Webb-Mitchell, *School of the Pilgrim*, 60–61.

barriers, which usually separate us, and to go forth together to encounter God in prayer—is this not the true meaning of the Christian pilgrimage?"[14]

In recent years at St. Benedict's Monastery, some of the women I have come to know have grown older, and their step slower. As we walk the streets of St. Joseph, Minnesota, around the Monastery, I have learned to slow down the pace of my walking, to walk in solidarity, in the company of, my sisters. On an actual pilgrimage, and the pilgrimage of life, there are times to walk by ourselves, but there are times that we may choose to walk with each other, not encouraging the other to walk at our pace, but for pilgrims to find the pace that works for one and all concerned. Finding such a pace is, after all, a gift of hospitality.

Summary

By welcoming the stranger among us, we, who are hosts, transcend our own needs and wants by putting them aside in welcoming Christ who resides in and is the stranger. By doing so, the community becomes the very living sacrament of human fulfillment and discovers a purpose in life: being and becoming a community of God's pilgrim people. By welcoming the stranger, the community broadens and stretches its soul, mind, and body, for we are not necessarily in control of what will occur in Christ-centered communities when we welcome the stranger, in whom the Spirit of Christ dwells among us, and who in turn enables us to be about something or someone greater than ourselves.

What the stranger—the one who is foreign to our gathering—does in effect is a very human thing: the stranger may be the stimulus for growth and change in a community's life. God may very well bring the stranger among us as we try to cling to old ways, knowing our propensity to change at a snail's pace as we cling to the sidewalk and stones on the pilgrim's path. Strangers call us to listen to one another anew, to sit silently and take in the stories of another, thus taking in the stories of God's people. The stranger, the pilgrim who visits—which may be us in a new setting—causes a ripple effect of change, calling a Christian community to truly be the body of Christ in ways that those who are already members no longer can do because of the stability or the ruts of our life in community. The stranger reminds us how we can be strangers unto our selves, pointing out parts of our lives that we fail tend to in our daily pilgrimage.

14. Quoted in Robinson, *Sacred Places, Pilgrim Paths*, 71.

Practicing Pilgrimage—Part I

In welcoming the stranger—be it in a church or a faith community—we welcome the outsider or visitor into our lives and make space for that person to grow. Jean Vanier writes that welcoming the other person, the newcomer, is to give space in our heart, where people know that they are accepted just as they are, with their wounds and their gifts. Welcoming the other, we no longer live in fear and insecurity, unclear about who we are and what our vocation in life is. It means to take time for aspects of a person's life. After some time, a surprising change happens: soon the stranger is no longer the stranger, the alien among us, but becomes a true travel companion. One may be simply an acquaintance, a friend for the day, or become our dearest love. Nonetheless, we now have a new friend who walks with us on this pilgrimage of life.

In the next section, the focus will be on the church, which is literally understood as "the pilgrims' house," and how worship is a kind of pilgrimage of the body, mind, and spirit, as we are transformed or converted once again through the practice of prayer, hearing the stories of God's pilgrim people throughout time, and celebrate the sacraments that enrich our very lives. The church or "parish" comes from the ancient Greek *paraikos*, which means "pilgrim, passing stranger," or, as some translations have it, the "house of the foot."[15]

---

15. Ibid., 61.

7

Being and Becoming God's Pilgrim People: Worship and Pilgrimage

> Weary pilgrim on life's pathway—
> Struggling on beneath thy load—
> Hear these words of consolation,
> Cast thy burden on the Lord.[1]

> Worship begins with God. God takes the initiative and calls us into being. In the name of Christ we answer God's call and assemble as the community of faith.[2]

> We are learning that unity at the font, pulpit, and table is the true road to healing the brokenness of Christ's church. —[3]

Worship on Pilgrimage

Worship is central in the life of many pilgrims on pilgrimage. Some of us find going to daily Mass or Holy Communion at day's end of walking a true joy. For the pilgrimage of everyday life, beginning each week with worship that includes the Lord's Supper is a helpful reminder for us to seek out the Christ in breaking bread with others throughout our busy week. As quoted

---

1. Verse 1 of "Weary Pilgrim on Life's Pathway," text by William J. Kirkpatrick, www.churchinmontereypark.org/Docs/Hymn/EnglishHymnal/html/hymns/697.html.
2. Presbyterian Church (USA), *Book of Common Worship*, 34.
3. Ibid., 7.

above from the *Book of Common Worship* from the Presbyterian Church (USA), it is at the font used at baptism, the pulpit where the Word of God is proclaimed and exclaimed, and the Lord's Supper table—or for others the altar—where Communion is celebrated, that we all find the "true road to healing the brokenness of Christ's church."[4] It is in worship that we discover, are reminded, or redirected to be on the *true* road, the pathway of Christian pilgrims, towards healing the brokenness of the body of Christ. The world—which is forever rebelling against the ways of God, undermining the love of Christ, and bringing destruction upon the ecological gift we have been given—looks in astonishment as we walk forward toward healing as a body of members.

Worship usually comes at the end of pilgrimages for me, either at day's end or at the end of the journey itself, though there are a few where the worship starts the whole shebang. Morning, midday, and evening prayers are staples of an actual pilgrimage and everyday pilgrimage. For example, at the end of the pilgrimage to Chimayo, worship is a large homecoming event, with five groups of pilgrims who started at five different geographical places around Chimayo (Bernal, Estancia, Costilla, Albuquerque, Chama), meeting at El Santuario de Chimayo, the old adobe structure that is the sanctuary of Chimayo. Each group comes in separately around 9:00 a.m. on a Saturday morning, going by a statue of the Blessed Virgin Mary, kissing the hem of her skirt. When walking through the doors of the sanctuary itself, each group is welcomed by a band of guitars and other instruments, playing songs from the pilgrimage. The first group of pilgrims warmly welcomes the incoming group until all five groups of pilgrims have entered the small sanctuary. Rosaries are placed around each pilgrim's neck by the Catholic Archbishop, followed by more hugs and kisses. Having gone on several pilgrimages to Chimayo, I enjoy seeing pilgrims I walked with in the past at these reunions. We then stream out of the intimate historic church to a large open plaza in the back of the church that can hold not only the pilgrims assembled, but friends and families as well for Mass. We gather our five crucifixes, our five images of Our Lady of Guadalupe, our five bags of collected soil, and bags of prayer requests. The Spiritual Director of the pilgrimages reminds us of the blessed time we had together. We listen to a person from each band of pilgrims tell a story from their time on pilgrimage, with much laughter and tears shared among us all. The music, the sense of relief and release, having walked over one hundred and ten

---

4. Ibid.

miles in five and a half days, the welcome arms of family and friends, and the celebration of the Eucharist, feeds body, mind, and spirit not only of individual pilgrims, but the body, mind, and spirit of Christ.

Or consider worship at the end of walking the Camino de Santiago de Compostela. I remember walking into the large Cathedral of Santiago, with the front of the sanctuary illuminated by a gold and marble screen, and the chandelier lights above, along with spot lights, showing off the elaborate gold finery. The reliquary of St. James is located in the front, near the altar. Around me are other pilgrims, our backpacks lined up against the stonewall or surrounding the base of the stone columns that hold the building up. The liturgy—meaning literally the "work of the people"—is spoken in Spanish of course. There are two highlights of worship, along with the Eucharist: one is the reading out loud of one's nationality the day after you turn in your credentials. It was a moment of pride to hear *el Carolina Norte*. The other was watching the huge incense burner or *Botafumeiro* swing after the Eucharist. It takes up to six men to swing this large pendulum-like structure, filled with burning incense. The incense was initially used to debug the pilgrims who came with all kinds of insects on them, along with the hope of killing the stench of pilgrims who had not taken a shower or bath along the Camino. The large incense burner is magnificent, and a great addition to worship.

Another story: on the way along Hadrian's Wall in England, with the group of pilgrims from the University of North Carolina-Chapel Hill, on the second day of the pilgrimage we were blessed with a drier day than the first, when we were all soaked (it was typical English weather). Gathered around a picnic table at a campground, we paused on Pentecost morning for worship. Celebrating Eucharist on a wooden picnic table, all were given red threads and wore red shirts, hats, or bandanas that day as a symbol of the fire that came down upon those early disciples gathered together as the Spirit filled their lives. And then, like the pilgrim disciples before us, we went out and embodied the Gospel that day with other people we met along the pilgrims' way, practicing gestures of hospitality of Jesus, the Pilgrim God.

Finally, it is a Sunday morning. Several hundred people from around the Chapel Hill area gather together at United Church of Chapel Hill (UCCH) for Sunday worship. One has a choice for times of worship: 8:45 a.m. worship includes Eucharist regularly, while 11:00 a.m. offers Eucharist once a month. The congregation is a rich blend of our liberal bubble, in which Jesus is preached: white and black families sit next to each other; lesbian couples with their newborn rock in the rocking chairs provided in the back of the sanctuary (all children welcome of all ages); there is a person who knows American Sign Language who is interpreting worship for those who are deaf. There are children throughout the congregation, seated by those people in their eighties an nineties. Music will often include many anthems and hymns written in the nineteenth and twentieth century, but now and then a more contemporary song squeezes in, along with blue grass and folk, and occasionally a song from the African continent. United Church is well known in the community for integrating people of different races, genders, sexes, sexual orientations, ethnicities, ages, educational backgrounds, and abilities. The concerns of the many are integrated in sermons weekly. Worship is reflective of a Protestant worship service, beginning with Call to Worship, then right to Confession, followed by the Word of God read and interpreted in a sermon, with a chance to respond to the Word read with the sacraments of the church, along with offering. And causes of justice are celebrated and blessed within the body of believers within worship. For example, during North Carolina's Moral Monday marches in 2013 and 2014, in which many Carolinians protested against the actions and policies of the General Assembly, numerous people from this congregation went to the march and were arrested for civil disobedience. Toward the end of worship, as a response to the Word of God read and exclaimed, numerous people would go to the front of the sanctuary and receive a blessings from the congregation for the work of justice that they were about to partake in on the following day in Raleigh. After worship, food and drink would be provided in the large fellowship hall, with time to chat with other congregants before going back on the pilgrimage of life.

In these four stories—from New Mexico's Chimayo, the Cathedral of Santiago de Compostela, the campground along Hadrian's Wall, and United Church of Chapel Hill—worship during an actual pilgrimage and the pilgrimage of life was central. That was because the one who called us to be pilgrims of Christ was none other than the God of creation.

Worship Is at the Heart of Pilgrimage

Let me reiterate: worship is at the heart of all Christian pilgrimages, whether it is an actual pilgrimage or the pilgrimage of life. Why is that? Because worship is at the very heart of a church's life—church being where two or three are gathered in Jesus's name. And the church, the body of Christ, is on a pilgrimage throughout time in all places. To reiterate: "All that the church is and does is rooted in its worship of God, who in turn invites us to live, enact, share, and walk in the way of Christ Jesus. The Christian community of faith, gathered in response to God's call, is formed in its worship. Worship is the principal influence that shapes (and nurtures) our faith, and is the most visible way we express faith." These are the opening lines of the Preface to the Presbyterian Church (USA) *Book of Common Worship*.[5] Worship reflects and is the embodiment of the theology of the various denominations and churches. Or as I've heard more than one Episcopalian or Anglican say: our liturgy is our theology. Sound theology is incorporated in sound liturgy, and vice versa. As a "cradle Christian," raised from infancy in the worship of a church, through countless moments of worship in various Protestant denominations, along with Roman Catholic and Greek Orthodox churches, I follow more closely the distinct trail of liturgies used in worship, because the liturgy or order of worship reveals the ways that the spirits, minds, and bodies of "us" modern day pilgrims are being nourished or, in some cases, not being nourished. For worship is a way for us to serve the Creator, the One who created us for the purpose of worshipping the Holy One.

What is worship? Presbyterian writer Frederick Buechner discusses worship as the following:

> Phrases like Worship Service or Service of Worship are tautologies. To worship God means to *serve* him. Basically there are two ways to do it. One way is to do things for him that he needs to have done—run errands for him, carry messages for him, fight on his side, feed his lambs, and so on. The other way is to do things for him that you need to do—sing songs for him, create beautiful things for him, give things up for him, tell him what's on your mind and in your heart, in general rejoice in him and make a fool of yourself for him the way lovers have always made fools of themselves for the one they love.
>
> A Quaker Meeting, a Pontifical High Mass, the Family Service at First Presbyterian, a Holy Roller Happening—unless there is an element of joy and foolishness in the proceedings, the time would be better spent doing something useful.[6]

---

5. Ibid., 1.
6. Buechner, *Wishful Thinking*, 98.

Practicing Pilgrimage—Part I

Worship is our way of serving or praising God and reminds us that we are part of a community greater than ourselves. Christian pilgrims on an actual pilgrimage or the pilgrimage of everyday life not only need and want worship: in both actual pilgrimages and the pilgrimage of everyday life, worship gives us hope when we are weary, reminding us what we are doing is for a greater good, and keeping us grounded and on the road when we would rather be off the road. We look forward to a day of rest, of Sabbath, during a pilgrimage on the road of life or life on the road. If we consider Hape Kerkeling's suggestion, which I mentioned earlier in this book, where he sees his walk on the Camino de Santiago de Compostela not as one long 300- to 500-mile walk—depending on where you start—but as a one-day pilgrimage made up of a thousand days of pilgrimage, then imagine that each day of our lives as Christians is a day of our pilgrimage toward the greater goal of being part of the realm of God's love. And during a week of seven days of pilgrimage, on one day a week we get a day of rest, of Sabbath, in which we worship God. In other words, our life as Christians may be perceived as a pilgrimage, in which we *are* pilgrims *becoming* or growing into our understanding of what it means to be one of God's pilgrim people on this earth. On this pilgrimage, our worship of God—daily or weekly—gives us, first, focus for why we are on the journey; second, a map for where we are going; and third, the liturgy of worship itself in which there is a pilgrimage logic.

The *focus* that is needed on the journey—knowing who and whose we are, a sense of vision about our community on the move—is both beautiful and mystifying, real and intimate yet also elusive, because we are on a journey of faith. Regrettably, there are few pastors or priests who point out that worship is, itself, a process of nurturing "us pilgrims" for our week-long walk in the world because this is not a common concept taught in many churches or seminaries. But there is an easy connection that can be made between worship as a place to nurture the mind, body, and spirit of pilgrims on an actual pilgrimage or the pilgrimage of life. As has been mentioned earlier in the book, the word *parish*, which is commonly used to talk about a church, means literally "pilgrim house." *Parish* comes from the ancient Greek word *paroikia* or *paraoikos*, which is translated as *sojourning*, dwelling in a strange land; or the life of a person here on earth is likened to a sojourning. Pilgrims are given an opportunity to come to worship in the parish, the pilgrim house. And this connection and focus is important because we need to be told and reminded during this period of time together in worship that we are God's pilgrim people in this world.

Second, worship provides for us a map for our sojourn. To quote the simple song, "God's got the whole world, in God's hands." We are all sojourners upon a world of God's creation. Granted, we have dominion over much of God's creation, but that doesn't make it ours per se, because we did not create it. God created it. A hunch: God has a better idea of where we are headed and a better sense of the lay of the land than we do. Granted, we have freedom of choice, but it is helpful to have a sense of direction, of knowing where we might be going, from time to time. As God's pilgrim people, in this life we are sent on an extraordinary journey, with new tales and old sagas being lived out through our lives during a week's time. It is in worship, with the reading of the Hebrew Scripture, Epistles, and Gospel, along with the preached word and sacraments, that we place our individual pilgrim story into the larger meta-pilgrimage story of God's people from the past as well as in the present. This provides a kind of "map" of sorts, letting us know where we are and giving us a sense as to where we should or should not be going.

Third, Sabbath and worship become "bookends" of our week, as it were—a convenient way to bracket our lives. By the end of the week, we may be ready to welcome the help of our community of faith to refocus on what matters, grateful for the good company of others who can join with us in the act of being community, being Christ, with and for one another.

In reflecting upon the place and presence, the act, of worship on pilgrimage, it appears that one can see a sort of "pilgrim logic" in the order of worship, the very liturgy, itself. There is the genesis of the journey in the "Gathering," with the "Call to Worship," followed by our spirit experiencing the ups and downs of the journey—through Confession. There is "The Word," including Scripture reading, which is enlivened by the sermon (a "feast of words" for the mind), and then the nurture of the body (Eucharist). And there is "Sending", the dismissal of people as they leave, charged and blessed for the journey ahead away from others we love dearly, but never out of each other's reach or contact.[7] In this chapter, the focus is on the way worship of God is a pilgrimage, in which we, who *are* God's pilgrim people, are nurtured, converted, or transformed over the course of worshipping God, who, through the Spirit, deepens and strengthens our

---

7. This framework of "Gathering; The Word; Sending" is found in Presbyterian Church (USA), *Book of Common Worship*.

faith so that when we leave our time of worship we are prepared to more closely follow Jesus, the Pilgrim God.

Below, I describe the movement of a pilgrimage found in or based upon the outline of the Order of Worship according to the Presbyterian Church (USA) *Book of Common Worship*. I chose this Order because it is the one I am most comfortable with as an ordained clergyperson. Other Protestant denominations, the Anglican or Episcopal churches, and the Roman Catholic and Eastern Orthodox churches have variations on the basic structure of worship suggested below. The parts of worship reflect the very movements of a pilgrimage itself, whether it is an actual pilgrimage or the pilgrimage of life.

Ringing of the Hour

It is no surprise that many churches in various countries around the world use bells to announce the hours to a larger town or village, as well as for musical interludes and concerts from a bell tower. But bells have also been commonly used to let the people know that worship was about to commence, and to summon us from our pilgrim trail and gather us to worship God.

Call to Worship and Prayer of the Day

The words of a "Call to Worship," often done antiphonally within and among a congregation, can be envisioned as a way of summoning or calling pilgrims from the dusty road of life to be present at a communal gathering of other pilgrims as we begin our worship of God.

This seems like a simple expectation: to call people to come worship God, or to welcome people to come in and worship God, without assumptions of who is or is not coming. The doors of a church are to be opened wide, and all pilgrims are to be welcomed from their pilgrimage, however they are dressed, smell, look like, act like, able-bodied and disabled alike, regardless of who they love or how they love, what they eat, smoke, or inhale. The openness of Jesus to one and all in Jewish society—including the outcasts—is to be emulated by the body of Christ today. Usually words of

Scripture are spoken or sung to proclaim who God is and what God has done.[8]

The Call to Worship is often followed by a Prayer of the Day or Opening Prayer, in which pilgrims pray a prayer of adoration. This is followed by an opening hymn of usually joyful praise. The focus is on the God of our pilgrimages throughout time, who created us to worship, made possible the trail we are on, and leads us forward this very day.

A word about the Opening Hymn. Numerous social-science studies show that there are few places in which a community or group gathers to sing en masse: sports events, e.g., baseball games where people sing "Take Me Out to the Ball Game," and worship in the context of a church or parish. The opening hymn may itself be a continuation of the opening movements of worship, as people find strength in numbers in knowing we are not the only ones who are walking with the Spirit. There are many others, our sisters and brothers, who have joined in song. This song unifies the various "I's" who come off the road into solidarity as a more communal "We."

Confession and Assurance of Pardon

The words of Jesus from the Gospel of Matthew seem to capture this moment in worship, practiced right after we gather together in the name of God: "Come to me, all you that are weary and are carrying heavy burdens, and I will give you rest. Take my yoke upon you, and learn from me; for I am gentle and humble in heart, and you will find rest for your souls" (11:28–30). In Confession, pilgrims literally and figuratively have a chance to unload those things that have weighed heavy upon heart, mind, and body, and are invited to recognize in what ways we have taken on the troubles of the world, trying to become Jesus, solving all the world's problems. It is a chance to take off our "backpack" of life and do some rearranging of the contents before we go back out into the world.

We are inspired to confess our sins from our personal and communal life because of the claim of the promise of God, sealed in our baptism. We do so knowing the promise of God's redemption for all human life. Grace is declared in the name of Jesus, and we accept that we are forgiven, confident that in dying to sin, "God raises us to new life."[9]

---

8. Ibid., 35.
9. Ibid., 35.

Practicing Pilgrimage—Part I

Sharing the Peace of Christ

On a pilgrimage there will be a rush of emotions and spiritual angst with one's self and others on the journey. The litany of shortcomings, bad decisions, and lists of failed relationships come to the fore. Our sins are ever before us on pilgrimage, to use Christian language. The aftereffects of these struggles in relationships with our inner selves, God, or others, often leave us battered and bruised. What we desire is not necessarily more uneasiness, but a peace that often passes human understanding, since we seem more able to create friction than exercise forgiveness. In worship, we are given an opportunity to reach out and literally grab that peace, take hold of it in our hands, in the time of "Sharing the Peace of Christ." Literally taking the hand of another, the physical touch, or extending a hug, a kiss on the cheek, are all ways of enfleshing the words, "Peace of Christ," embodying the gesture of peace with a physical act, in which the Spirit of Christ is present, fulfilling the Scripture, "Wherever two or three are gathered in my name, I am there" (Matt 18:20). In other words, our brokenness having been healed, we are made into agents or pilgrims of God's love in the world.[10]

Scripture: The Word

Worship ideally involves spirit, body, and mind. One of the key ingredients of worship is the reading of Scripture, sacred text of a community of faith. In all of the major religions of the world mentioned earlier, a religious text holds the story or history of the people and their relationship with creation, one another, and the Holy Other. These stories provide a road map of sorts for the pilgrims of these faiths. Or as it is written in the *Book of Common Worship*, "The God who acted in biblical history acts today. Through the Holy Spirit, Christ is present in the sermon, offering grace and calling for obedience."[11] This is what we yearn for on pilgrimage: direction, a pattern of habits that helps us negotiate the day-to-day changes.

Usually the reading of Scripture comes right before the sermon preached, steering the collected pilgrims attention to the ways that God has worked in the past, is present with us right where we are today, and guiding us into the future. In many churches, there is a reading of Hebrew Scripture, otherwise referred to as the Old Testament; the recitation of the

---

10. Ibid., 36.
11. Ibid., 37.

Psalms that echoes the message of the Old Testament and is often recited or chanted antiphonally; and the reading of one of Paul's Epistles or Letters, followed by the reading of the Gospel. In some churches, the importance of the Gospel is highlighted by the Gospel being read in the middle of the people assembled together, with those who are able or wishing to participate in spirit, rising to stand. It is a sign of honor, recognizing the centrality of the good news in the life of the people of God.

Sermon

It is the role of the one who is preaching to read the text carefully and provide for the congregation a reading that will challenge as well as give support to the pilgrim, feeding us intellectually and spiritually. Like any preacher worth her or his salt, we desire to connect the experiences of the people of God in their ordinary lives with the Scriptures, which are always in the process of being interpreted and reinterpreted, with the Spirit providing new insights into what is being read. We pilgrims never hear the same Scriptures read the same, because not only are we different when we hear it anew, but God's Spirit seems to be communicating something anew in each reading of Scripture. The hope is that at the end of the sermon we, the people, will be given some guidance as to how we should live in the coming week on our pilgrimage, with a word of support, courage, and love.

Hymn

Throughout worship, there needs to be a liberal use of music. Many pilgrims are dependent upon music, whether singing along or listening to it along the pilgrimage, actual or everyday alike. First, music includes many people who are unable to necessarily use words well or think or process linguistically (e.g., people with intellectual challenges). Second, music is part and parcel of any pilgrimage, whether it be the "song of birds" in the air, or the whistling or singing one does when all alone on the road. It simply sets a mood, and hopefully lifts the spirit. Third, there is one thing that most military bands have discovered in regards to music: groups move faster when walking, marching, or running to the beat of music. This is why, in worship, music that has more of a steady four-four beat works, while there is a slower hymn in the middle of worship, with another four-four beat hymn at the end of worship. Likewise, while on the road of pilgrimage, we depend upon the beat of the music to either pick up the pace of the walk or to slow us down.

Affirm the Faith: Creed

We respond to the Word read and proclaimed through affirming the faith. Or another way of saying this is stating what we believe. We are answering the questions: Why are we on this pilgrimage? For what end or purpose? The *telos* or *raison d'etre* of the pilgrimage is foremost in the pilgrim's mind. In other words, what do we believe is the purpose of our gathering together as pilgrims, and where in the heck are we going? While the words can sound dogmatic and doctrinaire, nonetheless, they provide a framework, the words of faith, that, at the end of the day establishes a pattern for uttering what we believe.

Offering

All pilgrimages cost blood, sweat, tears, laughter, gladness . . . and money. The question is always do we go with the cash in hand, or do we depend upon the goodness of strangers to meet our needs along the pilgrim's way? I hold up Jesus's example as a model: when sending out the seventy disciples as pilgrims, he sent them two by two with no knapsack, sandals, or walking sticks and with instruction to greet no one on the road (Luke 10:4). He follows this up in Luke 22:35, asking them: When I sent you out with no sandals, backpacks, or bag of money, you lacked for nothing, is that true? In other words, they relied on the friendship and hospitality of others.

Sacraments

In large part, up until now worship revolved around feeding of the mind and spirit through the use of words and participating in the communal activities. The body has been involved in such acts as passing the peace of Christ, speaking in the recitation of psalms, perhaps standing for the reading of one of the Scriptures, along with rising if able or participating in anyway possible with the singing of hymns.

But with the sacraments of baptism and the Eucharist or Holy Communion, the body along with the mind and spirit are being stimulated, fed, marked, and nurtured in tangible, concrete ways. The splash of water when being poured into a baptismal font, or the water running through the pastors hands, the toe touching the edge of the baptismal pool before going deeper into the water, the immersion of the body into the pool, marked with a wet finger with the sign of the cross as one hears these words, "In the name of the Father, the Son, and the Holy Spirit." When entering a strange chapel on the Camino or on the way to Chimayo, there is usually a small dish or bowl in the back of the church or chapel, in which a pilgrim touches a finger in the bowl and crosses one's self as a reminder of the baptismal vow. For we were marked at baptism with the sign of the cross as a public display of grace that has acted on our lives. And for some pilgrims, the scallop shell is itself a sign of the pilgrimage, a reminder of water from the ocean, and of the one who is the everlasting fountain of life.

Likewise, with Eucharist, there is literally a feeding of people in the middle of worship as a thankful response to the Word of God proclaimed and exclaimed. My Greek Orthodox, Catholic, and Episcopal sisters and brothers often use bread in the form of a flat wafer and often wine, and celebrate the Eucharist often, while my Protestant brothers and sisters share Holy Communion with chunks of bread and grape juice. What is key is the nurture of the body with actual food, and done in such a way that reminds us of the one who is Creator, Redeemer, and Sustainer of life. Broken bread, broken body, the cup of salvation, the blood of Jesus, poured out, filling us: in this sacrament "the bread and wine, the words and actions, make the promises of God visible and concrete."[12] And while we begin by eating the bread and drinking the cup, soon the bread within us breaks down and nurtures us and we literally and figuratively become the bread of life, the cup of salvation coursing through our veins.

What is especially powerful is when the meal itself becomes a moment for a pause in the stream of worship, and people gather more food, an actual meal, and feed one another and are fed, perhaps an evening meal together, in community. The Holy Trinity, Father, Son, and Holy Spirit or Creator, Christ, and Sustainer feed body, mind, and spirit.

Finally, on pilgrimages, I have experienced Pentecost and most often Holy Communion, along with a service to remind us of our baptism, including now and then a time of washing of pilgrims' feet. On the road, the setting is often outside, or in a small chapel, with only a few people gathered

---

12. Ibid., 41.

together in the name of Jesus. But these are often the most intimate and dearest experiences of the sacraments in a pilgrim's life.

Closing Hymn

After a prayer of Thanksgiving for this communal feast, along with the opportunity to be made whole through the singing of hymns, confession, assurance, receiving the Scriptures, and reflecting upon the message of the day, there is the hymn that literally sends us out onto the road of life. The tune and words of this hymn hold the possibilities of staying within us like an earworm, reminding us who and whose we are. And many times, announcements may be made before the closing hymn, or even at the beginning of worship. News about pilgrims is always welcome.

Charge and Benediction

Oftentimes, in worship, this part of our time together is done with a lighthearted spirit, if not blithely. Yet the words of the Charge are meant to last with us for the week. In this regard, the religious leader (pastor, priest, or minister) charges us or calls us to consider what is most important for us to remember that week. The "I charge you" words should be thought out carefully, with a sense of command, so that we, the pilgrims, remember and hold on to them. Perhaps we should write them down so as to remember them. This is what is written in the *Book of Common Worship*, which sounds appropriate for a pilgrimage:

> A charge [is given] to the people to go into the world in the name of Christ . . . [renewing] God's call to us to engage in obedient and grateful ministry as God's agents to heal life's brokenness. . . . God sends the church in the power of the Holy Spirit to proclaim the gospel, to engage in works of compassion and reconciliation, to strive for peace and justice in its own life and in the world, to be stewards of creation and of life, caring for creation until the day when God will make all things new.[13]

In the Benediction, the blessing, the way that someone gives and receives the benediction is with a priest or pastor putting her or his hand on our head, and reciting, "in the name of the Father, Son, and Holy Spirit." On

---

13. Ibid., 45.

the way to Chimayo, oftentimes before or after worship, people in churches we would visit would line up along the pathway from which we would exit a church. They would ask us to lay a hand on them and bless them, for we were holy ones on this exceptional journey. In worship, with many people, the pastor holds her or his hands up and blesses us for the road ahead that week.

Good Bye

Frederick Buechner reminds us of the origin of "goodbye": "It was a long while ago that the words *God be with you* disappeared into the word *goodbye*, but every now and again some trace of them still glimmers through."[14] At the end of worship, we are off again on our pilgrimage of life. Maybe there was a time of fellowship with cookies and coffee, punch for the children, after worship. Soon we leave this gathering and engage again with the pilgrimage of life. On both an actual pilgrimage and the pilgrimage of life, who knows what will happen in the week or span of time ahead. But this we do know: we go with a profound sense that we are not alone. God set us on this pilgrimage, accompanied by the Spirit, as we follow Jesus, the Pilgrim God.

In the next chapter and part of the book, the focus is on actual pilgrimages of God's people, right where we live, on the pilgrimage of life.

---

14. Buechner, *Whistling in the Dark*, 56.

PART II

Practicing Pilgrimage

All journeys begin with a single step.
All adventures begin with fear.
Within the unknown is understanding.
Each day is the beginning
of a season of growth or each of us.
—Book of Reflections.[15]

The first part of this book was dedicated to making the theological and practical argument that, for Christians, all of life is a pilgrimage. Each day, from the moment we wake up in the morning to the moment that we go to bed at night, is a part of the pilgrimage of life. Sleep is the time in which we are renewed to begin the next leg of our journey of faith the following day. This concept of pilgrimage is still foreign but gaining interest among many Christians, especially those in the Protestant denominations. In the Roman Catholic, Anglican/Episcopal, and eastern Orthodox churches, the opposite is true: they are well aware of the practice of pilgrimage. The reason for this split is because of the Protestant Reformation. Reformer Martin Luther condemned the practice primarily based upon the collection of financial indulgences, which was meant to help one's way out of Purgatory. Yet as was cited earlier, other Reformers, like John Calvin, continued to use the language of pilgrimage to describe Christians place in the world.

---

15. From Curry, *Way of the Labyrinth*, 45.

Being and Becoming God's Pilgrim People: Worship and Pilgrimage

To enable people to see in what ways the Christian life *is* a pilgrimage, there are several options available to awaken this state of being. First, one can read a book on pilgrimages, like this one, and be persuaded by words that life is a pilgrimage. Second: one can go on an actual or intentional pilgrimage here or abroad. But as I have heard from many over the years, they cannot afford to go on a pilgrimage either in terms of money or time, or are simply unable to walk long distances. This leads to the third option, which is to consider one of these small experiences of pilgrimage as a way of realizing that the Christian life is a pilgrimage.

In this second half of the book is a series of practices that a person can easily pursue, either individually or as a group. They cost little in the way of money and can take place right in one's backyard or neighborhood church, in rural, suburban, or urban enclaves. I will provide a bare-bones outline and theological topic for the pilgrimage, and it is up to you, dear reader, to fill in the blanks.

So as they say on the way to Santiago de Compostela: *Buen camino!*

8

Labyrinths

> Why labyrinths? Why all of a sudden
> are people everywhere walking the labyrinth?
> Because people are lost.
> Because the chaos is too much without the order of form.
> —Donna Schaper and Carole Ann Camp[1]

> Why does the labyrinth attract people? Because it is a tool
> to guide healing, deepen self-knowledge, and empower creativity. Walking
> the labyrinth clears the mind and gives insight into the spiritual journey.
> —Lauren Artress[2]

First Labyrinths

The first labyrinth pattern I remember seeing was on a T-shirt that was given to me after my initial pilgrimage to El Santuario de Chimayo in 1999. The labyrinth pattern was very basic and in a sense emblematic of the pilgrimage that I just took. While the pilgrimage route was more or less linear, walking from point A to point Z (Costilla to Chimayo), the circuitous route of the labyrinth caught my attention because it reminded me of the ups and downs of my spiritual, emotional, intellectual, and physical experiences of this trek. I was drawn to the curves, my eyes following the open pathways made by the dark lines of the outline of the labyrinth. I was mesmerized by the pattern, which is better known as the seven-path or circuit labyrinth

---

1. Schaper and Camp, *Labyrinths from the Outside In*, 1.
2. Artress, *Walking a Sacred Path*, 20–21.

Labyrinths

pattern, whose origin is among the Hopi Native Americans. While there were no labyrinths around the churches and chapels we visited on the first pilgrimage I took in 1999, in the years to come on other pilgrimages I would see a labyrinth situated usually in a garden on the grounds of the sacred site.

Introduced to the pattern of the labyrinth at Chimayo, the first time I ever walked a labyrinth was at the Trappists' Mepkin Abbey in Monck's Corner. It was a pattern that was also of the sevenfold pattern or circuit, located in a field not too far away from where the free-range chickens were once kept when Mepkin was selling eggs as part of their income base. Shrubbery and flowers helped make up or delineate where the path lay. I was free to simply walk around it, with no book of prayers or a pamphlet explaining the mystery and practice of walking a labyrinth. As a part of landscape, being somewhat symmetrical, the very design of the labyrinth brought a sense of peace and calm to my always-restless soul.

In the last few years I've noticed a surprising increase in the presence of labyrinths in and around the Research Triangle area of Raleigh, Durham, and Chapel Hill/Carrboro. United Methodist-related yet interdenominational Duke Chapel in Durham hosts a labyrinth during the holy season of Lent, as do many other smaller faith communities and retreat centers in the area. At the United Methodist's retreat center in Junaluska, North Carolina, there is a labyrinth in the earthen ground beside the main chapel. Binkley Baptist Church in Chapel Hill has a labyrinth stretched out in its fellowship area during one of the holy seasons too. Labyrinths are an interdenominational as well as inter-religious spiritual practice that is very popular in the United States. And this is great! Because the first step towards an actual pilgrimage is practicing the walk of spirituality on a labyrinth.

Labyrinths and Pilgrimages

Carole Ann Camp writes that the labyrinth walk represents "a journey, a pilgrimage, a conscious taking of time to seek God."[3] Labyrinths are a *form* of pilgrimage among Christians. Indeed, there is a direct link between labyrinths and pilgrimages. For many Christians, the first pilgrimage is going to be walking a labyrinth in which, with the slow meditative or contemplative walk that is an embodied prayer, the one walking is able to draw on some similar insights as pilgrims on a pilgrimage experience. When Christians

3. Schaper and Camp, *Labyrinths from the Outside In*, 62.

could no longer make a physical or intentional pilgrimage to Jerusalem, the home of the Christian faith, especially during the days of the medieval Crusades, many walked a symbolic pilgrimage in the form of a labyrinth built into the floors of the naves of many cathedrals. In a sense, people made believe they were walking to Jerusalem while walking the labyrinth.[4]

Other similarities between a pilgrimage and labyrinth are too numerous to count. For example, like a pilgrimage, one has to intentionally want to do it, and do it with a certain method in mind, in order to accomplish or achieve a kind of spiritual "zen" on the path. Labyrinths have a beginning, middle, and an end, just like a pilgrim's sojourn, in which the one who walks a labyrinth is often disappointed to see this time in the labyrinth draw to an end. Labyrinths include mind, body, and spirit, giving the one who walks freedom to stop worrying as to where one is walking and the ability simply to move almost effortlessly along while quieting the voices within us that take us away from focusing on the purpose of the labyrinth: our relationship with the Holy and with one another. And labyrinths also include various rituals and prayers that assist us in focusing or channeling our energies toward a deeper awareness of the God who is among us.

Helen Curry writes that for some, the labyrinth pattern is often considered the final steps of a pilgrim's journey:

> [The pilgrim often takes the last steps] on the knees in worship. The journey symbolized the twists and turns of life as well as an unmediated experience of the mystical itself, a torturous pathway that could not be traversed without the support of the church. In this final leg of the journey, Christian pilgrims took the symbolic trip to the center to touch the divine. . . . [Pilgrims] opened their hearts to the truths of the divine on such pilgrimages under the close watch of the mother church.[5]

These two theological practices—an actual pilgrimage and walking a labyrinth—are closely akin and entwined together throughout the ages.

~

In this chapter I simply want to more carefully draw the logical connection between the labyrinth and an actual pilgrimage, along with the pilgrimage of life, because they work so well hand in hand with each other. I will

---

4. Ibid., 6.
5. Curry, *Way of the Labyrinth*, 32.

explore the root of the labyrinth, the history of the labyrinth, and the theological practice of the labyrinth, along with possible designs. The first order, then, is to explore what a labyrinth *is*.

What Is a Labyrinth?

Lauren Artress describes labyrinths as being in the form of a circle with a meandering but purposeful path, from the edge to the center and back out again, large enough to be walked into. Though most labyrinths take the form of a circle, some earlier labyrinths were not circular but square.

Within the labyrinth itself, there is only one path, and when we enter it there is only one way to go, sending us into the very center or heart of the labyrinth. The one walking may spend some time there, at the heart of the labyrinth, in deeper prayer, pausing to reflect upon all that they have considered as they were drawn to the middle. Once a person senses that they are sated, or when time has drawn to a close, then people will turn around and head out of the labyrinth, following the path before us.[6] She writes,

> The labyrinth is a spiritual tool meant to awaken us to the deep rhythm that unites us to ourselves and to the Light that calls from within. In surrendering to the winding path, the soul finds healing and wholeness. . . . The labyrinth is a sacred place and can give us firsthand experiences of the Divine.[7]

An important distinction needs to be made: a labyrinth is different than a maze. A maze is meant to be a puzzle, with all kinds of possibilities for getting through it to the other side or to the center. Mazes are intellectually stimulating and can be physically exhausting. A labyrinth is not intended to be a mind-bending, physically wearying maze. Instead, the labyrinth is to be a place of healing for some, of expanding and deepening spiritual awareness for others, and it creates a place for rituals and prayers that are effectual in the context of a labyrinth.

---

6. Artress, *Walking a Sacred Path*, xxii.
7. Ibid.

Practicing Pilgrimage—Part II

Story of Labyrinths

While I was introduced to the labyrinth in a Christian context, the first labyrinths were not necessarily Christian in nature. Instead, they were more indigenous, created by those who practiced a religious faith whose name is lost in our day and age. Some archaeologists think the first labyrinth was created in Egypt and Ertruria (now central Italy) around 4,500 BCE.[8] There is a clay tablet from Pylos, Greece, which contains the design of a labyrinth that is thirty-two hundred years old. A Syrian potshard showing a labyrinth is believed to be of the same age. And from Tragliatella, there is a seventh-century BCE wine jar that depicts armed soldiers on horseback riding from a labyrinth that has the word *Truia* or Troy inscribed in the outermost circuit.[9]

But the Mediterranean region was not the only place where labyrinths were found. In Peru, the Nazcan people of about 500 BCE constructed a labyrinth-like figure on Pampa Ingenio, an extremely dry, flat desert. And the Hopi American Indians used a symbol known as the seven-path labyrinth, mentioned earlier in this chapter.[10]

Some think "labyrinth" comes from the word *labrys*, which is the sacred double-headed axe associated with the Minoan palace of Knossos on the isle of Crete. King Minos was said to have had Daedalus build a labyrinth, a house of winding passages to house the Minotaur (half man, half bull), which is the beast his wife, Pasiphae, bore after having sex with a bull.[11]

These early labyrinths were made of various materials. Some labyrinths are outlined with stone, while others are actually carved in stone. Many of the early Roman-style labyrinths were made of mosaic tiles, while there are turf or sod labyrinths throughout the United Kingdom, the countries of Scandinavia, and Germany.

Many of the labyrinths in churches throughout Europe and the British Isles appeared in the twelfth century and are usually formed based upon a kind of sacred geometry. Artress writes that sacred geometry is based on ancient, sacred knowledge that was uttered in architecture. "Through proportion, placement, and position of stone, wood, and mortar—using

---

8. Schaper and Camp, *Labyrinths from the Outside In*, 2.
9. Curry, *Way of the Labyrinth*, 21.
10. Schaper and Camp, *Labyrinths from the Outside In*, 4.
11. Ibid., 3.

a complementary system of numbers, angles, and design—the mind can find rest, comfort, and harmony. This leaves the mind open to other levels of awareness," write Artress.[12] She continues: "Sacred geometry is the key to creating 'an abode of eternal truth.' The architects approached this lofty ideal by embracing the concept and experience of unity, something we know little about in this postmodern age."[13] One of the earliest is in the Church of Reparatus, Algeria, around the fourth century, with others like the cathedral in Rheims, France, built in 1240, made mostly of blue stones.[14]

The most famous labyrinth among Christians is that of Chartres Cathedral in France. Schaper and Camp write,

> The paving stones that make up the illustrious labyrinth trace a pattern that spans the entire width of the nave. Those who know of its existence and its history can find it hidden under the wooden chairs that litter it. The circle on the floor repeats the pattern of the stained-glass circle of the western rose window. This sort of architectural analogy of the medieval builders was essential to the thinking of the mathematicians and mystics who made up the school of Chartres. In the view of these Platonic philosophers, whatever existed on earth could be only a dim reflection of a higher reality that existed on another plane, but the reflection had to remain true to the original in number and proportion. People were going to a real city called Jerusalem, in a faux pilgrimage, but they were also imitating a journey, which was understood as eternal and celestial.[15]

While many Christian cathedrals used this sacred geometry, some churches used non-Christian symbols, like the church of San Savino at Piacenza, Italy, which used the twelve signs of the zodiac that circles the labyrinth. And in the middle or central stone at the Chartres labyrinth, there is a legend that the stone represented the Cretan's labyrinth, which those who entered cannot leave unless they are helped, like Theseus, by Ariadne's thread.[16]

The story of the labyrinth continues today, as more retreat centers, churches, and other faith communities create and re-create their pattern in various parts of the geography of these institutions.

12. Artress, *Walking a Sacred Path*, 48.
13. Ibid., 49.
14. Schaper and Camp, *Labyrinths from the Outside In*, 6.
15. Ibid., 6–8.
16. Ibid., 8.

The Theological Practice of the Labyrinth

Labyrinths are more than simple symmetrical patterns in the floor of a cathedral, out in the garden of a retreat center, or a simple pattern on a piece of muslin in the fellowship hall. There is theological weight to the practice of walking the labyrinth, which is connected to the larger or meta-practice of pilgrimage.

In the Middle Ages, labyrinths were powerful theological practices and tools, as were the stone statues and stained glass windows of cathedrals, which are carved and patterned theological or biblical stories in stone and glass. The labyrinth was a symbolic trip to the underworld and resurrection. Heaven and hell were both invoked in the pattern of the labyrinth itself. With a Platonic mindset, it was believed that whatever existed on Earth could be a dim reflection of the higher reality of the heavens. To walk the labyrinth was to imitate a journey that would connect the believer with the eternal and celestial City of God.[17] Some penitents who entered the labyrinth would do so on their knees, going to the center and then back out again.

The pattern is as follows. First, the labyrinth has only one way or direction to enter it and proceed along it. And the person follows a single path. With the kind of multitasking of our daily lives, if not crisis and chaos, the single path is a wonderful gift. We walk or crawl on our knees, following the open path before us. Some people will even push along on their abdomens. We move slowly, maybe walking with a step where the heel of the foot going forward strikes the ground close to the toe box of the foot in front of it. Maybe you say a prayer for each step, or list those things you are grateful for, or are worried about. Some people will take a Rosary with them, or a version of prayer beads. It is both a path to the holy place in the center of the labyrinth, and the holy place inside of us where our true self or authentic self is one with God. The thrust is that we are leaving the life we lead, moving toward the Holy located in the center of the labyrinth, where, once arriving, we may sit down or simply bow and remain silent before the Holy Other. Once we sense that our time there has come to an end, that we are satiated, we slowly make our way from the center of the labyrinth toward the outer ring again, following the circuitous path, going back to the life we lead. But now we re-enter life with a sense of inner calm, knowing

---

17. Ibid., 6.

physically, mentally, and spiritually that the love of God is with us as we embrace the full life we live.

There is no doubt that labyrinths have taken hold of the church's imagination once again among this generation. Along with Roman Catholic churches, Protestant churches of various denominations are investing in making earthen labyrinths, purchasing cloth labyrinths, or making building floors with the labyrinth as an inset design. Perhaps Lauren Artress has her finger on what is attractive about labyrinths:

> [A labyrinth is a] tool to guide healing, deepen self-knowledge, and empower creativity. Walking the labyrinth clears the mind and gives insight into the spiritual journey. It urges action. It calms people in the throes of life transitions. It helps them see their lives in the context of a path, a pilgrimage. They realize that they are not human beings on a spiritual path but spiritual beings on a human path. To those of us who feel we have untapped gifts to offer, it stirs the creative fires within. To others who are in deep sorrow, the walk gives solace and peace. The experience is different for everyone because each of us brings different raw material to the labyrinth. We bring our unique hopes, dreams, history, and longings of the soul.[18]

This brings us to an important point: the outer labyrinth we walk reveals in a way the labyrinth within us, between self and God, self and love, self and community or body of Christ, and maybe light and darkness. In praying or meditating as we walk the labyrinth, the walk becomes an embodiment of prayer or gestured prayer.

Labyrinth Designs

There are various labyrinth designs that are used by various faith communities, some of which you enter in and turn to the right, and others in which you turn to the left. When entering a building like a church, a supermarket, or school building, people tend to turn to the right when they first enter rather than the left, though left-handed people tend to turn to the left. As mentioned earlier, the most famous labyrinth design is from Chartres Cathedral. This pattern, or a version of this pattern, has been replicated in many churches and faith communities, either as part of a floor design or on a piece of canvas or muslin, making the labyrinth transportable.

18. Artress, *Walking a Sacred Path*, 20, 21.

Practicing Pilgrimage—Part II

The classic Chartres design is here:

However, the three- or seven-circuit labyrinths are below:

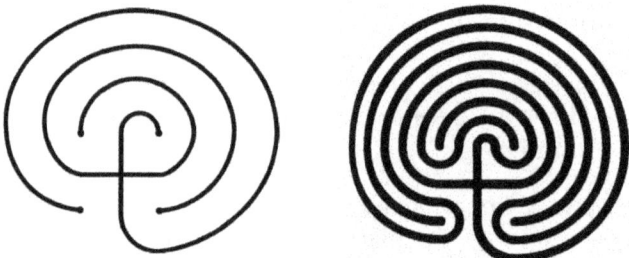

What is important about these bottom two designs is how portable they are. I have seen people draw out a labyrinth on a sandy beach, or create interesting mounds of dirt and other debris on an open patch of forest floor. I have also seen these designs in fellowship rooms in churches, designed using blue painting tape, flour, or sand from an outdoor backyard or playground. Others have used yards of butcher paper and painted the design of these labyrinths in watercolor paints, throwing it away after use. In other words, refashioning this design is easy for people who are interested in this ritual of walking a labyrinth. What is fun is using all kinds of materials to build the pathway of the labyrinth.

The other components that lend themselves to the labyrinth include the use of candles to create a certain atmosphere, along with calm, contemplative music, either recorded or live. Sometimes, there are flowers at the center of the labyrinth, or an icon of a saint or perhaps Jesus Christ. Walking the labyrinth is usually possible during certain times outside of worship, so that the one walking may walk at her or his pace.

Again, there are many ways to travel the labyrinth. Some choose to take a slow step, walking heel to heel with a few seconds in between each step, praying a prayer or repeating a mantra for each step. This helps silence some of the other voices that may be demanding our attention in our heads. When walking a labyrinth, some softly sing a favorite hymn, or a refrain from a hymn, or a simple song, like this from the Taizé community: "Jesus, remember me when you come into your kingdom." Others may choose to kneel and move forward on one's knees. Others may choose to crawl or move along on their abdomen in a prostrate posture. In other words, there is no "right" or "normal" way to walk a labyrinth, except not to do it quickly.

Summary

Again, labyrinths, like pilgrimages, are an allegory of the religious or spiritual life we live. Labyrinths and pilgrimages are invitations and practices that are a kind of invitation to a believer to a deeper, more meaningful experience of God.

I conclude this chapter with a few thoughts about the advantages of a labyrinth over a pilgrimage: unlike some pilgrimages, what is important to remember about a labyrinth is that anyone who wants to do it, can. Physically, people who may use a walker, cane, or wheel chair may participate, depending on one's need or sense of independence or dependence. People of all ages, of educational backgrounds, sex, gender, sexual orientation, ethnicity, or nationality may participate in walking a labyrinth. Again, one big hurdle or obstacle to many people doing an actual pilgrimage is the issue of financial cost, life priorities, and time: they simply do not have the funds or ability to take time off for a certain pilgrimage. A labyrinth is both affordable money-wise and time-wise. One doesn't have to travel a long distance to walk a labyrinth, spending countless hours and days away from work, nor does it cost anything to walk a labyrinth. As mentioned above, some labyrinth patterns, like the three-circuit or seven-circuit or pattern labyrinth, can be drawn in the sand on a beach, or on the dirt floor in a forest. One can walk a labyrinth in one's back yard!

Because anyone can walk or move along a labyrinth, the next chapter's focus makes sense thematically: life is a pilgrimage! The challenge is how to wake or reveal how our daily life is a pilgrimage.

9

Teaching the Pilgrimage of Life

> We each come to the path bringing our many realities,
> our individual histories, the unique journeys we have traveled.
> —Helen Curry[1]

> We always know which is the best road to follow,
> but we follow only the road that we have become accustomed to.
> —Paulo Coelho[2]

A Gathering of Strangers Who Become Pilgrims

One of the greatest joys I have in life is working with a small church or faith community, middle- and high-school youth gatherings, college and university gatherings, church boards and Sessions, as well as Bible studies and workshop gatherings on the practice of pilgrimage in life generally, and for their group's aim or mission specifically. The joy comes with watching and listening as we all teach and learn together about the art and practice of pilgrimage through the actual practices of a pilgrimage.

    This section is a basic teaching outline I use for teaching a group of people that life is a pilgrimage, based upon the experiences I have on an actual pilgrimage. This is where the text of teaching *about* everyday pilgrimage involves being on an *actual* pilgrimage. By working with a group on the concepts or ideas of what it means to be a pilgrim and what a pilgrimage is, my hope is that a group will raise some old and new ideas of

---

1. Curry, *Way of the Labyrinth*, 16.
2. Coelho, *The Pilgrimage*.

Teaching the Pilgrimage of Life

these concepts that benefit the entire group. While I resist the simplistic educational formulation of "short-term objectives" and "long-term goals," or "behavioral objectives," most of the material in this chapter falls under "long-term goals," because my hope, as an educator, is that we think of these ideas, stimulated by pilgrimage from the session provided below, for a long time. The pilgrimage workshop provided below comes in five parts that are easily replicated and can be added to or streamlined, depending on the aims or purposes of the group. The steps I follow in teaching a group about the practices of pilgrimage include written material found in my books *Follow Me* and *School of the Pilgrim* as well as material from films like *The Way*.

The format below may be used for a group as small as five or six people, to a group as large as twenty-five. Depending on the group's schedule, I have compacted this schedule for an afternoon or morning workshop time (three hours), and also expanded it to a two-day activity. I have also shaped the format so that it fits the theme of a group, from a church's leadership council or Session using the experience of pilgrimage as a visioning activity, to a time of team building. The format below is broad and loose enough for a person to use the outline for her or his own purpose, or group's goal.

Part I: The Storied Journey of Our Lives

Like all good educators, the first thing I like to do is have a chance for people to get to know one another in a group gathering. Name games and other icebreakers are helpful.

One idea is for people to bring a personal token, symbol, or sign that is from their pilgrimage of life that is meaningful. This practice hearkens back to pilgrimages I have made to Esquipulas, Guatemala, in which pilgrims come from all over Central America—bringing with them items like a child's shirt, a jeweled cross, a Bible, or a hat blessed by the priests with holy water—and then hold the item up to the sight line of the eyes of the statue, El Cristo Negro, confirming the blessings of the Almighty upon this item. These items were simply known as *recuerdos,* or reminders of the pilgrimage they made to Esquipulas. In our own lives, we all have *recuerdos* or reminders, symbols that are reminders of where we were when something special happened in our lives.

Practicing Pilgrimage—Part II

The other activity that is helpful is providing people with a four- or five-foot by three-foot piece of butcher paper or newsprint, and crayons, pens, or markers. Have the gathering create a timeline map of their lives, marking it off by five-year increments on the path. Start a line—a pathway—with one's birth, then mark down where one lived and what was happening in five years, then in ten years, and so on. Bring the timeline "path" to the day of the gathering. Perhaps people can write a small narrative on each five-year mark, or if there was an important event, e.g., a wedding, a funeral, a birth, a graduation, and mark that down in between the five year marks. Bring these time-line paths to the group and compare and contrast the various pathways our lives have taken. No matter how small or large three group may be, what is striking is seeing all these pathways in their beauty, and that they all now converge for a brief moment in the time and space where people are gathered! You can even spread the various time lines on the floor like the spokes of a wheel converging in the middle.

Another idea is giving a person a small map of the United States with the goal of having them identify which state or states they have lived or visited. This may also be done with a world map. Have people draw circles around the places where they've lived in their lives. Maybe take a marker or pen and draw a line between the places where you've lived. The idea is to show movement in a person's life between towns, cities, subdivisions, and rural locales where one has lived. You can continue this project with people mapping out where they'd like to live, which gets a whole new response and discussion going for a group of people.

Finally, you can pass out large white circles of construction paper and ask the participants to make the disk into a clock hand with a marker or pen. Have the participants then fill in the clock hand for when the gathering of pilgrims met. Have the participants now go back to when they woke up this morning and fill in the white clock face of the clock with all the places and people that they have met that day. It is a way of reminding people of how many times they have physically moved that day within a twelve-hour span of time as a daily pilgrimage in one's everyday life.

This opening exercise gets people talking about the journey or pilgrimage that is their very lives. It usually takes such an activity to spark people's knowledge that they have been on a journey for most of their lives. What is even more amazing is the realization that the journey is continuing on right after they leave the gathering of pilgrims for a quick break for coffee or tea.

Part II: Basics of Life as a Pilgrimage

Having had everyone discuss their life as a pilgrimage, with interest piqued as to the movements of our daily lives, turn then to the question, What is a pilgrimage? And are we all pilgrims? Many of these answers are found not only in the beginning of this book, but also in my other books on pilgrimage. For this section, I usually use a PowerPoint presentation on the characteristics of pilgrimage mentioned in chapter 5 of this book. In the PowerPoint, I go over each characteristic of pilgrimage, tying together an actual story or incident from an intentional pilgrimage, an encounter in daily life with the characteristic, with the overall theoretical and theological or philosophical description of the aspect of pilgrimage. By using all three sets or pools of knowledge, my aim is to show that these characteristics are not merely theoretical but tangible and accessible to each person in one's daily life.

Part III: Movie Time!

I have found that there are special "travel" films that may help with a discussion of the pilgrimage of life. I include this activity after the initial "Opening Activity," and discussion of the characteristics of "The Pilgrimage of Life." One movie that is obvious for a discussion of pilgrimage is *The Way*.[3] I have found this film by Emilio Estevez and Martin Sheen to be helpful in teaching a group about the contours of an actual pilgrimage, specifically the Camino de Santiago de Compostela in Spain. Martin Sheen literally picks up his deceased son's backpack at the beginning point of the pilgrimage in St. Jean, France, and off he goes to Finnisterre, where he empties his son's ashes into the Atlantic Ocean. I have shown bits and pieces of the film, and I usually encourage a group to watch the film to the end since there is such a great feast of pilgrimage themes and images to be discussed at various moments.

There are other films or movies, television shows as well, that may be used for discussing the basics of pilgrimage, like *The Trip to Bountiful*,[4] in which an elderly woman relives the rich yet often distressing memories of her earlier life as she makes her way back to Bountiful, Texas. In one group

---

3. *The Way*. Directed by Emilio Estevez. United States and Spain: Filmax: 2010.
4. *Trip to Bountiful*. Directed by Peter Masterson. United States: 1985.

Practicing Pilgrimage—Part II

I used the film, *Lars and the Real Girl*,[5] in which a young man, who found it hard to come out of his inner shell, embraces a life-size mannequin, which guides him to discover the young woman who is in love with him, and right before him! This is a pilgrimage of his inner life. As for television shows, there are quite a few episodes of *Northern Exposure*, set in Cicely, Alaska, that would be a great jumping-off point for discussing pilgrimage. A few television episodes of any of world-class chef Anthony Bourdain and his journeys in search of great food abroad could also stimulate a discussion on pilgrimage.

Part IV: A Pilgrimage

It is important not only to listen and watch the general description *about* a pilgrimage; it is even more important to actually *do* a pilgrimage! There are many working parts to this activity of walking an actual pilgrimage:

- Constructing a crude cross. On my first pilgrimage to Chimayo, New Mexico, I was smitten with the idea of carrying or bearing the cross of Christ on pilgrimage. The crosses constructed for Chimayo are usually six feet tall, and would bear the wooden sculpted figure of a bleeding and beaten Jesus on the cross. For Protestant groups, a simple cross without the figure of Jesus is often used. My partner, Dean, gave me an idea years ago of having a group construct a cross out of branches and twigs from around a church, a faith community's building, or a retreat center. The branches and twigs should be no longer than from one's hip to the ground, and no thicker than one's forefinger. Simply break the twigs to size. Gather two handfuls of branches and tie them together. Take these two bound gathering of twigs and branches, and have them cross in the middle of each other, or perpendicular to one another. Then, with a ball of yarn or jute or twine, start to bind the two bundles of twigs and branches together, making an improvised "God's eye" in the middle. This means going around the four points where the wood is gathered many times, until the "Eye" truly binds the wood together. Along the pilgrimage, have each person in the group carry the cross for a distance, depending upon one's ability to carry the cross. There will be stations or milestones or markers along

---

5. *Lars and the Real Girl*. Directed by Craig Gillespiel. Beverly Hills, CA: 20th Century Fox Home Entertainment, 2008.

Teaching the Pilgrimage of Life

the way of a short pilgrimage, in which the group may stop, practice one of the activities listed in the chapter 15, "Daily Pilgrimage" in this book, and people can switch carrying the cross. At each stop, pick up another smaller branch, a flower, even garbage, a leaf, or other road debris, and nestle these pieces in between the branches. By doing so, the cross soon has the marks of where the community has trod.

- Copy off some of the practices, exercises, or prayers in "Daily Pilgrimage" and other chapters in this book, and make a small booklet or simply staple some of the practices together, which can easily be carried by the pilgrims. For example, start with the prayers for pilgrims upon their departure and conclude with prayers for pilgrims upon their return. Depending on the distance and time on pilgrimage, break the pilgrimage up so there is time to do a few exercises. For example, for an hour pilgrimage, break it up every fifteen minutes with an exercise, regardless of the length; signing the senses is very powerful outdoors, as is the Navajo prayer of seven directions, mentioned earlier in this book.

- Some pilgrimages can be led outside around a suburban neighborhood, on a rural path, a hiking trail, or through an urban section of a city within certain city blocks, or within a church or retreat center on a rainy or snowy day. When walking, intersperse times of walking two by two, allowing people to chat. Then every fifteen minutes a group could be spread out in single file and walk silently. When leading pilgrimages over a period of days, I like to begin the morning with a pilgrimage of silent contemplation, in which everyone is quiet, focused on a prayer being prayed repetitively, or giving a person a word to focus on for the next thirty minutes.

- I have done pilgrimages in which people wore shoes. I've also done group pilgrimages in which every one walked barefoot, especially in an area where there was a lot of grass. The touch or feel of the earth can be important. I picked up this idea from walking barefoot on St. Patrick's Purgatory and Croagh Patrick in Ireland.

- Some pilgrimages may be done where people walk at a normal pace, while some pilgrimages may be done where people walk slowly, heel-to-heel, pausing between steps, and silent, as one would walk a labyrinth.

Practicing Pilgrimage—Part II

- I've prayed many kinds of prayers on pilgrimage. I've used Catholic rosaries on pilgrimage, with the practices and words written out for a group, along with prayer beads given to me by my Episcopal friends. There is also the famous "Jesus prayer," which comes from Russia in the nineteenth century, and is simply a repetition of this line: "Lord Jesus Christ, Son of God, have mercy on me, a sinner." The idea behind this prayer is that it literally covers all the bases: praise of God, acknowledgment of Jesus as Lord and Savior, confession, and thanksgiving for being saved.

- Sometimes, at the end of a pilgrimage, there may be a "sense" that a group is open to having a washing of the feet. Use John 13:1–17 as our guide, where Jesus lifts up the lowly act of washing the feet. It can be quite powerful to wash another person's feet, especially among a group of pilgrims at the end of a day of walking.

- In many mainline denominations there are hymnbooks or songbooks that may be brought along and used. Sometimes there is a guitarist who brings along a guitar on a pilgrimage and leads and accompanies the group; other instruments I have used on pilgrimages include a violin or a flute.

Part V: The Concluding Session
Tying It All Together

At the end of our time together, it is important to have a recap, pulling together the varied experiences of pilgrimage—as a personal reflection on pilgrimage of life, a presentation of a way of living the pilgrimage life, a movie, and an actual pilgrimage—with assisting a group to make the connections between the theory "out there" to life where we live. At the very end of the session together, I like to divide people into groups as small as two or three, or as large as five or six individuals, depending on the size of the group. Provide each group with a piece of butcher paper or large newsprint, along with a magic marker, and tape these pieces of paper on a nearby wall. Re-visit chapter 5 list of characteristics of the Pilgrimage of Life (via PowerPoint or on a separate piece of butcher paper or newsprint). If the group is from a church, like a board of lay leaders or a Session, have them focus on where the church will be in five years' time on its pilgrimage. Ask them to use resource material from the first opening session, e.g., welcoming practices, the "Pilgrimage of Life" PowerPoint discussion, the movie *The Way*, and the actual pilgrimage. For the discussion, you may start off with "Hospitality," and ask some questions: How does the church need to make some modifications in its current program or practice of inviting and welcoming strangers on their respective journeys? Does the church need to work on inviting and welcoming people from different races, ethnicities, or nationalities of those who currently attend? If the church is largely heterosexual couples, does the church look for ways that it can be more inviting and welcoming of LGBTQI individuals, couples, and families? Go through each one of the characteristics in each small group. This will take up to 10 to 20 minutes. Then bring all the groups together into one large group. Have a spokesperson from each group share their response to each characteristic and how they do or do not see it practiced within the church's life. If not, how would they like to add it among their repertoire of activities?

For the end of this time together, I have concluded such group activities with celebration of Holy Communion, since Jesus actually shared his Last Supper at the conclusion of Passover Seder, itself a celebration of pilgrimage. I've also begun the time together with "Blessing of Pilgrims upon Departure" at the very beginning, and then used the service of "Blessing of Pilgrims upon Return," both in the Daily Pilgrimage chapter (chapter 15); at this concluding time, gathering everyone into a circle and celebrating our time together.

Closing Thoughts

Again, the above activities can be modified in all kinds of ways:

- I've used this basic framework for a group of ten and a group of fifty people, and it seems to work well for all group sizes.
- This framework can be stretched out to cover a morning or afternoon workshop schedule, or can be spread out over a series of days, with other readings, movies, art and recreation activities brought into the day.
- I've used this framework while walking and leading a group on part of the Appalachian Trail and Pacific Crest Trail, and I've led groups using this framework in churches and retreat centers, as well as in urban centers.

- Leaders should feel free to adapt to the needs of the group, and have fun!

Conclusion

When leading a group on the characteristics of pilgrimage and the movie, the people participating in this activity are more receivers of the information than participants on the pilgrimage. I usually find that it is in the actual pilgrimage that people become "alive" to the possibility of seeing their life as a pilgrimage that is being lived out daily. Indeed, out of all the sections provided above, the most important part or activity is probably the actual pilgrimage. It is in the actual making of the cross, the walk, and the practice of activities and prayers along the way that pull people in deeper into the life of a pilgrim. So when shaping or guiding a group through this format, the highlight or where the most time should be spent is on the actual pilgrimage itself.

As I've cited before, Phil Cousineau, a veteran pilgrim, writes that the true pilgrimage is the "undiscovered land of your own imagination, which you could not have explored any other way than through these lands, with gratitude in your satchel and the compassion for all you see as your touchstone."[6] Hopefully by taking this pilgrimage with a group of people, the group may discover the pilgrimage that this group has already been on, and that the way forward offers a new way of being in this world.

---

6. Cousineau, *Art of Pilgrimage*, 225–26.

10

A Pilgrimage of New Beginnings

> What is the difference between a pilgrim and a tourist?
> I sat in a church in Prague contemplating this question. . . .
> I observed that tourists take pictures. Pilgrims may also, but they go farther:
> they sit and meditate, some kneel in prayer, some light candles. . . .
> The pilgrim participates. The tourist observes.
> —Lauren Artress[1]

> Listen, God, I want very much to be a pilgrim,
> in order to get to you by a long journey,
> and in order to be a large piece of you:
> you garden of living avenues.
> —Rainer Maria Rilke[2]

> Walk as if you are kissing the earth with your feet.
> —Thich Nhat Hanh[3]

New Beginnings

As I write this, I am preparing for my daughter's wedding to her boyfriend of seven years. As the dad of the bride, I will officiate the wedding, so the next question was, "Who will walk the bride down the aisle?" This is a

---

1. Artress, *Walking a Sacred Path*, 35.
2. Rainer Maria Rilke, Book Two, *The Book of Pilgrimage*, www.walkingfarfromhome.com/rilke-on-pilgrimage.
3. Quoted in Shaw, *Thich Nhat Hanh: Buddhism in Action*.

Practicing Pilgrimage—Part II

tradition that harkens back generations, when the patriarch of the family literally and metaphorically handed the bride over to the next man in her life who would now care for her. When I wed my daughter's mom, we decided to do things differently. Both my parents walked me down the aisle first, and then both her parents walked her down the aisle. We clearly saw that both of our parents were handing us off to each other.

For my daughter, there is really no sense that her mom and I are giving her away per se. Rather, we are seeing that she is joining with a man whom she has loved for more than seven years (and counting). My daughter decided that the ones to take her "down the aisle" would be my partner and her mom. Why my partner? Because he helped raise her since she was seven years old. Yet what is significant in this ritual of a wedding is the entrance of and walking in of the bride in a heterosexual wedding.[4] While the groom gets equally gussied up, as do the groomsmen and the bridesmaids, it is the bride that receives the most attention at that hour as she walks in and takes her place in the front of the family and friends gathered that day. Equally striking is the time at the close of worship, when the couple walks out of the worship space, hand in hand or arm in arm, legally and symbolically now a unit of two people, wedded or united together. With this new beginning of life, the married couple walks out of the ceremony together, either hand in hand or arm in arm, off on their pilgrimage of life together.

The other time that I remember the act of walking forward during worship was for the baptism of both my children when they were infants. Each child wore the same baptismal gown that was made from fine Liberty of London linen cloth, with tatted crochet lace around each cuff and the lower hem of the gown that was made by my grandmother. There is something symbolic about going forward with one's child in one's arms, taking the baby forward to be baptized. With both children, I was the pastor who would both say the prayers and perform the holy sacrament of baptizing the baby with these words, "I baptize you in the name of the one who creates, redeems, and saves, Father, Son, and Holy Spirit," or "Creator, Christ, and Sustainer." Sometimes the new young infant is then carried by a pastor down an aisle of a church, with the congregation singing something like "God's got the itsy bitsy baby in God's hand," or the pastor saying, "Welcome your new sister (or brother) into the life of the household of faith." Baptisms are, after all, the beginning of a person's public walk or pilgrimage

---

4. Given that marriage between two adults of either gender is now possible in most of the United States, some of this ritual has changed, so that everyone simply stands up when a couple to be wedded enters into the room where they are to be wed.

of faith, in which the entire congregation witnesses the baptized one's place among the throng of other pilgrims who are already on the journey.

In both weddings and baptisms, as well as other ceremonies in the life of a church that celebrate new beginnings, such as confirmation classes or the welcoming of new members, a community of faith makes public what God's Spirit is already doing in the lives of those gathered. We worship a God who is making "a new heaven and a new earth" (Rev 21:1). Or to quote Ecclesiastes, "There is a time for everything, and a season for every activity under heaven. A time to be born, and a time to die, a time to plant and a time to uproot" (3:1–2). There is no doubt that God is a God of new beginnings.

Consider all the other "new beginnings" that occur in the life of a family, among friends, and a congregation that could be memorialized with a pilgrimage. For example, a "House Blessing" is a pilgrimage of sorts, as people walk behind or with a pastor or priest, who blesses the house, which is becoming a home for a family. Various denominations like the Episcopalians, Roman Catholics, and the Evangelical Lutheran Church of America (ELCA) have House Blessings as part of their liturgical tradition. Other churches will have a worship liturgy that is designed for a new church beginning, perhaps meeting in a school's auditorium or fellowship hall of another church, as well as a pilgrimage-like ritual that honors the building and completion of a church's sanctuary. Of course, there are also worship liturgies for the time that a congregation leaves a sanctuary, in essence desanctifying the space, making it "less holy" perhaps, though nothing can block or forbid God from entering any space.

Life is full of new beginnings and that often requires and asks for an initiation rite of passage, which is similar to the beginning or departure of people on a pilgrimage. The beginning of a significant relationship is often given the date of when a couple either first met, were engaged, or were married, which, with time, becomes an anniversary date. Moving into a house or a community has a starting date. Joining a religious community may have a date when a novice makes a committment to the gathering's greater life. Beginning a new job, starting a new enterprise, a baby's birth into the family, learning yoga, entering college—all of these "firsts" and "starts" and "beginnings" often require or beg for a ritual to celebrate the significance of the occasion.

In this chapter, the focus is on ways to celebrate or mark a new beginning in one's life or the life of a community. After all, we are simply

Practicing Pilgrimage—Part II

participating in the dawning of what God is creating: "a new heaven and a new earth" (Rev 21:1).

Activities

Making a Mandala of New Habits, New Practices, or New Traditions

Every New Year's Eve and New Year's Day some people make lists of things they will do differently in the coming year. Some take up a new exercise activity; others simply take up exercise. Still others try a new diet, promise to dance more in the coming year, take an art class, or finish a degree.

For this activity, take a piece of construction paper or newsprint. Flip a large bowl over and place it on the paper. Take a pen or pencil and trace around the bowl, so that there is a large circle left on the paper. Take a pair of scissors and cut out the circle. Divide the circle into three zones or four quadrants. In each section draw a picture, a symbol, or a few words that express a new habit or ritual, a new practice in your daily or communal life, or a year's goal and hopeful accomplishment. You may draw more zones, but know that one can only achieve so much "new" activity in any year. You may draw pictures around the word, making this truly a work of art. Contemplate and meditate on what you are drawing or writing. If you are doing this as a group project, share with others what your goals are. If not sharing with others, then go on to the next part of this project: cut out the three zones or four quadrants. Consider in what ways you can achieve these goals along the pilgrimage itself, or within the coming year. Place the cut pieces in your backpack or pocket, and carry them with you on the pilgrimage, looking at the pieces from time to time, contemplating ways of achieving them. At the end of the pilgrimage, you have a choice: either be like the Tibetan Buddhist monks who ceremoniously destroy their mandalas and sweep their sand art away; burn the pieces of paper, letting them go. The other option is to place the pieces into a memory box (see chapter 11 on remembrance) and remember from time to time what your goals and dreams were for the coming year.

Journaling and Sketching

I usually take a pad of paper, notebook, and plenty of pens and pencils with me on a pilgrimage, along with a decent camera. Journaling—the old fashion way—includes writing up stories from the day at the end of a long daily walk. Sometimes I'll simply record the highlights of the day, promising myself to go back and fill in the blanks another day. Sketching is a "lost art" some say. In the journal I also may draw or sketch something significant from that day. I sketch in a notebook along with an account of the day because sketching involves stopping, sitting down, and focusing on an object, person, or landscape, rather than taking a quick picture with a camera. Writing and sketching force a person to slow down and reflect upon the day.

Collecting Prayers

I try to be a conscientious prayer-lists person, though I fail miserably in keeping up with the list. On the pilgrimage to Chimayo, the habit is to invite congregations to give us slips of paper upon which people have written prayer concerns. I usually stuff the slips of paper into my pocket of the pants or shorts I'm wearing, and I am able to get them out and read them from time to time. At the end of the day, we give back the slips of paper and get new slips of prayers for the next day, which keeps the prayers fresh.

A Tin Cup or Water Bottle

On the Camino to Santiago de Compostela, one carries a passport or *credencial* showing where one has been along the way. A "virgin" (unadorned) tin cup or new water bottle can serve the same function wherever you go; simply collect stickers from the various places you visit while on pilgrimage. It is modeled on the Olympics, in which people gather inexpensive pins. I have seen water bottles and tin cups plastered with all kinds of stickers at the end of a pilgrimage.

Likewise, I have learned that when people ride bicycles from one end of the United States to the other, they dip their back tire in the ocean prior to leaving and then dip their front tire when they get to the opposite coast. I have blessed people with water, reaffirmed their baptismal promises at the beginning of a pilgrimage, as well as washed feet toward the end of such sojourns. Water matters!

Practicing Pilgrimage—Part II

Taking on a New Name for the Journey

Some communities of faith have naming ceremonies in inducting new members into a gathering. For example, in becoming an oblate of St. Benedict's Monastery in St. Joseph, Minnesota, I took on the name "Alcuin," who was the educational reformer under Charlemagne. While not quite a "saint," he did achieve the status of "blessed Alcuin." The question on pilgrimage is this: is there a saint or a person you admire greatly who you think is incredibly charitable, just, courageous, or patient that you would like to emulate? What would it mean to walk in her or his steps? What ways have they changed you? Changed the world? Changed people for the better?

Name Game

How about remembering our ancestors, traditions and homes, loyalties and love, and the kind on a pilgrimage. In introducing ourselves to one another in beginning a pilgrimage, we can go around a group and see how far back we can go in our memory of our lineage. Who are the people who have brought us to this pilgrimage? How were they pilgrims before us? Again: are we walking in their footsteps? For example, this is a little of my lineage: "I am Brett, brother of Todd, son of Liz and Don of Brooklyn, New York, who were daughter and son of Alice and Paul of Brooklyn, NY, and Evelyn and Porter of Brooklyn, NY . . ." How many of your ancestors can you remember? What do you remember? What habits or behaviors did you inherit from these ancestors? Which habits or behaviors of theirs do you practice that you would like to leave to the side of your lifelong pilgrimage? What new habits might be good for you to pick up?

Packet of Wildflowers!

New beginnings seem to include flowers a lot of the time. Going to a wedding there are flowers in the sanctuary, among circle of friends, in garlands, boutonnieres, bouquets, and tables. In the beginning of holy days of a church year, there are flowers. Consider carrying with you a packet of wild flower seeds that are native to the land where you are walking. In strategic places where you think there needs to be a few flowers, feel free to spread some of the wild flower seeds. This may or may not be legal, so check forestry agencies and other authorities before you do it!

A Pilgrimage of New Beginnings

Re-affirmation of Baptism

I have mentioned this several times throughout this book: baptism matters. Consider baptism as a beginning of sorts, in which a person is starting her or his public walk of faith. Grace has already done the most important work, and baptism is a sign and seal of the work of God already done. In the reaffirmation of baptism, we are simply remembering our baptism, and are joyful because we know whose we are: we are God's people. This service comes from the *Book of Common Worship* of the Presbyterian Church (USA).

> Leader: Jesus said: "I am the light of the world. Whoever follows me will never walk in darkness, but will have the light of life" (John 8:12). The call of Christ is to willing, dedicated discipleship. Our discipleship is a manifestation of the new life into which we enter through baptism. It is possible because in Jesus Christ we have been set free from the bondage of sin and death.
>
> Leader: Discipleship is both a gift and a commitment, an offering and a responsibility. It is marked by change, growth, and deepened commitment. It is lived out of a renewing sense of God's calling to us, and of God's claim upon us made in our baptism. On this occasion we celebrate with all the pilgrims in renewing our baptism.
>
> Leader: Profession of Faith: The grace bestowed on you in baptism is sufficient because it is God's grace. By God's grace we are saved and enabled to grow in the faith and to commit our lives in ways which please God. I invite you now to claim that grace given you in baptism by reaffirming your baptismal vows: to renounce all that opposes God and God's kingdom and to affirm the faith of the holy catholic church.
>
> Leader: Trusting in the gracious mercy of God, do you turn from the ways of sin and renounce evil and its power in the world?
>
> People: We do.
>
> Leader: Who is your Lord and Savior?
>
> People: Jesus Christ is my Lord and Savior.
>
> Leader: Will you be Christ's faithful disciple, obeying his Word and showing his love?
>
> People: I will with the help of God.
>
> Apostles' Creed (Traditional or ecumenical; all recite.);
>
> Leader: You have publicly professed your faith. Will you devote yourself to the church's teaching and fellowship, to the breaking of bread, and the prayers of the Church?
>
> People: I will with God's help.

Practicing Pilgrimage—Part II

(At this point, you may use a bowl with water in it, and either let each individual come forward and apply the sign of the cross on a forehead with water, or take a branch, and dip it in water, and spray the heads of many with water, saying the words, "Remember your baptism and be thankful!")

All Pray: Faithful God, in baptism you claimed us, and by your Spirit you are working in our lives, empowering us to live a life worthy of our calling. We thank you for leading us to this time and place of reaffirming the covenant you made with us in our baptism. Establish us in your truth, and guide us by your Spirit, that, together with all your people, we may grow in faith, hope, and love, and be faithful disciples of Jesus Christ, to whom, with you and the Holy Spirit be honor and glory, now and forever. Amen.

Conclusion

Life has many beginning moments, like birth, the opening day of school, the first day at a job, or confirmation in a church, which includes lots of rituals of initiation. There are also certain stretches of the everyday pilgrimage life, covering a span of time, in which one may feel lost or in a period of discernment regarding "next choices" or "new chapters" that are more intense; there may be a sense of pilgrimage or wandering in life, with accompanying rituals of intensification. And there are moments when one realizes that there are certain endings to life as well, like graduation from a school, the last day of employment, and the time when our earthly pilgrimage has come to an end, with sets of rituals of passage. In this book, the accompanying chapters on the daily walk of pilgrimage can serve as a chapter on the intensification of pilgrimage, and the chapter on remembrance focuses on the conclusion of life's pilgrimage for pilgrims. For now, enjoy the pilgrimage practices of a new beginning in one's life, or the life of a community!

11

Pilgrimage of Remembrance

> There are two ways of remembering. One is to make an excursion
> from the living present back into the dead past. . . . The other way is to
> summon the dead past back into the living present. . . .
> When Jesus said, "Do this in remembrance of me" (1 Corinthians 11:24),
> he was not prescribing a periodic slug of nostalgia.
> —Frederick Buechner[1]

> There is a time to weep and a time to laugh,
> a time to mourn and a time to dance.
> —Ecclesiastes 3:4

Homecomings, Funerals, Memorials, and Pilgrimages

A pilgrimage is largely learning to walk or move in the footsteps or paths of others who have preceded us for a higher, holy, or spiritual reason or purpose. But this is not merely following footsteps, but also listening to the chatter that comes along with it, for we listen and read the saintly stories because, as Patricia Hampl writes, we desire to listen "to the gossip of the ages."[2]

Along the way of an actual pilgrimage or the pilgrimage of life, we may stop at various milestones or memorials, chapels or shrines, built by human hands to memorialize an "event" that happened on the way to one's destination. These memorials along the way are a sign or symbol, referencing us to

---

1. Buechner, *Wishful Thinking*, 58.
2. Hampl, *Virgin Time*, 56.

the past in which we place our present lives as we move toward the future. Another way of saying this is that a pilgrim wants to bring one's life story to God, no matter what has occurred, placing it in the larger context of God's story in the present, which is still unfolding today in our very midst, leading us into the future. After all, God calls us from the future, keeping watch over our every footstep in the present, forgiving us for our past errors, and often cleaning up after us.

Consider homecomings at churches, a tradition that is very popular in the American South. While I was used to family reunions and gatherings of former high school and college classmates for class reunions with high school and university connections, it was not until I moved to the South that I was baptized into the ritual of a church's homecoming celebration, usually held in the fall months. They are sometimes a mixture of a reunion of sorts and an old fashion tent revival, depending on who is planning the event. When I was a pastor of a church with a homecoming event, I usually planned for the whole weekend to be taken up with good Southern food (e.g., fried chicken, okra, grits, hush puppies, and sweet tea) and various choirs singing, usually inviting one of the former pastors to preach, maybe read from the lectionary during worship on Sunday morning, or assist with Holy Communion.

What is powerful in these gatherings is that there is a confluence of both the saints and sinners today who gather to remember the days of a church's history, and who bring along with them the memories and thus the spirits of those who are now numbered among the "cloud of witnesses" (Heb 12:1). Maybe it is in worship, with everyone gathered together, that a hymn evokes a memory in a person's or community's life. Or maybe memories are sparked by a certain Scripture passage, a sermon's theme, a prayer prayed. Maybe a member who has been absent for a while comes one Sunday and sits in a pew or chair where she or he had always sat for many years before leaving a congregation.

Another memory or example: I have served churches in which there is a cemetery maintained by the church in the back or on the side of the sanctuary. I find in the celebrating of the sacrament of baptism, which reminds us of our baptism of course, as well as in celebrating the Eucharist that there is an invocation of the memory of the saints of the past to join the saints in the present. One of my most intense experiences of the power of memory of those who have passed away was at Ernest Myatt Presbyterian Church, at Easter sunrise worship. The congregation would gather in

Pilgrimage of Remembrance

the cemetery, located behind the church building itself, usually gathering around a large, old oak tree in the middle of the acreage. Early in the morning, before sunrise, people walked out from the warmth of the sanctuary into the dark, where the air was cool outside, and gathered under the tree in a circle. I would read the Gospel, which is either one of the verses about an angel surprising the women who came to prepare Jesus's body, or the story of the gardener telling Mary about the resurrection. There was a mysterious power that would embrace us all as I then intoned the story of Jesus's Last Supper with his disciples, reading the words from 1 Corinthians in which Jesus took the bread, blessed, and broke it, poured the wine into a cup, saying "do this in remembrance of me."

In this section on remembrance, the focus is on literally re-membering or bringing back to memory, again, the stories, ideas, feelings, and thoughts of those who are not necessarily with us today yet whose stories and presence we embrace today. For example, every time we recite the words of the Apostles' Creed we acknowledge the presence of the saints when we say that we believe "in the Holy Spirit, the holy catholic church, the *communion of saints* [my emphasis], the forgiveness of sins, and life everlasting."

Activities

At my dad's memorial worship service, I was amazed at all the ways we signified his life among us. We had a constant slide show of his life playing on a computer monitor; we displayed all his kitschy art projects next to his various framed works of art with stamps and coins; there was an elaborate presentation of his "military miniatures" or toy soldiers; and there were framed photographs and albums of photos of the family for people to look at as we welcomed friends and family members in a reception line. These "relics" are more like *recuerdos* in Spanish, reminders or relics with memories of who and whose we are in life. In this section, I will suggest ways that we may remember—or literally be re-membered—with the memory of others no longer with us in this time and space.

All Saints' Day

In the United Church of Chapel Hill, the focus was on All Saints' Day and the relics of those departed, and the remembrance of those no longer with us was more than "in the air," but rather an intrinsic part of worship. We did a short litany that affirmed the lives of those who recently departed, with people invited to name aloud those no longer with us. My friend Jane Day decorated the chancel space in the front of the sanctuary nearest the Lord's Supper table, with a lot of bric-a-brac from her mom's house, like vases, wheat, pottery scraps, two different scarves, and in the middle of it all a small framed picture of her mom.

In other churches, during the worship processional, people carry in handmade banners with symbols of those departed since the previous All Saints' Day as a way of recognizing the beloved no longer with us. These small two-feet-by-two-feet felt banners may then be taken back to the family's home after being used in worship. Still others bring forward pictures and photographs—framed and unframed—of people who have died, placing them on a table in the front of the sanctuary. Included sometimes during this collection of memorabilia are small votive candles, which are lit by members of a congregation as a way of remembering others.

On pilgrimage, consider bringing pictures of the departed. Place these photos in a backpack's pocket, or in a pocket that can easily be taken out along a pathway, igniting a spark of memory. We may say a prayer for the recently departed daily, or leave mementos of our beloved along the trail. Sometimes I've collected a small stone with the person's name on it to remember them. Other times I've built a cairn: a tower of stones and rocks with the bottom rock the biggest as a base, putting smaller stones on top of it, as a solitary reminder of someone who has passed away.

Building a Cairn

As mentioned above, one of the most powerful signs of remembrance is the building of cairns on a pilgrimage. A cairn is quite simple: in a location filled with different sizes of stones and rocks, one simply stacks up rocks and stones. The very stopping to build a cairn, maybe praying for or remembering the person to whom the cairns is in memory of, is a rich spiritual tradition. The cairn needs not stand more than a few feet, or maybe a foot. It is a marker, remembering someone beloved.

Candles

Along many pilgrimage routes there are plenty of church sanctuaries, along with many small shrines, in which the lighting of a votive candle might come in handy. I know some pilgrims who carry votive candles with them for such purposes of creating or improvising a memorial in someone's honor along a pilgrimage. At St. Benedict's Monastery, the monks actually put small pictures of the deceased monks on the dinner tables on the anniversary of their deaths, lighting a small votive candle that is nearby to remember that sister's presence in the life of the community.

Talismans, Symbols, and Signs of the Past

Some pilgrims take a coin, stone, leaf, an old postcard of those who are recently departed, and carry it with them on an actual pilgrimage. In a sense, we are bringing the memory of these people with us on pilgrimage. In my case, I usually take a scallop shell, shoved in the pocket of my pants, along with a large scallop shell tied to my backpack. Some people carry a small, smooth stone to remember a river they walked over and loved. Others will purchase a cheap stack of postcards on the pilgrimage route and, for old times' sake, send the cards to friends and family members who are not with them on pilgrimage. I've known people to carry puzzle pieces, Monopoly tokens, which are all relics of where people come from. They want these small items to be easy to get to in order to remember why they are on the pilgrimage.

Veneration of the Cross of Christ

On pilgrimage to Chimayo, one of the practices I have come to respect is the time of veneration of the cross. On the pilgrimage, we have a tall cross with a hand-carved statue of the crucified Jesus on it, created by a local artist. On the first and last night of the pilgrimage, pilgrims gather around and venerate the cross in this simple way: with the lights dimmed, candles around the room, and Christian music on in the background, there is a large quilt placed on the floor in front of the cross, which has been placed in a wooden stand. Each pilgrim takes turns sitting on the quilt, reflecting upon the pilgrimage and one's life, considering why the Holy Spirit has brought us on this pilgrimage, and what lessons we are to learn (the focus is on the departure of pilgrims), and then what was learned on the pilgrimage as we were accompanied by the Spirit of the Christ. This can go on for roughly forty-five minutes, depending upon the size of the group, as some pilgrims kneel in front of the cross, while others lie prostrate before the cross.

Practicing Pilgrimage—Part II

Create an Original, Creative Photo Album

Though this may seem old-fashioned, some people still create photo albums that capture their journey their own way. Take some of the photos, newspaper and magazine clippings, rose petals and leaves, and other flora and fauna from the pilgrimage you were on, and either start to build this photo album chronologically or thematically. At some craft stores, there are easy to apply bric a brac that could adorn the edges of the photo album.

Blogs and Websites

Like a photo album, one can create a website, blog, Instagram account, or Facebook page that is specific to the pilgrimage a person or group is on for others to sign in and keep track of others on a pilgrimage. Then, when the pilgrimage is over, a person or group has an easy to read website or blog they can refer to from time to time to remember the pilgrimage they were on in the not too distant past.

Memory Boxes

For each and every pilgrimage, create a "box" of memories from old shoeboxes. The shoebox can be decorated on the outside with images from the pilgrimage, and filled inside with various rocks, shells, menus from restaurants, receipts, photos, hats, buttons, or other items that provide an emotional resonance with the pilgrim.

Tattoos

This may seem far-fetched, but I observed a lot of people getting tattoos of scallop shells on their arm, on their calf, or on their back after the pilgrimage to Santiago de Compostela. There are other symbols for other pilgrimage routes that a pilgrim might find endearing, and the pilgrim gets a tattoo of the symbol as a reminder of the pilgrimage.

Pilgrimage of Remembrance

A Prayer for Healing

Many people go on pilgrimage in order to be healed of a past affliction, either emotional or spiritual. Here is a prayer used on the way to Chimayo:

> Lord, you invite all who are burdened to come to You. Allow Your healing hand to heal me. Touch my soul with Your compassion for others. Touch my heart with Your courage and infinite love for all. Touch my mind with Your wisdom, that my mouth may always proclaim Your praise. Teach me to reach out to You in my need, and help me to lead others to You by my example. Most loving Heart of Jesus, bring me health in body and spirit that I may serve You with all my strength. Touch gently this life that You have created, now and forever. Amen.[3]

A Litany for Life

L: For moms and dads
P: God be with them,
L: For the gift of compassion
P: God be with them,
L: For the gift of patient love
P: God be with them,
L: For a growing love of life
P: God be with them,
L: For new moms
P: God be with them,
L: For teenage moms
P: God be with them,
L: For moms who are beaten
P: God be with them,
L: For moms who are afraid
P: God be with them,
L: For moms who are alone
P: God be with them,
L: For moms with broken hearts
P: God be with them,

---

3. *Archdiocesan Pilgrimage for Vocations Handbook*, 43.

L: For moms who have no one to love them
P: God be with them,
L: For moms who need us
P: God be with them,
L: For unborn babies
P: God be with them,
L: For innocent children
P: God be with them,
L: For children with disabilities
P: God be with them,
L: For new dads
P: God be with them,
L: For teenage dads
P: God be with them,
L: For dads who are addicted
P: God be with them,
L: For dads who are angry
P: God be with them,
L: For dads who are alone
P: God be with them,
L: For dads who love their children
P: God be with them,
L: For dads who have no one to love them
P: God be with them,
L: For dads who have run away
P: God be with them.
Amen

Conclusion

Having walked countless miles—or ridden a camel or horse, kayaked, flown, biked—I want first to remember the very physical aspect of what I have accomplished. To that end, I have actually practiced many of the activities listed above, including getting a tattoo of the School of the Pilgrim logo on my left arm. Second, I want to remember those who I once walked with in this life but who have since deceased. We need to keep record of their names, their stories, their pictures in order to keep their memories alive for the next generation of believers and pilgrims. Finally, we remember others because we wish to be remembered as well by those who follow in our footsteps. This book is a way of keeping a legacy of this pilgrim's life.

12

A Pilgrimage of the Earth

> For the beauty of the earth,
> For the beauty of the skies,
> For the love which from our birth
> Over and around us lies:
> Lord of all to thee we raise
> This our hymn of grateful praise.
> —"For the Beauty of the Earth"[1]

> The earth is the Lord's, and everything in it.
> The world and all its people belong to God.
> —Psalm 24:1

> Yours is the day, yours also the night;
> you established the luminaries and the sun.
> You have fixed all the bounds of the earth;
> you made summer and winter.
> —Psalm 74:16–17

For the Beauty of the Earth

While this may seem rather obvious, it should nonetheless be pointed out that most actual pilgrimages are more or less outdoor activities. As a child, I spent a great deal of time outside, playing in a wonderful municipal

---

1. Nineteenth-century hymn, text by Folliot Sandford Pierpoint, tune by William Chatterton Dix.

playground right behind my parents' house in Maplewood, New Jersey. When our family moved to Portland, Oregon, I was soon immersed in outdoor activities, including downhill and cross-country skiing during the winter months, water skiing and canoeing in summer, along with hiking various trails around Mt. Hood and Mt. Jefferson. My time with Civil Air Patrol also brought me to the outdoors, as I participated in a search and rescue team in which I spent several hours hunting for survivors from small aircraft crashes. I also spent a great deal of time in the air as a passenger in small aircrafts flown by Civil Air Patrol personnel, which was one of the perks of being in Civil Air Patrol in Portland. Unlike flying in a jet plane around 33,000 feet above ground, when flying in a small aircraft, I appreciated the rich diversity of the terrain under my feet: square lots of varied colors of land hedged in by green trees, meandering rivers and creeks, small dots of houses, with cars traveling slowly along the black ribbon of roadway, with Mt. Hood off in the horizon.

What was interesting to me is that the land, sky, and water were never truly part of my experience in a church per se. The environmental or ecological movements of the 1970s never came into the discussions of Sunday school or youth groups, let alone Reformed worship in the 1960s. It wasn't until the advent of Earth Day on April 22, 1970, that this country slowly started to turn and look around us and see what was happening to this planet, with our polluted rivers, rising oceans, smog-filled air, destruction of the ozone, destruction of the soil with over planting, and with new concerns about extreme weather patterns with what we now call global climate change. To this day, I remember serving a congregation in rural North Carolina in which many tobacco farmers' acreage around the church were experiencing a drought one summer, and the prayer request was simply for rain, and lots of it! This was a prayer request I never received or heard about while serving congregations in suburban or urban parishes.

With my first pilgrimage to Chimayo, I was reintroduced to the centrality of earth, sky, water, and fire on pilgrimage. Getting up at 3:00 a.m. in Costilla, and walking at 5:00 a.m. along the side of the road *before* sunrise—and thus in the dark, when it hasn't yet reached the coldest part of the night—quickly reconnects a person's mind, body, and spirit to the earth, sky, water, and fire. Whether I am walking the Camino de Santiago de Compostela, riding on a camel's back in the middle of the Sinai desert and sleeping under the canopy of stars at night, walking barefoot among the ruins of St. Patrick's Purgatory, skimming in a kayak along a watery route of a pilgrimage, or walking and tenting along the remaining bits and pieces of Hadrian's Wall in England, whenever my feet hit earth or I sense the push of water against the floating craft, I feel most connected to the Creator God.

In this section, the focus is on the way we honor earth, sky, water, and fire as parts of God's good creation while on pilgrimage. We honor these elements of life through our faith in Christ. In Esquipulas, Guatemala, home of El Cristo Negro, they taught me this saying about pilgrimage: "The Christ you seek you will not find unless you bring him with you." Through the practice and prism of faith, everyday occurrences are occasions in which the Spirit of God may be made manifest. For example, the earth we walk upon becomes sacred ground mid-stride as we pray. The water we travel upon becomes the fount of everyday blessings as we sing the old hymn, "Come Thou Fount of Every Blessing." Feeling a cool breeze on a hot, muggy North Carolina night in August, stirring into motion a set of chimes on a breezeway reminds us of the movement of God's Spirit, which flows and refreshes our sweat-soaked bodies. What makes a chapel, a shrine, or a sanctuary sacred space are the people within whom the sacred resides. The pilgrim's very body touching earth, sky, water, and feeling rays of heat from the sun, becomes a conduit of knowledge, a medium of communication, and the means of connecting with others and creation around us. We are, as pilgrims of Christ, agents of social change.[2]

Soil, sky, water, and fire play a prominent role in the Christian narrative. It is important to remember that Jesus preached outside, and not necessarily indoors within a home or synagogue. He met his disciples and followers on the side of hills (Sermon on the Mount) and from a fishing boat in the Sea of Galilee. Jesus refers to himself as "living water" and the "light of the world" throughout the Gospels, especially in John. Also in John, Jesus refers to himself as a vine, one of several agricultural metaphors used by Jesus to enable us to understand our relationship to God. One of the most repeated connections that Jesus makes between the Creator's care of the creatures of the earth and God's care of humanity is in this simple illustration from Matthew 6:26: "Look at the birds of the air; they neither sow nor reap nor gather into barns, and yet your heavenly Father feeds them. Are you not of more value than they?" To quote Reformed theologian Abraham Kuyper, "There is not a square inch in the whole domain of

---

2. Webb-Mitchell, *School of the Pilgrim*, 126.

A Pilgrimage of the Earth

our human existence over which Christ, who is Sovereign over all, does not cry: 'Mine!'"[3]

What follows in this section are some activities that will hopefully direct pilgrims' attention to the power and place of earth, sky, water, and fire on pilgrimage as we walk in this "Christ-haunted" and blessed landscape.

Activities

Prayer

This is a prayer that may be prayed antiphonally with another person or with a group:

> Leader: In the fading of the summer sun,
> the shortening of days, cooling breeze,
> swallows' flight and moonlight rays,
> **People: We see the Creator's hand.**
> Leader: In the browning of leaves once green,
> morning mists, autumn chill,
> fruit that falls, and frost's first kiss,
> **People: We see the Creator's hand.**
> Leader: Creator God, forgive our moments of ingratitude,
> the spiritual blindness that prevents us
> from appreciating the wonder that is this world,
> the endless cycle of nature,
> of life and death and rebirth.
> Forgive us for taking without giving,
> reaping without sowing.
> Open our eyes to see,
> our lips to praise,
> our hands to share
> and may our feet tread lightly on the road.
> **Amen.**[4]

---

3. Quoted in Bratt, *Abraham Kuyper*, 488.
4. From a Christian liturgy for Samhain; see http://www.faithandworship.com/Samhain_praying_though_the_Celtic_year.htm#ixzz3HgyjSzVG.

Practicing Pilgrimage—Part II

Collection of Soil or Waters

One practice that I appreciated in walking on pilgrimage to Chimayo was the collection of soil from the various places where we stopped along the way. I learned quickly not to call it "dirt" but either earth or soil, as a form of reverence for what God made. We collected about one or two kitchen cups of earth from each place we visited, collecting it in a muslin bag. Over a week's period of being on pilgrimage, the bag became heavier as we walked. The goal? At the end of the pilgrimage, when five groups of pilgrims gathered at El Santuario de Chimayo, we had a large mound of earth that would be blessed and honored by the group of pilgrims as a visible testimony to the places we had visited along the way.

On other pilgrimages I could see people doing something similar in other locales, and not only with soil, but also with water. For example, many people enjoy taking small bottles to the river Jordan in Israel and scooping up water, bringing some of the water back home for special purposes. I have mixed water from the river Jordan into the water in a baptismal font and used the water for baptisms, which was special for the family whose baby I baptized.

Colored Sand

In recent years in Chapel Hill and Carrboro, we have been blessed by a group of traveling Tibetan Buddhist monks who spend over a week in one of the towns and create a beautiful sand mandala painting. The sand mandalas are created with a certain balanced composition in which a figure of a certain deity resides. The mandala shows a kind of labyrinth in which people may travel from having a closed mind to an enlightened mind. The monks consecrate the site where the mandala is to be created with sacred chants, prayers, and trumpetlike instruments, accompanied by drums. Likewise, once the mandala is completed, there is a large ceremony with much music and lots of chants in which the mandala is destroyed by the head monk taking a large paintbrush and going through the sand. Soon, more paintbrushes come out and the mandala is destroyed, but not all is lost! The mandalas are said to transmit a positive energy to the environment and to the people who view them. The swept up remains are now put in small bags and, with the deity's healing blessing, the people take the sand

and deposit it around their homes for a blessing, or the nearest waterway as an expression of sharing the mandala's blessings with all.

On a pilgrimage, a group could create a crude mandala or circle of colored sand, maybe painting an image of Jesus or Mary with sand before the pilgrimage begins. After a blessing upon its completion, then sweep up the sand and place in small bags. Now, along the pilgrimage route, deposit the sand at places where the pilgrims stop, or in the waterway, thus blessing each place and source of water.

Ashes of Our Beloved

The only person I know personally who has been cremated is my dad, whose ashes are interred at Willamette National Cemetery in Portland, Oregon. I know other friends who had a loved one—a parent, a child, a partner—whose bodily remains were cremated, and they have taken the remains with them on pilgrimage, depositing some of the ashes along the way. This was dramatically portrayed in the movie *The Way*, in which the character played by Martin Sheen takes his son's remains along the Camino and throws them into the waters of the Atlantic Ocean at Finnisterre, the "end of the earth." It is a dramatic moment that reminds us we are made of the stuff of the stars.

Ladybugs

This is a cool activity I've done on Earth Day: take a box of ladybugs along with you on pilgrimage. Like the ashes, feel free to share the ladybugs along the way, which are a way of healing the earth.

Banners

Banners are festive but also send a message. Imagine creating a banner that celebrates the beauty of God's creation, and also communicates to others to be good to the earth, and carrying that with you on a pilgrimage. The banner might have the image of John Muir or Rachel Carson on it: Muir helped create the national park system in the United States, and Rachel Carson's book *Silent Spring* was one of the catalysts for the environmental movement here and in the wider world. Perhaps surround their images with words from their writings, and on the other side, quote one of the psalms at the top of this chapter.

Walking Sticks

At home, I have three large wooden hand-carved walking sticks that were given to me by students who took my Duke course on pilgrimage and education. I've used metal and fiberglass walking sticks on pilgrimage. I've also made crude walking sticks with groups as we walked a route through a national park or along the Appalachian Trail, with people carving and smoothing their walking sticks at campfire. I've brought bells to put on the walking sticks that make a nice little chime sound when walking, as well as yarn to decorate their walking sticks. I know of some groups who allow the members to take the walking sticks home as a relic and reminder of the pilgrimage. And I've known groups who, on the last night of the pilgrimage, burn them in a fire as a celebration of completing the pilgrimage.

Greening of the Cross

At Easter sunrise and Easter morning worship, I invite congregants to bring flowers from home to decorate or "green" a cross made of a simple wood frame with chicken wire around it. People may then stick cut flowers through the chicken wire, creating a floral or green cross.

As I mentioned in the section of working with a group on the characteristics of the pilgrimage of life, I usually make a cross with the group, using fallen twigs and branches from around the area where the pilgrimage is to take place. The branches are no longer than my hip to the floor or ground, and no fatter than my pointer finger. Binding these sticks up to make a cross works by creating two bundles of equal thickness. I use the story that Christ's wooden cross fragments are not in a souvenir shop in Jerusalem, but spread through all creation. Criss-cross the bundles, then bind them together with jute or colorful yarn, making a God's eye. You may choose bare branches, but some groups I've done pilgrimage which have simply left the leaves on the branches in making a cross and carrying that cross with them on the pilgrimage route.

A Pilgrimage of the Earth

Tobacco, Water, and Blessing the Earth

Father Ed Savilla, the Spiritual Director of the Pilgrimage to Chimayo, usually conducts a powerful devotion to the earth when he leads pilgrimage, celebrating the earth outside of Taos Pueblo. He will have someone read a psalm, like those included at the top of this chapter, along with both a reading of one of the creation stories in Genesis 1 and 2, and a reading of a creation story of the Navajo people. Along the way, there is a distribution of tobacco to the earth, and a pouring of water on us and upon the earth as part of the ceremony, along with a distribution of ashes. After all, as we remind ourselves at Ash Wednesday worship, we are nothing more than merely earth, dust, ashes, with lots of water added into us, made in the image of God, who gives us life.

Rose Compass Cross: The Four Directions and Four Seasons of Creation

Some groups create T-shirts, or small metal or clay crosses the size of one's palm to be carried in a pocket. Some crosses may be fashioned in the shape of a rose compass that can also remind people of the four seasons of the year.

Picking Up Trash and Recycling while on Pilgrimage

This seems so simple yet it is also so important: bringing a bag for garbage and a bag for recycling on a pilgrimage. I've learned to do this while hiking, and there is no doubt that along pilgrimage routes the garbage is omnipresent. Likewise, the food that I carry in bags I usually place in containers that need to be thrown away or better yet, recycled. I carry a plastic BPA-free bottle of water on pilgrimage that I fill up with water along the trek too.

Signing of the Senses

One prayer I especially like to pray on pilgrimage, either by myself or with a small group, is the "signing of the senses." In the Catholic, Eastern Orthodox, and Episcopal/Anglican tradition, the signing of the body is a ritual

Practicing Pilgrimage—Part II

used widely in their churches. On pilgrimage with a small group, I will gather everyone together and pair people up, or get individuals into a group of three people. Then I will read the following prayer, asking each person in the group to sign the senses on their pilgrim partner.

> Receive the cross on your forehead. It is Christ himself who now strengthens you with this sign of his love [sign the cross of Christ on the forehead].
>
> Receive the sign of the cross on your ears, that you may hear the voice of God [using your thumb, sign the cross of Christ over each ear].
>
> Receive the sign of the cross on your eyes, that you may see the glory of God [sign using your thumb or forefinger].
>
> Receive the sign of the cross on your lips, that you may respond to the word of God [again, administer the sign].
>
> Receive the sign of the cross over your heart, that Christ may dwell there by faith [sign].
>
> Receive the sign of the cross on your shoulders, that you may bear the gentle yoke of Christ [sign].
>
> Receive the sign of the cross on your feet, that you may walk in the way of Christ [sign].
>
> Leader: I sign you with the sign of eternal life in the name of God, Creator, Redeemer and Sustainer. Amen.[5]
>
> [This can be closed with a passing of the peace: L: The peace of Christ be with you. P: And also with you.]

Conclusion

In this day and age in which we live, where there is a threat of climate change, the activities of the pilgrimage of the earth may be exciting for a group to take on as they work on getting others to attend to the theological issues that are pressing for us as a community of faith. To add to the activities, a group may also include literature, talks about the issues of climate change, and suggestions for how we can change our lives for the good of all creation. Enabling people to attend to and be mindful of nature around us—from birds and bees, to flora and fauna, the quality of air we breathe and the water we drink—will add to the benefits we derive naturally from taking a walk in the woods.

5. "Archdiocesan Pilgrimage for Vocations," in *Archdiocesan Pilgrimage for Vocations Handbook*, 39.

13

A Pilgrimage of Justice and Peace

> Guide my feet while I run this race,
> guide my feet while I run this race,
> guide my feet while I run this race,
> For I don't want to run this race in vain.
> —"Guide My Feet"[1]

> Forward together, not one step back![2]

Marches and Pilgrimages for Justice and Peace

I once attended a rally against climate change in the plaza of the Orange County Courthouse and Chapel Hill Post Office on Franklin Street. This brick-and-stone plaza outside of the courthouse and post office is the site of many public protests in Chapel Hill. Located across the street from the campus of the University of North Carolina-Chapel Hill, the plaza is well known in the area as a safe zone for rallying groups of people on many issues, both liberal and conservative causes (and everything in between). Trying to post letters in that post office, I have been given brochures on numerous worthy and questionable causes. Most recently, I was there on the plaza with over a thousand people to bear witness to the Moral Monday rallies that have energized North Carolinians in light of the regressive politics of the General Assembly legislators. I've given out food to those who

---

1. African American spiritual. See *The New Century Hymnal*, no. 497.
2. This was a chant often used during the Moral Monday marches in Raleigh, North Carolina, during the summers of 2013 and 2014.

occupied the plaza in small tents and lean-tos on cold evenings during the Chapel Hill Occupy movement.

I began this book with a story of a march for justice and peace in Raleigh, North Carolina, known as "HKonJ." This was part of the larger "Moral Monday" movement based in North Carolina as a result of the radically new and severe laws and budget priorities of the North Carolina General Assembly. More recently, a similar march has taken place in other state capitols in which legislators have passed what feel like draconian bills on topics like the environment and fracking, voting rights and civil rights, health care in general and women's health care in particular, LGBTQ discrimination and marriage equality, and education in the public schools or public university system. These protests usually include a march or pilgrimage against the laws passed or being debated. More than three hundred thousand people marched or went on pilgrimage as part of the People Climate March in New York City on September 21, 2014, protesting the lack of movement of the governments and multinational corporations of this world in doing anything significant about climate control. And then there are those witnessing against increased police violence in cities like Ferguson, Missouri—"Ferguson October"—with people protesting the rise in the number of deaths of young African American men such as Michael Brown. These walks and marches—a.k.a., pilgrimages—are reminiscent of the 1960s pilgrimages or marches that Dr. Martin Luther King Jr. and other members of the Southern Christian Leadership Conference (SCLC) led in the South and other parts of the United States against the injustices suffered by African Americans in this country. Consider the power of a march or a pilgrimage of people to change a culture by reflecting upon the march from Selma to Montgomery, Alabama, after Bloody Sunday helped usher in the new Voting Rights Act of 1965. The inspiration for this pilgrimage of justice was inspired by other such marches and pilgrimages, like Mahatma Gandhi's Salt March in the earlier part of the twentieth century that brought down the British colonial rule of India. The presence of so many people moving en masse demonstrated that there was a critical mass of people that no military force could stop, or diplomatic and political bodies could ignore. There is a sense of goodness or rightness, a powerful sense of energy, emerging from a group of people dedicated to righting a wrong, to healing a culture's wound, when people gather together as a group with a common cause in mind. There can be a shift of public opinion when a gathering of individuals become a group with one focus in mind, like the

A Pilgrimage of Justice and Peace

Solidarity movement in then-communist Poland, in which people started to literally move en masse from one location to another, practicing nonviolence. Maintaining a central, core vision of justice and peace before them, a people with such a vision will not perish (Prov 29:18).

I usually join with the North Carolina Central University group of students, staff, and faculty lesbian, gay, bisexual, transgender, queer, questioning, and intersex (LGBTQI) groups that will be marching in the statewide Pride Parade. The first Pride Parade was in New York City, and started soon after the famous Stonewall protests, in which a group of bar patrons—many of whom were drag queens—objected to and protested against the police intimidation and brutality they received nightly, based largely upon homophobia among those who are sworn to defend and protect us. Pride parades were—and still are—political along with being a festival of sorts, as the LGBTQI community is out and proud, no longer hiding in various closets. While there will be many floats, bikes, dancers, clowns, nuns-in-drag, and bands sporting rainbow colors—the unofficial flag or banner of the LGBTQI movement—there will be many people who are carrying protest signs calling for justice in terms of marriage equality, options for medical care for partners and spouses along with children, and equal housing opportunities, to name a few issues. But the common vision, the common cause, is equality in all arenas of civil life.

On the campus of the University of North Carolina and in the community of Chapel Hill-Carrboro, there is a pilgrimage or "walk" of sorts, called the "Black and Blue Tour." This "tour" or pilgrimage leads participants through the campus of the University of North Carolina, starting at the "Unsung Founders Memorial" at McCorkle Place on the campus, and walking through the campus and downtown area. Since much of the early campus buildings were built by slave labor, it is powerful to walk among buildings built and cared for by African Americans who could not attend the University until the 1960s. The tour or pilgrimage continues through parts of Chapel Hill and Carrboro that once housed segregated black communities like Northside in Chapel Hill, along with the segregated schools like Lincoln High School. But there is also evidence of the black civil rights movement, with a symbolic metal marker near University Presbyterian Church that recognizes the Freedom Riders who came through the area in the 1960s on their way down to Mississippi. This "tour" is a pilgrimage, of sorts, reminding people of the struggle for equality in this region, which is

Practicing Pilgrimage—Part II

saturated with the blood and sweat of those denied basic liberty and freedom in this land.

Finally, I recently went walking along Boston's Freedom Trail. This trail is self-guided, though one can either purchase a $3.00 map or pay to be guided by a person dressed in colonial garb (women in large flowing dresses and women and men dressed as militiamen, wearing knickers and tri-corner hats). Starting at the "new" Boston State House, I follow a trail that is marked by red brick buried in the cement sidewalks and city streets. I walk past Park Place Church, famous for its role in the abolition movement in the nineteenth century, next door to a cemetery that contains the remains of Sam Adams and John Hancock, Philis (an African American free woman), and Paul Revere, to name a few. Those who have walked this trail know that within a rather short distance—the distance that a horse could travel in a day or so—the cradle of freedom and liberty of the colonies is traceable by foot. On this trail, I read plaques and laminated sheets describing the history of certain areas. I listen to a young man in the Old North Church giving yet one more short lecture on the history of the church and its connection with Paul Revere. I listen to a gentleman dressed as Ben Franklin tell of the historic events, like the Boston Massacre and arguments that John Adams and John Hancock made in defense of the act of treason they were committing against the British crown. In a sense, the Freedom Trail is another pilgrimage of justice and peace, as the colonial powers were invested in liberty and freedom. From the Tea Party and Boston Massacre to the battles of Concord and Lexington, this trail connects contemporary history buffs to the nitty-gritty story of our early founders. We contemporary walkers are reminded that these people were united with a common vision, captured in the Declaration of Independence, that "all men [sic] are created equal, that they are endowed by their Creator with certain unalienable rights, that among these are life, liberty and the pursuit of happiness."

I could continue discussing other marches and pilgrimages for justice and peace that I've been part of for the last forty years of my life. All these marches are pilgrimages, given the description I offered in the first part of this book. The marches involve people walking a certain distance, from point A to Z, for a specific political aim or purpose. The people marching on such a political pilgrimage have an agenda, like addressing the plight of prisoners in a faraway land, curing AIDS in our lifetime, or speaking out against those forces who cause poverty or unhealthy living conditions in a country. The people in the march or pilgrimage are involved in the political movement by simply walking with their feet, desirous of wooing and persuading others to join their cause, inviting individuals to become part of the larger "we-ness" of the group. With songs, placards, speeches, and written addresses, the people's minds, bodies, and spirits are engaged. While people will think strategically of ways they can shape a march or pilgrimage, in the end, the very mass of people themselves will shape the agenda, and will alone decide the success or failure of the march. And there is the spiritual aspect of such pilgrimages. Both Hebrew Scripture and the New Testament are full of passages on justice and peace, letting one and all know that we worship a God who demands nothing less of us than justice and peace for all: "But let justice roll down like waters, and righteousness like an ever-flowing stream" (Amos 5:24); "For I the LORD love justice" (Isa 61:8); "Will not God bring about justice for God's elect who cry to God day and night, and will God delay long over them?" (Luke 18:7). In other words, by participating in marches and pilgrimages of justice and peace, we are placing our individual or smaller communal story into the larger narrative of God and God's people throughout time who advocate with those who have been discriminated against, denied basic rights, or been treated in an unjust manner, where hate and violence were allowed to grow and where peace was pushed to the side in place of a corrupt and corrosive power. By placing our story-fed action—a.k.a., pilgrimage—in the larger narrative of God's justice and peace, we are embodying God's justice and peace.

In this chapter, I will first look at the history and theological importance of a pilgrimage or march for justice and peace. Following this will be a quick checklist of what to bring, sing, or focus on for such a pilgrimage so that it might become more than just a moment in a social calendar, a social movement.

History of Marches or Pilgrimages of Justice and Peace

There is a rich history of marching or walking for the cause of justice and peace throughout time and around the world. Some could make the argument that the biblical story of Passover and the Exodus of the people Israel, who moved en masse to the land of "milk and honey," was a religious and political movement against Pharaoh and for freedom of the people in a new land. Such a mass movement with a common goal or vision would be intimidating.

Practicing Pilgrimage—Part II

There is no doubt that the other source of marches as pilgrimages comes from a military background. Throughout time, the presence of a large group walking together with a kind of uniformity, e.g., marching in lock step, with weapons, could be an intimidating presence to those people on the opposing side. The presence of a large number of people marching for a common purpose could easily swamp and take over a loose gathering of individuals.

In historic protest marches—from the Suffragette movement in the early part of the twentieth century, to the modern National Organization of Women (NOW) marches for the Equal Rights Amendment, and the march of migrant farm workers with Cesar Chavez in the 1960s in central California—it has been the sheer number of individuals marching together, in step, that has brought a sense of fear to the powers opposing the granting of liberty and freedom to those oppressed. Or consider the pilgrimage of peace workers at Ft. Benning, Georgia, and other military bases, where in the sixties and seventies people objected to the rise of nuclear weaponry, or to the teaching of torture techniques by U.S. military personnel to international military servicemen and women. I have been part of these demonstrations, in which people plant small white crosses along the pilgrimage route, with the names of those killed by torture written on them in black ink. Candlelight vigils continue in the evening as people encamp around the margins of these military bases, protesting the infringement of human rights. And the more people who are there to bear witness to the injustice, to march or be on pilgrimage against the powers, walking without weapons, thus powerless, cause the powers-that-be great fear and intimidation, because it is the rising up of a people who are willing to risk everything that will conquer even the most well equipped armies.

Theological Reflection on Pilgrimages of Justice and Peace

Marching or going on a pilgrimage dedicated to issues of peace and justice is profoundly theological—a kind of theology-in-action. Christians engage in such profound movements because our lives are not about us per se. Instead, we are interested in life in general, for we are part of a larger community of God's creation, both human life as well as life throughout the cosmos.

In this Christian context, we are "church" with each other, as in, wherever two or three are gathered in the name of Jesus. Or as Paul describes the church, it is the body of Christ, in which we are individually members, one of another (Rom 12). In this body, the weakest or least strong member, or the member who is not held up to the spotlight, is as important as the brightest among the many in the body of Christ. In other words, we are as strong as the weakest link. And in the suffering of humankind, there are the wounds within the body, borne by our sisters and brothers either geographically close or faraway, who share in the divine nature of being created in the image of God.

What is crucial here is mindfulness of the network of relationships that connect us with the greater world in which we live. Pilgrimages with a political and religious cast provide opportunities for teaching and learning with others who are not as well-informed on current events. By marching and going on pilgrimage, like CROP walk, sponsored by Church World Services, we not only raise money to help feed the world, but also teach others about the economics of food and fresh water. By going on a march or pilgrimage around issues of race in the United States currently, with marches sponsored by groups like Black Lives Matter, the hope is that people will not only show their interest in struggling with racial inequality in the U.S., but also show solidarity with those who feel oppressed, solely because of the color of their skin. Or as a white middle-class male, if my sister is receiving unequal pay for the same kind of work I'm doing with the same background, or if a person who is black and young is facing suppression at the polls, I should be incensed. Awareness of the ties that bind us together will change my politics, my economic perspective, and my opinion on race, sex, and sexual orientation, to name a few areas. With contemplation and such exposure to the realities of this world, one sooner or later may let go of one's own agenda and one's focus on the self, and focus instead on the Christ within us, who connects us to the world of others around us, or to quote Paul, "I, yet not I, but Christ within me" (Gal 2:20). As Richard Rohr has written, "Our Western culture leans toward self-sufficiency and independence, and we often need to be reminded that we are part of a greater whole, that we are not alone in our longings and efforts for peace, justice, and healing. This is one of the great gifts of what we usually mean by 'church'—a gathering of people in solidarity of purpose, praying and seeking God's presence together."[3] Rohr even suggests that we could expand our awareness into action: "Find some way in which you can join in the life that is greater than your own. Participate in a vigil, sharing the grief and hope

---

3. Rohr, "Life as Pariticipation."

Practicing Pilgrimage—Part II

of your neighborhood or world. March with others to bring visibility and voice to an important issue. Make a pilgrimage to a sacred or violated site to connect your small place in time with a history and a broader meaning."[4]

In an attempt to work toward justice and peace not because it is the "right" thing to do but the Godly thing to do, consider creative ways of making a march or pilgrimage of justice and peace happen in this next section.

Creating a Pilgrimage of Justice and Peace

The first task for any movement of justice or peace—consider the role of nonviolence in the modern civil rights movement—is a quieting of both the angry heart and the restless mind. Inner peace brings about outer peace. In order to prepare for and conduct a march or pilgrimage of justice and peace, be sure to address some of the following aspects of a pilgrimage:

- The focus of the march or pilgrimage: be sure you know what the focus of the march is about, which usually falls in place with a simple "bumper sticker" logo that can be repeated and chanted, time and again. The issue is one of focus: know what you're protesting against and for.

- Designate stations or memorials: along with focus, what helps are "stations" or memorials along the way. Consider the "stations of the cross," which reveal the various places that Jesus stopped on his way to die on the cross; each station reveals a new part of the story. On a pilgrimage of justice and peace, have preset stations for tribute or memorials to be read, crosses to be planted in the ground to remember those who walked in the way of justice before us.

- Songs: no march or pilgrimage would be complete without songs or a song sheet, with such favorites as "We Shall Overcome," "If I Had a Hammer," and other tried-and-true songs, as well as new ones.

- Placards and signs: have a trove of signs and placards available for the marchers and pilgrims to carry along the way, or pens and paint, along with paper and sticks to create banners.

- Speakers: at the beginning and end of a march or pilgrimage, have speakers lined up to, first, establish the reason for the march or

---

4. Ibid. As Hune Margulies insists, inner peace brings outer peace. See Margulies, "On Moses and Jesus and the Purpose of Religion."

pilgrimage, and at the end to rally the marchers or pilgrims, congratulating them for their efforts and asking them to go home and continue to fight the good fight.

- Literature: be sure to have literature available to inform the marchers and pilgrims, as well as those who are watching the pilgrimage, about the background and purpose of the march this day.

- Water and food: be sure there is water and food available to help those who are feeling thirsty or tired and who will need some nutrition.

- Emergency personnel and communication: it is said that Martin Luther King Jr.'s friend Bayard Rustin coordinated the March for Jobs and Freedom in Washington, DC, in 1963 with phone calls and telegrams. Be sure that you have modern technology at hand to be sure everyone is all right throughout the pilgrimage.

- Crosses and physical markers: at protests and rallies at Ft. Benning, Georgia, and on peace marches I've gone on for those who have died in Central America fighting for justice and equal rights, participants have carried one- or two-foot white crosses with the names of those who have died painted on them with black ink. The bottom tip of the cross is usually sharpened, making it easier to plant the cross into the ground at the conclusion of the march or pilgrimage, leaving a statement behind.

Forward Together, Not One Step Back!

These marches and pilgrimages of justice and peace are necessary in a world in which those in power are not always mindful of those in great need. We engage in such pilgrimages because we serve a God who is all about justice for all people (Isa 45:19–21). As we walk and protest in such pilgrimages, sometimes for those who cannot for various reasons walk or protest for themselves, or whose voices have been stymied, we are reassured that we are not alone. The Spirit of God is the thread uniting us all together to the Creator, who is the source of Life.

14

Pilgrimages of Advent and Lent

> This Advent I invite you to set out on a pilgrimage—a journey towards a renewed and deeper encounter with God—something active, not simply read about, so there will be things to do each day. Let us set out together and may God be with us on the road. —Paul Nicholson[1]

> The spiritual pilgrimage of Lent begins with closing our mouths.
> —The Right Reverend Richard Chartres[2]

Journey

Walk into any United Methodist, Presbyterian, Episcopal, Lutheran, Moravian, Catholic, Baptist, or United Church of Christ education building, fellowship hall, church library, youth group room, or hallway going toward the sanctuary, and the word *Journey* may be posted on a corkboard around the season of Advent or Lent. There are usually images of biblical figures on a road or dirt path. Perhaps someone made a crude pair of brown paper sandals from paper bags and taped or stapled it onto a bulletin board in a rather colorful, eye-catching display. In many of the church buildings I have been to of various denominations, there is usually one or more bulletin boards with a message of "journey" or "footsteps of Jesus" or "faith walk."

The seasons of Advent and Christmas, ending with Epiphany, along with the seasons of Lent and Easter, including the season of Pentecost, are themselves a pilgrimage through a set span of days according to biblical, historic events. Advent's four Sundays can be a set of pilgrimage events that

1. Nicholson, "Advent Pilgrimage."
2. "Spiritual Discipline of Lent."

Pilgrimages of Advent and Lent

lead up to the Christmas narrative, continuing into the Epiphany story. The Epiphany narrative is a mix of two pilgrimage tales: the Three Wise Men, the Magi, arrive from the East on a pilgrimage following a star, and the Holy Family soon departs from Bethlehem to Egypt, knowing the infant Jesus would be put to death were the family to stay in Jerusalem. Lent is well known as a season for following many practices that are also found in pilgrimage. For example, the feast of Shrove Tuesday, a.k.a., Mardi Gras, followed by fasting beginning on Ash Wednesday, is reminiscent of many pilgrimages that ask pilgrims to feast the day they go on a pilgrimage, and then fast the following Wednesday on beans, rice, and water. This was a similar practice of St. Patrick's Purgatory's pilgrimage, in which pilgrims were told to eat heartily before they came on pilgrimage on the holy isle on Lough Derg, where we feasted on a diet of dry bread and black coffee or tea once a day. The readings during this season touch on the basic practices of the Christian life, calling us to reflect upon our lives in the great story of the Jesus narrative. It culminates on Palm Sunday with Jesus entering Jerusalem as he came to observe the annual pilgrimage of the Jewish people over Passover. Jesus was literally *on pilgrimage* in his last week of earthly life. The meal that he shared with his disciples, what we call the Last Supper, was made up of the elements of a Seder meal. Not only was Jesus observing the pilgrimage of his people, but was also on his pilgrimage towards the cross, culminating in his death on Good Friday, in which many congregations observe the fourteen stations of the cross. After a period of deep reflection on Holy Saturday, which culminates in the Easter vigil, there is the joyous resurrection. Easter is also a season for pilgrimage, as is Pentecost (fifty days).

In this short chapter, I will merely cover the basic elements of the two seasons around Jesus's birth, death, and resurrection. Unbeknownst to some in a congregation or parish, they have been honoring and celebrating two long and important seasons of the church year that are oriented around the theme of pilgrimage. In highlighting what are probably common practices in many congregations and parishes, my hope is simply to illumine how these activities are part and parcel of the pilgrimage of life.

Activities for Advent, Christmas, and Epiphany: Light

On an actual pilgrimage, light is very important, especially when leaving early in the morning and arriving late at night. Many pilgrims either hold and use small flashlights, or have flashlights that are strapped around their heads, used to illuminate the material in a backpack when it is dark in a dorm or outside, as well as to help illumine a path before us. I remember many mornings leaving an Albergue on the Camino, with a path in front of me lit up by individual lights strapped upon people's heads as we made our way to the Albergue in the next town.

With a church on pilgrimage, light plays an important role during both Advent and Lent. In the seasons of Advent and Christmas, light plays a special role as Jesus is considered the light of the world (John 1:4–5), who tells his followers not to hide their light under a bushel (Matt 5:15). This is why light plays an incredible role on pilgrimage. Light summons or announces the presence of the Holy in small-group devotions or congregational worship, which is the aim or end of our Christian pilgrimage. I've been on pilgrimages in which churches welcomed pilgrims (church members) using paper-bag luminarias. Having the trail lit through the darkness gives a certain warmth to the life of the church.

During Advent there is also the lighting of the candles around the Advent wreath each Sunday, where an individual or a family unit proceeds to the front of a sanctuary and lights the candles for each Sunday of Advent. For many congregations and parishes, there is also a Christmas tree that may be lit.

Finally, during the pilgrimage of the church toward Christmas through Advent, there is Christmas Eve worship, traditionally a candlelight service. Individual candles are handed out to members of a congregation that evening during worship, and during the singing of the hymn "Silent Night," candles are all lit.

The Four Sundays of Advent: A Pilgrimage

In trying to bring the theme of pilgrimage to Advent, a church may choose the four Sundays as stepping stones, a pathway towards Christmas. The circle of the wreath symbolizes the eternal love of God, much like a wedding ring does, for there is neither a beginning nor an end in a ring, and through the center of the ring is the portal through which the Holy enters our lives, and the unknown is then free to roam. The first Sunday is the theme of "Hope," followed by "Peace," "Joy," and "Love." The lighting of the candles for each successive Sunday (four, with the Christ candle making it five candles), around an Advent wreath shows this progression or movement towards Christmas. Some churches focus on the individuals who will make up the Nativity story, including the Angel Gabriel one Sunday, John the Baptist the next Sunday, Joseph and Mary another Sunday. For each Sunday, invite members of a church to portray these characters, discussing their pilgrimage towards Bethlehem, building up to Christmas.

Processional

To enable a congregation to have the feel of being on an actual pilgrimage, invite the members not to go into the sanctuary but to gather in the Narthex or some outside meeting space like a church's plaza or porch. With perhaps a large banner for the season, and acolytes with candles, maybe with instrumentalists like guitarists and other musical instruments, enter the sanctuary singing a hymn of Advent. This can also be done throughout the rest of the year, including Lent.

On Christmas Eve, some churches also include a procession of the members of the Holy Family during the opening hymn, along with shepherds and perhaps some of the animals nestling around a Christmas tree, which may be placed in the front of a sanctuary. They each take their place in a tableau in the front of a sanctuary. Likewise, on Epiphany, some churches have the Three Wise Men or Magi, along with someone bearing the Christ candle, to come marching forward in a sanctuary during the singing of the opening hymn, "We Three Kings of Orient Are."

Activities for Lent, Palm Sunday, Maundy Thursday, Good Friday, and Easter Vigil

Jesus spent forty days in the wilderness fasting, reflecting, being tempted by the evil one. During Lent, we reflect upon this passage of time; we not only remember what Jesus has done and is doing in our lives but also reconsider in what ways our lives reflect—or don't reflect—a Christ-centered life. Lent leads us through Holy Week to Easter morning when we hear "He is risen! Alleluia!"

Practicing Pilgrimage—Part II

Ash Wednesday

The imposition of ashes starts with a pilgrimage as people line up to have ashes placed upon their foreheads, hearing the reminder that we are made up of ashes and dust, and to dust we shall return. We begin this season from our ground zero, in which we realize that who we are is dependent upon whose we are, and we are God's creation, created in the image of God. Throughout the day, we continue the pilgrimage of life with the mark of the cross clearly seen on our foreheads for the public at large to see who we are.

Forty Days of Lenten Prayer Beads

In the Roman Catholic Church and among many Anglican churches, there is a practice of using prayer beads to focus one's prayers. Go to a local craft store and get some beads and string, dental floss, or light wire that is easily tied. In some traditions, people use a medallion in the middle of the strings. There are six Wednesdays in Lent. Be sure each person has six large beads. In between may be ten smaller beads, separating the larger beads. Place these prayer beads in your pocket, using them as a way of focusing on the six things we are grateful for, or six things we are asking forgiveness for. Keep these prayer beads in your pocket for the season of Lent, on your pilgrimage of life, walking around with them and remembering that we are loved each step of the way.

Palm Sunday

Palms are an appropriate symbol for this day. I tend to be a gatherer of palm fronds, and hold on to palm fronds throughout the year. When I am a pastor in a church, I use those almost-one-year-old palm fronds for ashes for Ash Wednesday the following year. Palms remind us that Jesus entered Jerusalem willingly, knowing full well what was ahead of him that week.

Maundy Thursday

Foot washing! John 13:1–17 is all about foot washing. This is the penultimate symbol of pilgrimage with Jesus and of following the Pilgrim God. I realize that Holy Communion was first celebrated during this time, and this is the meal giving spiritual as well as physical sustenance to our lives, becoming the very paradigm of how and why we extend hospitality to strangers. But here it is the foot washing that is central for the church and that helps us focus on our pilgrimage today. With the washing of the feet as an example of what Jesus did with his disciples, engaging in the practice today as he did, we take care of the lowly foot. After all, wearing sandals was a luxury during the days of Jesus, and he commanded his disciples to walk barefoot. The touch of the hands of someone else on our feet, washing our feet, and vice versa, reminds us of the pilgrim life we lead today.

Among Roman Catholics, Maundy Thursday is also the beginning of the Triduum, the three days in which the church observes the concluding hours of Jesus's earthly ministry. Many believers simply put all work aside in order to focus upon the hours and minutes that are ticking by that signal the ending of the Pilgrim God's last moments on earth. In terms of the language and practice of pilgrimage, this is a rich opportunity to turn people's attention to the realization that we are participating in a real, live, intentional, pilgrimage as a body of believers, remembering the sacrifice that God withstood and made, witnessing his only begotten Son's death.

Good Friday and Tenebrae

With some churches, there is a "stripping of the altar" at the conclusion of worship, in which the stoles, altar cloths, and other elements of worship located in the sanctuary are removed. Others choose to do this on Good Friday, or over Tenebrae worship. The most moving part of Tenebrae is the extinguishing of the candles, one by one, as the hours of Jesus's life on earth are remembered before he breathed his last breath. In this powerful moment, in which the Tenebrae worship is in the evening, the pilgrims move into darkness, in which, stripped of everything, we who are believers are given an opportunity to cling to the One remaining hope: God.

Holy Saturday

Among Roman Catholics, this is where the line from the Apostles' Creed comes into play: "He descended into hell." It is a time of quiet reflection after Maundy Thursday, Good Friday, and Tenebrae. Usually, Holy Saturday is a day of prayer and supplication, in preparation or in contrast with the exultation of Easter Vigil.

Practicing Pilgrimage—Part II

Easter Vigil

I was first introduced to the pilgrimage aspect of the Easter Vigil at Princeton Theological Seminary, under the artful direction of Dr. Arlo Duba. The Vigil of Easter is usually held as a build up to Easter sunrise service at the crack of 12:01 a.m., in which Easter begins. At Princeton, a person carries a singular candle, a.k.a., the Christ candle, leading pilgrims to different stations of the stories that led to the crucifixion of Jesus, but also to the after effects of the death and resurrection of Jesus. This would all lead to people coming into Miller Chapel, lights blazing, with a seminarian reading the Easter sermon of St. John Chrysostom.

Likewise, I have been to Chapel of the Cross, an Episcopal church in Chapel Hill, North Carolina, in which Easter Vigil is around worship, in which people wait outside the sanctuary around a small Hibachi-like grill, warming us up until someone lights the Christ candle. The person with the Christ candle leads the congregants on a pilgrimage into the sanctuary for the beginning of worship, with lights low, the brightest light in the entire room being the Christ candle, as it should be. The Scriptures read that evening—beginning with the creation of the world in Genesis—lead us to the reading of the Easter story, around midnight, at which time the lights then break forth, and the "Alleluias!" are shared.

I want to take this Vigil one step further: at St. Benedict's Monastery in St. Joseph, Minnesota, the women also share a devotion in the practice of waiting through the night until Easter sunrise comes and wakes us all up. The sisters and other guests sign up for a vigil at the large baptismal font, where there is a singular light—the Christ candle again. I signed up for the 2:00 a.m. shift, and stayed an hour. These women play out this practice of waiting while on pilgrimage, powerfully.

Easter Sunrise

Pilgrims gather for an early morning Easter sunrise service, usually beginning at 5:00 or 5:30 a.m. at the latest. The idea is that we pilgrims are gathered together as God's people as the rooster crows in the morning, observing and honoring the pilgrimage of the Pilgrim God from life, to death, to life anew. Breakfast casseroles, coffee, tea, and orange juice await those who gather early. At two congregations where I was pastor—Ernest Myatt Presbyterian Church and First Presbyterian Church, Henderson—we celebrated Easter sunrise with Holy Communion in the cemetery (Ernest Myatt) or columbarium (First), witnessing among the deceased about the good news of the resurrection of all believers, for "death has lost its sting." It is an incredibly rich, thick experience to be on pilgrimage through the heralding of Jesus on Palm Sunday, moving to the somberness of Maundy Thursday, the tragedy of Good Friday, concluding with the celebration of Easter Sunday.

Conclusion

While many Protestant and Roman Catholic Christians see pilgrimage as a new experience in today's plethora of activities for churches and parishes, it is an ancient practice that resonates with so many of us because every year we practice aspects of it in the seasons of Advent and Lent. Hopefully, given the ancillary activities I have provided above, more congregational and parish leaders will intensify the "pilgrimage" and "pilgrim" aspects of these seasons, enabling others to see that *all* of Christian life is a journey, following the thick yet long arc of the Christian narrative.

15

A Daily Pilgrimage

> In the tender compassion of our God
> the dawn from on high shall break upon us,
> to shine on those who dwell in darkness
> and the shadow of death,
> and to guide our feet into the way of peace.
> —Canticle of Zechariah[1]

> To be pilgrims walking on a path, we need
> to participate in the dance between silence and image,
> ear and eye, inner and outer. We need to change our seeking
> into discovery, our drifting into pilgrimage.
> —Lauren Artress[2]

> The path around our home is also the ground of awakening.
> —Thich Nhat Hanh[3]

A Morning Walk

Here's the challenge of an actual pilgrimage, and one that I hope to answer with both the School of the Pilgrim workshops and experiences in general and this book in particular: How do you stay open and alive to all that you have experienced? It can be like watching a powerful play, hearing an

---

1. Luke 1:68–79.
2. Artress, *Walking a Sacred Path*, 24.
3. Quoted in Cousineau, *Art of Pilgrimage*, 225.

A Daily Pilgrimage

amazing work of music, or reading a fantastic book—one's life is changed for a while, until the ordinariness or normality of existence returns and closes the chapter of our life-changing, earth-shattering experience.

One of the ways that I keep the memories of my most recent pilgrimage alive and remember that life *is* a pilgrimage is to take a daily walk right where I live. Though at first much of the terrain around my home changes after going on a pilgrimage, because I see it with "pilgrim eyes," after a while the local walk may become rather "ordinary" and taken for granted. So I take a different path around a neighborhood. This idea came about during the earliest days when I was trying to wrap my mind around the idea of the School of the Pilgrim as a school without walls, and more an approach to life generally than a specific curriculum, and my friend and master potter Richard Bresnahan helped me host a meeting of like-minded folks who were interested in pilgrimage at St. John's University and Abbey in Collegeville, Minnesota. There was another writer, Sr. Stefanie Weisgram, OSB (a Benedictine monk), Patrick Henry, formerly of the Ecumenical Institute at St. John's Abbey and University, who had great skill in development work, and Richard. We met around a perfectly square table in his pottery studio that had four benches around it. In the middle of the table was a hot steaming pot of green tea, along with a fruit pie, with other fruits on the table. The question that we raised was not only about the structure of the School of the Pilgrim, but about how we help people understand that their daily life, their walk with Jesus, is a pilgrimage.

The ideas started flooding in, many of which have found their way into this chapter. For example, one idea was taking a short walk in the morning, listing and praying things I was thankful for in terms of both small and large blessings in life. Even looking up into the blue yonder or saying aloud to the higher power, "Thank you for a good night's sleep." This was made easier when our two dogs were alive, and we would all three go down the long driveway to pick up the newspapers in all kinds of weather, with me muttering prayers down the path.

Over the morning cup of coffee and bowl of oatmeal, I mutter a three-part prayer that I learned on the way to Chimayo, included in this book. The first part of the prayer is said in the preparation of the meal; the second part right before consuming it; and the third part is uttered at the end of the meal.

As I get into my car on my way to work I find a scallop shell in my glovebox. As I have written earlier, the scallop shell is a symbol of the pilgrimage to Santiago de Compostela. Scallop shells are also in my backpack and are part of a insignia for the School of the Pilgrim, which is also tattooed on my upper left shoulder muscle. Now and then I will put a small seashell in my pant's pocket.

For a daily pilgrimage that I may take without a group of people I know, like when I began the Camino de Santiago de Compostela, where there are no prayers listed along the way, no app (yet) that can be downloaded along a pilgrimage route, I have collected some written prayers from various liturgical texts I have used and modified them with the language of pilgrimage. Many of these prayers, rituals, and suggested songs come from the Roman Catholic Archdiocese of Santa Fe, New Mexico, in a little handbook they publish every year for the Archdiocesan Pilgrimages for Vocations. I have used this book on many of the solo pilgrimages I have taken, and have used many of the rituals, prayers, and songs with groups.

Blessing of Pilgrims upon Departure

This prayer is from the Roman Catholic Archdiocese of Santa Fe, New Mexico, Pilgrimage for Vocations booklet, as are many of the other prayers in this section. One speaks this blessing when the pilgrims depart for the 120-mile sojourn before them:

> ALL: In the name of the Father, Son, and Holy Spirit. May God, our strength and salvation, be with you all.
>
> Leader: Sisters and brothers, as we set out, we should remind ourselves of the reasons for our resolve to go on this holy pilgrimage. The place we intend to visit is a monument to the devotion of the people of God. They have gone there in great numbers to be strengthened in the Christian way of life and to become more determined to devote themselves to the works of charity. We must also try to bring something to the faithful who live there: our example of faith, hope, and love. In this way both they and we will be enriched by the help we give each other.
>
> Reader: A reading from Luke 24:13–35
>
> L: God is the beginning and the end of life's pilgrimage. Let us call on him with confidence, saying: Lord, be the companion of our journey.
>
> L: God, all holy, of old you made yourself the guide and the way for your people as they wandered in the desert. Be our protection as we

A Daily Pilgrimage

begin this journey, so that we may return home again in safety. For this we pray:

People: Lord, be the companion of our journey.

L: You have given us your only Son to be our way to you; make us follow him faithfully and unswervingly. For this we pray:

P: Lord, be the companion of our journey.

L: You gave us Mary and Paul to be models for following Christ; grant that through their examples we may live a new life. For this we pray:

P: Lord, be the companion of our journey.

L: You guide your pilgrim Church on earth through the Holy Spirit; may we seek you in all things and walk always in the way of your commandments. For this we pray:

P: Lord, be the companion of our journey.

L: You lead us along right and peaceful paths; grant that we may one day see you face to face in heaven. For this we pray:

P: Lord, be the companion of our journey.

L: All-powerful God, you always show mercy toward those who love you and you are never far away for those who seek you. Remain with your servants on this holy pilgrimage and guide their way in accord with your will. Shelter them with your protection by day, give them the light of your grace by night, and, as their companion on the journey, bring them to their destination in safety. We ask this through Christ our Lord. Amen.

ALL: May the Lord guide us and direct our journey in safety: Amen.

ALL: May the Lord be our companion along this way: Amen.

ALL: May the Lord grant that the journey we begin, relying on him, will end happily through his protection. Amen.[4]

Morning Prayer

I use *A Shorter Morning and Evening Prayer*, published by Liturgical Press in Collegeville, Minnesota, which provides a daily list of psalms and other readings for a month-long period:

O Lord open my lips and my mouth will proclaim your praise.

O God, come to my assistance.

O Lord, make haste to help me.

---

4. *Archdiocesan Prayers for Vocation*, 3–6.

Practicing Pilgrimage—Part II

In the name of the Father, Son, and Holy Spirit. As it was in the beginning, is now, and ever shall be, world without end. Amen.

Two or three readings from the Old Testament (below):

Psalm 119:145–52 (Pray and reflect)
Exodus 15:1–4a, 8–13, 17–18 (Pray and reflect)
Psalm 117 (Pray and reflect)

Gospel Reading or Epistle Reading (New Testament): 2 Peter 1:10–11 (Pray and reflect)

Canticle of Zechariah:

> Blessed be the Lord, the God of Israel;
> he has come to his people and set them free.
> He has raised up for us a mighty Savior,
> born of the house of his servant David.
> Through his holy prophets he promised of old
> > that he would save us from our enemies,
> > from the hands of all who hate us.
> He promised to show mercy to our forbears
> and to remember his holy covenant.
> This was the oath he swore to Abraham and Sarah:
> to set us free from the hands of our enemies,
> free to worship him without fear,
> holy and righteous in his sight
> > and all the days of our life.
> You, my child, shall be called the prophet of the Most High;
> for you will go before the Lord to prepare his way,
> to give his people knowledge of salvation
> by the forgiveness of their sins.
> In the tender compassion of our God
> the dawn from on high shall break upon us,
> to shine on those who dwell in darkness and the shadow of death,
> and to guide our feet into the way of peace.
> Glory . . .

Intercessions:

> Let us all praise Christ. In order to become our faithful and merciful high priest before God's throne, he chose to become one of us, a brother in all things. In prayer we ask of him:
>
> Sun of Justice, you filled us with light at our baptism, we dedicate this day to you.
>
> Lord, share the treasure of your love.
>
> At every hour of the day we give you glory in all our deeds, we offer you praise.
>
> Lord, share the treasure of your love.
>
> Mary, your mother, was obedient to your word, direct our lives in accordance with that word.
>
> Lord, share the treasure of your love.
>
> Our lives are surrounded with passing things; set our hearts on things of heaven, so that through faith, hope, and love we may come to enjoy the vision of your glory.
>
> Lord, share the treasure of your love.

Lord's Prayer (pray the Lord's Prayer communally, then follow it with this prayer):

> God, free us from the dark night of death. Let the light of resurrection dawn within our hearts to bring us to the radiance of eternal life.
>
> We ask this through our Lord Jesus Christ, your Son, who lives and reigns with you and the Holy Spirit, one God, forever and ever.

Mealtime Prayer

This powerful prayer, set in three parts, has a way of slowing everyone on a pilgrimage from rushing into and out of mealtime:

> May our eyes be opened, and, in this act of common sharing, may we see the risen Lord of life in our food, our conversation, and lives shared in common. May the blessing of God, Christ's peace, and the Spirit's love rest upon this table. Alleluia! Amen.

Practicing Pilgrimage—Part II

> With the first taste, I promise to practice loving kindness. With the second, I promise to relieve the suffering of others. With the third, I promise to learn the way of simplicity and calmness.

(At the conclusion of the meal):

> The plate is empty. My hunger is satisfied. I vow to live for the benefit of all creation. Amen.[5]

Psalmody

During the day, pilgrims may want to pray the following Scriptures or prayers of saints and followers of Christ.

- Awake, O Sleeper, and arise from the dead and Christ will give you light. (Eph 5:14)

- Put to death, then, the parts of you that are earthly: immorality, impurity, passion, evil desire, and the greed that is idolatry. By these you too once conducted yourself, when you lived in that way. But now you must put them all away: anger, fury, malice, slander, and obscene language out of your mouths.

  Stop lying to one another, since you have taken off the old self with its practices and have put on the new self, which is being renewed, for knowledge, in the image of its creator.

  Put on then, as God's chosen ones, holy and beloved, heartfelt compassion, kindness, humility, gentleness, and patience, bearing with one another and forgiving one another, if one has a grievance against another; as the Lord has forgiven you, so must you also do.

  And over all these put on love, that is, the bond of perfection. And let the peace of Christ control your hearts, the peace into which you were also called in one body.

  And be thankful. Let the word of Christ dwell in you richly, as in all wisdom you teach and admonish one another, singing psalms, hymns, and spiritual songs with gratitude in your hearts to God.

  And whatever you do, in word or in deed, do everything in the name of the Lord Jesus, giving thanks to God through him. (Col 3:5–17)

---

5. Archdiocesan Prayers for Vocation, 30.

- "Lord, I thank you for the gift of my life and for accepting me as I am in my journey toward you. Be my companion whatever the journey, and draw me always nearer to your love" (Meister Eckhart).
- "We put our hands, our eyes, and our hearts at Christ's disposal, so that he will act through us" (Mother Teresa).[6]

The Canticle of the Creatures

Along with the song of peace, this treasured canticle is by St. Francis of Assisi:

> Most High, all-powerful, good Lord, all praise be yours, all glory, all honor, and all blessing. To you alone, Most High, do they belong. No mortal lips are worthy to pronounce your name.
>
> All praise be yours, my Lord, in all your creatures, especially Sir Brother Sun, who brings the day and light you give us through him. How beautiful he is, how radiant in his splendor! Of you, Most High, he is the token.
>
> All praise be yours, my Lord, for Sister Moon and the Stars; in the heavens you have made them, bright and precious and fair.
>
> All praise be yours, my Lord, for Brother Wind and the Air, and fair and stormy, all the weather's moods, by which you nourish everything you have made.
>
> All praise be yours, my Lord, for Sister Water. She is so useful and lowly, so precious and pure.
>
> All praise be yours, my Lord, for Brother Fire, by whom you brighten the night. How beautiful he is, how joyful, robust, and strong!
>
> All praise be yours, my Lord, for Sister Earth, our mother, who feeds us, rules us, and produces all sorts of fruit and colored flowers and herbs.
>
> All praise be yours, my Lord, for those who forgive one another for love of you and endure infirmity and tribulation. Happy are they who endure these in peace, for by you, Most High, they will be crowned.
>
> All praise to you, my Lord, for our Sister Physical Death, from whose embrace no mortal can escape. Woe to those who die in mortal sin! Happy are those she finds doing your most holy will! The second death can do no harm to them.

---

6. Ibid., 7–9.

Practicing Pilgrimage—Part II

> Praise and bless my Lord, and give him thanks and serve him with great humility.[7]

The Angelus

Among Roman Catholics, this prayer is prayed at 6:00 a.m., noon, and 6:00 p.m.:

> The angel spoke God's message to Mary and she conceived of the Holy Spirit.
>
> Hail Mary, full of grace, the Lord be with you. Blessed are you among women, and blessed is the fruit of your womb, Jesus. Holy Mary, Mother of God, pray for us sinners, now and in our death. Amen.
>
> "I am the lowly servant of the Lord. Let it be done to me according to your Word."
>
> Hail Mary . . .
>
> And the Word became flesh and lived among us.
>
> Hail Mary . . .
>
> Pray for us, holy Mother of God, that we may become worthy of the promises of Christ.
>
> Fill our hearts, God, with your grace: once, through the message of an angel you revealed to us the incarnation of your Son. Now, through his suffering and death lead us to the glory of his resurrection. We ask this through Christ our Lord. Amen.[8]

A Pilgrim's Companion Psalm

> The road home, O God, seems long
> and at times is difficult and painful.
> Grant me a holy communion, a companionship with others,
> as I journey homeward to you.
> I live in times of great trial:
> an age of change sits at my door.
> Without a community with others,

---

7. Ibid., 11.
8. Ibid., 29.

A Daily Pilgrimage

I can so easily lose the way,
can be led astray by illusions of holiness,
misguided by my ego's desires.
Open my eyes to your precious gift
of the Church's Communion of Saints.
"Saint" is a name I would never call myself,
but the treasury of my faith
teaches me about my holy birthright,
that I am part of the web of sacred communion,
uniting me with all other home-bound pilgrims
and with all who now rejoice
at their homecoming in you.
May I feed this day upon the food
of this mystic, holy communion
with those friends and fellow pilgrims
with whom I share this planet Earth,
as well as those saints now fully one with you.
May this awareness of my companion journey
with all the saints
deepen my life of prayer
and fertilize my faith in you, my Beloved.
By this communion of holy ones
may I be daily challenged
to greater compassion and charity
as I walk the way of the pilgrim.[9]
Amen

Stations of the Cross

Typically on Good Friday there is a vigil held that involves visiting the stations of the cross, typically a plaque commemorating the various places where Jesus stopped on his way to Golgotha. Here is a possible devotion for such a pilgrimage:

---

9. Ibid., 37.

Practicing Pilgrimage—Part II

Prayer: Almighty God, you have given the human race Jesus Christ our Savior as a model of humility. He fulfilled your will by becoming man and giving his life on the cross. Help us to bear witness to you by following his example of suffering and make us worthy to share in his resurrection. We ask this through our Lord Jesus Christ.

First Station: Jesus is condemned to death by Pilate.
Meditation: Jesus has been scourged and crowned with thorns. Now, Pilate unjustly condemns him to die on a cross.

Second Station: Jesus accepts his cross.
Meditation: Jesus is given a cross to carry on his bleeding and bruised shoulders. He takes this cross upon himself as he takes upon himself all of our sins.

Third Station: Jesus falls the first time.
Meditation: Jesus, weakened by all his suffering, stumbles and falls on the way to Calvary. He struggles and rises, despite his pain, to go onward toward his death.

Fourth Station: Jesus meets his mother, Mary.
Meditation: Jesus sees his mother. Both are stricken with grief. Her love for him is surpassed only by his love and concern for her.

Fifth Station: Simon helps carry the cross.
Meditation: Jesus is growing weaker. Fearing that he may not be able to go on, his executioners force Simon of Cyrene to help him carry his cross.

Sixth Station: Veronica wipes the face of Jesus.
Meditation: Jesus's face is bathed in sweat and blood. Veronica, moved by pity, wipes his face with her veil, and the image of his holy face is imprinted on the cloth.

Seventh Station: Jesus falls the second time.
Meditation: Jesus falls again under the weight of the cross. His executioners drag him to his feet and force him to go onward to Calvary.

Eighth Station: Jesus meets the women of Jerusalem.
Meditation: Jesus is so bruised and bleeding that the women of Jerusalem weep when they see him. He tells them, "Weep not for me, but rather for your children."

Ninth Station: Jesus falls the third time.

Meditation: Jesus, weak and exhausted, falls for the third time. Though he hardly has strength to move, his executioners try to make him walk faster.

Tenth Station: Jesus is stripped of his garments.
Meditation: Jesus has reached the summit of Calvary, the place of his execution. As they strip him of his garments, they reopen his bleeding wounds.

Eleventh Station: Jesus is nailed to the cross.
Meditation: Jesus is now thrown down upon the cross. His executioners violently stretch his limbs and fasten them with crude nails to the wood.

Twelfth Station: Jesus dies upon the cross.
Meditation: Jesus is crucified. After three hours of agony and pain, he commends his spirit to his Father, bows his head and dies.

Thirteenth Station: Jesus is taken from the cross.
Meditation: Jesus's lifeless body is taken from the cross by his disciples Joseph and Nicodemus. Tenderly, they place him in the arms of his sorrowing mother.

Fourteenth Station: Jesus is laid in the tomb.
Meditation: Jesus's body is wrapped in a shroud and placed in the nearby sepulcher of a friend. Then a large stone is rolled against the entrance and they depart.[10]

God, grant grace to those who follow the way of Jesus, through life, death, and life eternal. We pray these things in your beloved Son's name. Amen.

Evening Prayer

This is from the Benedictine *A Shorter Morning and Evening Prayer* as well. One may choose to read these psalms from the New Revised Standard Version of the Bible.

Psalm 11

> In the Lord I have taken my refuge.
> How can you say to my soul:
> "Fly like a bird to its mountain.
>
> See the wicked bracing their bow;

10. Archdiocesan Prayers, 69–77.

Practicing Pilgrimage—Part II

> they are fixing their arrows on the string
> to shoot upright people in the dark.
> Foundations once destroyed, what can the just do?"

> The Lord is in his holy temple,
> the Lord, whose throne is in heaven.
> His eyes look down on the world;
> his gaze tests mortal men.

> The Lord tests the just and the wicked:
> the lover of violence he hates.
> He sends fire and brimstone on the wicked;
> he sends a scorching wind as their lot.

> The Lord is just and loves justice:
> the upright shall see his face.

(Silent Prayer)

Psalm 15

> Lord, who shall be admitted to your tent
> and dwell on your holy mountain?

> He who walks without fault;
> he who acts with justice
> and speaks the truth from his heart;
> he who does not slander with his tongue;

> he who does no wrong to his brother,
> who casts no slur on his neighbor,
> who holds the godless in disdain,
> but honors those who fear the Lord;

> he who keeps his pledge, come what may;
> who takes no interest on a loan
> and accepts no bribes against the innocent.
> Such a man will stand firm forever.

Canticle: Ephesians 1:3–10

A Daily Pilgrimage

Reading: Choose a Gospel reading, or something from Paul's Epistles.

Canticle of Mary:

> My soul proclaims the greatness of the Lord,
> my spirit rejoices in God my Savior,
> for he has looked with favor on his lowly servant.
> From this day all generations will call me blessed;
> the Almighty has done great things for me,
> and holy is His Name.
> He has mercy on those who fear him
> in every generation.
> He has shown the strength of his arm,
> he has scattered the proud in their conceit.
> He has cast down the mighty from their thrones,
> and has lifted up the lowly.
> He has filled the hungry with good things,
> and the rich he has sent away empty.
> He has come to the help of his servant Israel,
> for he has remembered his promise of mercy,
> the promise he made to our forbears,
> to Abraham and Sarah and their children forever.

Intercessions:

> God has made an everlasting covenant with the people, and God never ceases to bless them. Grateful for these gifts, we confidently direct our prayers to him: Lord, bless your people.
>
> Save your people, Lord, and bless your inheritance.
>
> Lord, bless your people.
>
> Gather into one body all who bear the name of Christian, that the world may believe in Christ whom you have sent.
>
> Lord, bless your people.
>
> Give our friends and our loved ones a share in divine life, let them be symbols of Christ before people.
>
> Lord, bless your people.

Practicing Pilgrimage—Part II

Show your love to those who are suffering, open their eyes to the vision of your revelation.

Lord, bless your people.

Be compassionate to those who have died, welcome them into the company of the faithful departed.

Our Father . . .

Closing Prayer:

God, may this evening pledge of our service to you bring you glory and praise. For our salvation you looked with favor on the lowliness of the Virgin Mary; lead us to the fullness of the salvation you have prepared for us. We ask this through our Lord Jesus Christ, your Son, who lives and reigns with you and the Holy Spirit, one God, forever and ever. Amen.[11]

Night Prayer

Before turning in at night, light a candle and recite this prayer:

Jesus said, "I am the light of the world . . . whoever follows me will have the light of life and will never walk in darkness" (John 8:12).

(Pause)

A peaceful night and a perfect end grant us.

(Pause)

Let us reimagine our day now, and see everyone who was with us in this day, caught up in the same love as Christ. Let us especially focus upon people whom I might be tempted to call "least," and those who do not have an easy entry to my heart of love and compassion.

(Pause)

When today did I feel God's love?

(Pause)

How did I find God in touch? Smell? Taste? Sight? Sound?

(Pause)

How did I love God today?

(Pause)

How might God have suffered so that I might be born this day?

11. *A Shorter Morning and Evening Prayer*, 51–54.

A Daily Pilgrimage

(Pause)

How have I shown God's love to others?

(Blow out the candle)

The light of this candle is now out. But the light of Christ in each of us must continue to shine in our lives. Toward this end I pray, "Our Father, who art in heaven . . ."[12]

Blessing of Pilgrims upon Return

L: In the name of the Father, Son, and Holy Spirit. May God, our strength and salvation, be with you all.

May God, our hope and our strength, fill you with peace and with joy in the Holy Spirit. Glory to God, now and forever. Amen.

People, our pilgrimage has been a privileged period of grace given us by God. We who have come in trust to this holy place are moved with a new resolve to be renewed in heart. The sanctuaries that we have visited are a sign of the house not built with hands, namely, the Body of Christ, in which we are the living stones built upon Christ, the cornerstone. As we return home, let us live up to the vocation God has given us: to be a chosen race, a royal priesthood, a holy nation, a people God claims for God's own, so that we may everywhere proclaim the goodness of him who called us from darkness into his marvelous light.

A reading: Luke 24:28–35

L: The Lord of heaven willed that in Christ's humanity the fullness of divinity should dwell as in its temple. Let us pray to him, saying:

P: Look down from heaven, O Lord, and bless your people.

L: God all-holy, in the Passover exodus you prefigured the blessed road of your people toward salvation; grant that in all the paths we follow we may remain wholeheartedly faithful to you. For this we pray:

P: Look down from heaven, O Lord, and bless your people.

L: You set your Church in this world as a sanctuary from which the true light would shine for all to see; grant that many people will enter this sanctuary and walk in your ways. For this we pray:

P: Look down from heaven, O Lord, and bless your people.

12. Archdiocesan Prayers for Vocation, 32–33.

Practicing Pilgrimage—Part II

L: You have told us that here we have no lasting city; grant that we may always seek the city that is to come. For this we pray:

P: Look down from heaven, O Lord, and bless your people.

L: You teach all the faithful to perceive the signs of your presence along all the pathways of life. Grant that like the disciples of Emmaus we may come to recognize Christ as the companion of our journey and know him in the breaking of the bread. For this we pray:

P: Look down from heaven, O Lord, and bless your people.

L: Blessed are you, O God: from all races of the earth you have chosen a people dedicated to you, eager to do what is right. Your grace has moved the hearts of these, your friends, to love you more deeply and to serve you more generously. We ask you to bless them, so that they may tell of your wonderful deeds and give proof of them in their lives. We ask this through Christ our Lord.

P: Amen.

L: May God, the Lord of heaven and earth, who so graciously has accompanied you on this pilgrimage, continue to keep you under his protection.

P: Amen.

L: May God, who gathered all his scattered children in Christ Jesus, grant that you will be of one heart and one mind in Christ.

P: Amen.

L: May God, whose goodness inspires in you all that you desire and achieve, strengthen your devotion by this blessing.

P: Amen.

A Charge and Benediction

The resources shared in this chapter are ones I use throughout a pilgrimage, and usually use them more than once a day. I am also known for singing during a pilgrimage, with a rich variety of songs in my head and heart. The benefit of using these prayers, especially the "Prayer upon Departure" and "Prayer upon Return," is that it provides a "bookend," of sorts, a sense of "beginning and end" of the pilgrimage. Likewise, the Morning and Evening Prayers provide a "bookend" for the day, beginning and ending. The prayers in between help direct mind and heart to stay focused on the place where we are and are going to, and may perhaps enable us to reflect upon all the ways that God was with us on the pilgrimage that day. Likewise, the

A Daily Pilgrimage

other prayers and rituals throughout this book are meant to help us focus upon the incredible opportunity we have to be pilgrims of God. In the end, being a pilgrim of God is a special calling, and it is, in the words of many Benedictions, the grace of our Lord Jesus Christ, the love of God, and the sweet communion of the Holy Spirit that surrounds us each and every day of our journey.

EPILOGUE

The Church as Resident Pilgrims

> Hear my prayer, O Lord,
> and give ear to my cry;
> do not hold your peace at my tears.
> For I am your passing guest,
> a pilgrim, like all my forebears. (Ps 39:12 NRSV)[1]

> Not everyone will understand your journey. That's okay. You're
> Here to live your life, not to make everyone understand (Banksy)

The Church as Resident Pilgrims

In the introduction of this book, "Practicing Pilgrimage," I began with a story of an actual pilgrimage. I discussed throughout this book how an actual pilgrimage provides a portal or way of understanding better the pilgrimage of everyday life as a Christian. Throughout this book, I hope that I captured well a dialogue between actual pilgrimage stories and the pilgrimage of everyday life, and how both work well together, wherever we are in the pathway of life. An actual pilgrimage reminds me of the key components that are necessary to meet each day of my life as a pilgrimage in the quotidian or ordinary moments of everyday life as a follower of Jesus.

It seems fitting, then, to end this book with an Epilogue that discusses the pilgrimage of everyday life. After all, as the Psalmist reminds us, we people of faith in the Christian and Jewish traditions are all resident pilgrims, each one of us passing through the house of God. That's why the

---

1. The word for "pilgrim" in ancient Hebrew, *ger* or *gar*, can also be translated as "alien" or "stranger." I choose to use the word *pilgrim*, and that has made all the difference.

subtitle in this book is "Being and Becoming God's Pilgrim People." As God's people, we are already pilgrims. The thing is this: we are either not aware, or are rarely aware, of this reality. That's the reason for writing this book: to provide a way of educating people in the ways of becoming or living into the reality of being God's pilgrim people.

The concluding illustration for this book is based upon my work as a pastor—or pilgrim guide—with many middle-class and upper-middle-class, medium-size Presbyterian churches that I've worked with over the years. In these churches I emphasize that I am a pilgrim among the pilgrims of God. Every day I walk with the people in our sometimes ordinary and oftentimes extraordinary lives. Taking the various parts of pilgrimage characteristics found earlier in this book as a guide, I will describe how I understand the pilgrimage of everyday life with and as part of the body of Christ in general, a congregation in particular, and as a Christian personally.

We, Who Are Many, Are One Body in Christ

The Apostle Paul's description of the church universal as the one body of Christ lends itself beautifully to the concept that we who are members of this body are part of a larger body of people on pilgrimage. This body of Christ is not a stagnant body. There is nothing static about Christ's body. This is the body of the risen Christ, as Karl Barth would be quick to remind us, making it mystical but tangible, otherworldly but immanent. In his letter to Romans, Paul writes that we have many members in this body, who have all different roles and functions, yet are part of the one body of and in Christ. Some have gifts of prophecy, others, ministry, still others teachers, exhorters, givers, leaders, and compassionate ones (Rom 12:5–6). Paul reiterates this very point in 1 Corinthians 12:1–31: "For just as the body is one and has many members, and all the members of the body, though many, are one body, so it is with Christ" (v. 12). The theme? Many in the one, and one with many members. And it is a body with all kinds of movable parts, with working eyes and ears (v. 16), head and feet (v. 21), a nose (v. 17), and surely hands, and the list goes on. So the body of Christ, the church, the community that calls itself Christian, is a moving, dynamic, changing, walking entity in this world, with moving parts, inspired by the mind of Christ no less. And in this body there is to be no dissension, but we are to have the same care for one another: "If one member suffers, all suffer together with it; if one member is honored, all rejoice together with it" (v. 26). This is the

The Church as Resident Pilgrims

greater context in which we live as Christians whose forebears first called themselves people of "the Way" (Acts 9:2). Christians are part of a body that is moving along the pathway of life, stretched out to the four corners of the world, involving an incredibly diverse gathering of people who are called to work together for the greater good of the body.

The Church as a Community of Resident Pilgrims

The immensity and complex nature of this mysterious yet real body is too much for my little mind to wrap itself around. But in an individual congregation or parish I can identify the various macrocosmic parts of the body in the microcosmic reality of church life: leaders, teachers, compassionate ones, givers, healers, and prophets among women and men, young and old, able-bodied and people with certain challenges, LGBTQ and non-LGBTQ, wealthy and struggling families.

The current context that frames parts of the body of Christ on pilgrimage is the congregation of St. Andrew's Presbyterian Church in Portland, Oregon. This is the eighth church where I have been either pastor or interim pastor. It is here, with those who attend this congregation, that I can best practice the pilgrimage of everyday life. It is here, with the people of this congregation, that healing often happens, miracles take place, worship is practiced weekly, book groups meet, service unto others in the community and Cuba happens; Bible studies occur weekly; small and large groups meet; prayers are prayed; church grounds are beautified and fixed, hospitality is lavished upon strangers, those who struggle financially find assistance, and we sinners get a fresh stab at life again and again.

Pastor as Pilgrim Guide

My role as pastor is that of pilgrim guide, as accompanier, who walks alongside this congregation for a span of time and certain miles, before I take off to walk with others. Congregation and pastor alike follow the Pilgrim God, with the pastor more or less in charge of organizing the group of resident pilgrims along the way. I always appreciated Paulo Coelho's "Petrus" understanding of pilgrim guide, in which I am learning more, or a deeper learning is going on for me daily on the pilgrimage as a pilgrim guide. I see, hear, and feel the various levels of learning going on more acutely because I have walked with others along the way. Sometimes I am walking with those pilgrims in front of the line, and sometimes I play the role of "clean up" person. It just matters what day, which issue, and who is involved that dictates what I can do.

The four areas of a church's life that show how the resident pilgrims of a congregation participate in the life of pilgrimage every day include worship, fellowship, education, and service to the greater good of the body of Christ on pilgrimage.

Worship with Pilgrims

Week after week, we worship God, who created this pilgrimage and blesses our lives as resident pilgrims. We currently set 10:00 to 11:15 a.m. every Sunday as our primary time of worship, though we are discerning other days and times for opportunities to worship God. It is here, weekly, that the members of the body gather from around the Portland metro area to seek sustenance for their spiritual, emotional, relational, intellectual, and even sometimes physical, needs, desires, and wants. Our worship follows the pattern of worship established earlier in this book, in which members go through a kind of spiritual pilgrimage set in our very order of worship. People begin worship by coming into a common space and calling each other to worship God during our initial gathering. The Word read in Holy Scriptures, as well as exclaimed and explained in the Sermon comes next. Eucharist is celebrated once a month, in which people are fed spiritually, intellectually and physically. In the sending, the resident pilgrims of this church are sent back into the world with a charge and blessing. And as we leave, a reality sets in: the people who have just gathered together for worship will never all be there in the same place or as the same people again. It was a once-in-a-lifetime, Kodak moment, which has come and gone as people leave to go back on their individual pilgrimages.

Fellowship of Pilgrims

I am increasingly aware of the time of fellowship after worship for people to check in on each other regarding people's individual pilgrimage tales. Over a cup of coffee, tea, or juice, people share quickly about one's life, both its joys and challenges. This fellowship is crucial for the well being of a church as resident pilgrims. While we are a church that is well-structured in terms of social networking, it is still word of mouth that enables us to

The Church as Resident Pilgrims

be on top of the daily changes in people's pilgrim lives. The quote above by the elusive Banksy seemed fitting for this chapter: we are all on a journey, a pilgrimage. It is OK if not everyone understands the nature of my journey or your pilgrimage. Each one of us in the large band of resident pilgrims are given not only unique gifts and talents, but extraordinary and unexpected ways of practicing these gifts and talents, in which not everyone is going to understand, except for God who created us and calls us out of our surrounding culture to this unique gathering of resident pilgrims.

Pilgrimage Education as Discipleship

The word *education* comes from the Latin word *educare*, to draw out or unfold the powers of the mind. I want to broaden it here to call out, shape, form, and nurture the mind, body, and spirit of the one who is called out. Just now on my Facebook page, someone posted pictures of a confirmation class of Presbyterian students in California going on an "ecumenical pilgrimage" to a Roman Catholic church. On Sundays and during the week, there are classes, small group meetings, dinners, lunches, receptions, and ad hoc moments in which people are learning more about their individual pilgrimage of faith, and the larger pilgrimage of the body of Christ. To be truly educated in the way of the Pilgrim God is to be surprised with the grace of Jesus right where we are on our everyday pilgrimage.

Service

Hospitality is central to a group of resident pilgrims. The Rule of Benedict set a high standard or bar for us all to practice on life's everyday pilgrimage: "let all be received as Christ." When turning a coat over to a community clothes closet, we are to understand that we are giving this coat to Jesus. When we are called to participate in a soup kitchen, canned food drive, grow food for those who are hungry, we are to consider Christ as the who is receiving such food. And when there is an injustice in the world, in which people are treated unjustly because of who they are, e.g., race, gender, sexual orientation, ability, or age, it is important for us to pursue justice as a way of loving the Pilgrim God among us. It is in serving others, or being served to on pilgrimage, that we are allowed to meet God in a new and unexpected way.

Practicing Pilgrimage—Part II

≈

To embrace the Christian life as resident pilgrims means that we are moving through this world as a radical community of slightly subversive disciples, on a pilgrimage that we "get" as we follow the Pilgrim God, but is oblivious to others in this world. Each day on our pilgrimage, God remakes us more into the image of the Creator, whose image we bear. In our relationships, our spontaneous acts of creativity and imagination on pilgrimage, and in our practice of free will, we demonstrate to others that we are created in the image of God. Our daily pilgrimage enables us to experience grace that helps us rediscover our roots in the Christian community. At times, in this earthly pilgrimage, we will experience extreme challenges, and yet find that it is the Pilgrim God, made manifest through the Holy Spirit in the lives of others, who can best empathize with us, for Jesus knows the true destination. The path we are on may be clearly seen at times, and at other times it reveals itself as we take a step of faith and go forward, even though the path is not, at first, obvious. Walking or moving with each other, day by day, week by week, year by year, may our spiritual roots be strengthened on the Way; may we learn to live life daily as a pilgrimage; and may we always keep our eyes on our true destination: God.

Bibliography

Archdiocesan Prayers for Vocation. Archdiocese of New Mexico. Santa Fe, 1999.
Archdiocesan Pilgrimage for Vocations Handbook. Archdiocese of New Mexico. Santa Fe, 2009.
Artress, Lauren. *Walking a Sacred Path: Rediscovering the Labyrinth as a Sacred Tool*. New York: Riverhead, 2006.
Bratt, James D., ed. *Abraham Kuyper: A Centennial Reader*. Grand Rapids: Eerdmans, 1998.
Benedict, St. *The Rule of St. Benedict*. Translated by Anthony C. Meisel and M. L. del Mastro. New York: Image, 1975.
Berry, Wendell. *Jayber Crow: A Novel*. Washington, DC: Counterpoint, 2000.
Buechner, Frederick. *Whistling in the Dark*. New York: Harper & Row, 1988.
———. *Wishful Thinking: A Seeker's ABC*. New York: Harper & Row, 1973.
Carse, Henry. *Sinai: The Abundant Emptiness*. London: Ziggurat, 2013.
Chatwin, Bruce. *The Songlines*. 1st American ed. New York: Viking, 1987.
Coelho, Paulo. *The Pilgrimage: A Contemporary Quest for Ancient Wisdom*. Translated by Alan Clarke. New York: HarperOne, 2008.
Cousineau, Phil. *The Art of Pilgrimage: The Seeker's Guide to Making Travel Sacred*. Berkeley: Conari, 1998.
Curry, Helen. *The Way of the Labyrinth: A Powerful Meditation for Everyday Life*. Compass. New York: Penguin, 2000.
Dillard, Annie. *Teaching a Stone to Talk*. New York: Harper & Row, 1983.
Fisher, Mary Pat. *Living Religions*. 9th ed. Upper Saddle River, NJ: Pearson, 2014.
Hampl, Patricia. *Virgin Time: In Search of the Contemplative Life*. New York: Ballantine, 1992.
Jabr, Ferris. "Why Walking Helps Us Think." *New Yorker*, September 3, 2014. http://www.newyorker.com/tech/elements/walking-helps-us-think.
Joyce, Rachel. *The Unlikely Pilgrimage of Harold Fry*. New York: Random House, 2012.
Kerkeling, Hape. *I'm Off Then: Losing and Finding Myself on the Camino de Santiago*. Translated by Shelley Frisch. New York: Free, 2009.
Lewis-Kraus, Gideon. *A Sense of Direction: Pilgrimage for the Restless and the Hopeful*. New York: Riverhead, 2013.
Loder, James E. *The Transforming Moment: Understanding Convictional Experiences*. New York: Harper & Row, 1981.
Macfarlane, Robert. *The Old Ways: A Journey on Foot*. New York: Viking, 2012.
Machado, Antonio. "Proverbios y cantares XXIX" [Proverbs and Songs 29]. In *Selected Poems of Antonio Machado*, translated by Betty Jean Craige. Baton Rouge: Louisiana State University Press, 1979.

Bibliography

MacIntyre, Alasdair. *After Virtue: A Study in Moral Theory*. Notre Dame: University of Notre Dame, 1981.

Margulies, Hune. "On Moses and Jesus and the Purpose of Religion." *Tiferet: A Journal of Spirit Literature*. http://tiferetjournal.com/on-moses-and-jesus-and-the-purpose-of-religion/.

Merton, Thomas. *Thoughts in Solitude*. New York: Farrar, Straus and Cudahy, 1958.

The New Century Hymnal. Ecumenical ed. Cleveland: Pilgrim, 1995.

Nicholson, Paul. "An Advent Pilgrimage." *Thinking Faith*, November 25, 2013. http://www.thinkingfaith.org/articles/advent-pilgrimage.

Pohl, Christine D. *Making Room: Recovering Hospitality as a Christian Tradition*. Grand Rapids: Eerdmans, 1999.

Presbyterian Church (USA). *Book of Common Worship*. Louisville: Westminster John Knox, 1993.

Robinson, Martin. *Sacred Places, Pilgrim Paths: An Anthology of Pilgrimage*. London: HarperCollins, 1997.

Rodriguez, Richard. *Darling: A Spiritual Autobiography*. New York: Viking, 2013.

———. *Hunger of Memory: The Education of Richard Rodriguez; An Autobiography*. New York: Bantam, 1983.

Rohr, Richard. "Life as Participation." September 20, 2014. http://myemail.constantcontact.com/Richard-Rohr-s-Meditation--Sabbath----Life-as-Participation--Community.html?soid=1103098668616&aid=mh7pYeY7SnI.

———. "The Ultimate Paradigm Shift." Monday, August 18, 2014. http://myemail.constantcontact.com/Richard-Rohr-s-Meditation--The-Ultimate-Paradigm-Shift.html?soid=1103098668616&aid=Xd_qYFgg-wo.

Russell, Larry. "A Description of Pilgrimage." Personal paper. N.d.

Schaper, Donna, and Carole Ann Camp. *Labyrinths from the Outside In: Walking to Spiritual Insight; A Beginner's Guide*. Woodstock, VT: SkyLight Paths, 2000.

Shaw, Maura D. *Thich Nhat Hanh: Buddhism in Action*. Woodstock, VT: SkyLight Paths, 2004.

A Shorter Morning and Evening Prayer: The Psalter of the Liturgy of the Hours. Collegeville, MN: Liturgical Press, 1987.

Spalding, John. *A Pilgrim's Digress: My Perilous, Fumbling Quest for the Celestial City*. New York: Harmony, 2003.

"The Spiritual Discipline of Lent Begins with Closing Our Mouths." *Christian Today*, March 6, 2014. http://www.christiantoday.com/article/the.spiritual.pilgrimage.of.lent.begins.with.closing.our.mouths/36116.htm.

Vanier, Jean. *Community and Growth*. 2nd ed. Mahwah, NJ: Paulist, 1989.

Webb-Mitchell, Brett. *Beyond Accessibility: Toward Full Inclusion of People with Disabilities in Faith Communities*. New York: Church Publishing Group, 2010.

———. *Christly Gestures: Learning to Be Members of the Body of Christ*. Grand Rapids: Eerdmans, 2003.

———. *Follow Me: Christian Growth on the Pilgrim's Way*. New York: Seabury, 2007.

———. *School of the Pilgrim: An Alternative Path to Christian Growth*. Louisville: Westminster John Knox, 2007.

Young, William. *The World's Religions: Worldviews and Contemporary Issues*. 3rd ed. Upper Saddle River, NJ: Pearson, 2010.

www.ingramcontent.com/pod-product-compliance
Lightning Source LLC
Chambersburg PA
CBHW031426150426
43191CB00006B/417